Close Reading with Computers

CLOSE READING with COMPUTERS

Textual Scholarship, Computational Formalism, and David Mitchell's *Cloud Atlas*

> Martin Paul Eve

STANFORD UNIVERSITY PRESS
Stanford, California

STANFORD UNIVERSITY PRESS

Stanford, California

Printed in the United States of America on acid-free, archival-quality paper

Library of Congress Cataloging-in-Publication Data

Names: Eve, Martin Paul, 1986– author.

Title: Close reading with computers : textual scholarship, computational formalism, and David Mitchell's Cloud atlas / Martin Paul Eve.

Description: Stanford, California : Stanford University Press, 2019. | Includes bibliographical references and index.

Identifiers: LCCN 2018035887 (print) | LCCN 2018037273 (ebook) | ISBN 9781503609372 | ISBN 9781503606999 (cloth : alk. paper) | ISBN 9781503609365 (pbk.)

Subjects: LCSH: Mitchell, David (David Stephen). Cloud atlas—Criticism, Textual. | Criticism, Textual—Methodology—Computer programs. | Digital humanities—Research—Methodology. | Computational linguistics—Methodology.

Classification: LCC PR6063.I785 (ebook) | LCC PR6063.I785 Z59 2019 (print) | DDC 823/.914—dc23

LC record available at https://lccn.loc.gov/2018035887

Cover design: Anne Jordan

Text design: Kevin Barrett Kane

Typeset at Stanford University Press in 11/15 Minion

> To Nan, Ethel Gray.

Countless times since that day, a more experienced mechanic has pointed out to me something that was right in front of my face, but which I lacked the knowledge to see. It is an uncanny experience; the raw sensual data reaching my eye before and after are the same, but without the pertinent framework of meaning, the features in question are invisible. Once they have been pointed out, it seems impossible that I should not have seen them before.

—Matthew B. Crawford, *Shop Class as Soulcraft*

CONTENTS

ACKNOWLEDGMENTS

I came to the computational study of novels through a chance intersection of two of my main life interests: literature and computer programming. Before I was an academic, I was a computer programmer. At age seven I was incredibly lucky to have an information technology teacher—Andrew J. Read—who had written a book to teach children to program in the BASIC language.[1] When I asked "what is computer programming?" I was immediately taken off the standard course of learning Microsoft Word (the dreadful syllabus that so often works its way into school-level Information Technology courses) and transferred to study *Mars and Back* for the remainder of the year. I have never stopped my programming activities, and I find the process deeply satisfying in a very different way from that of writing literary criticism. I would like to thank Andrew for recognizing this interest and for nurturing it. A good teacher can make all the difference in life.

When I found myself conducting so-called digital humanities research on not just a single author but a single novel, I initially fell into a slump of despair. Who, I wondered, was going to publish this monograph that was both esoteric in subject and unconventional in method? Some colleagues expressed disbelief that I would pursue so unpublishable a project even while applauding my integrity (though I think they might have meant "On your head be it"). Fortunately, Emily-Jane Cohen at Stanford University

Press did not toss this manuscript onto the reject pile, and for recognizing the potential here, as well as for all of her other editorial help and work, I thank her, along with Faith Wilson Stein, Jessica Ling, Stephanie Adams, Joe Abbott, Anne Jordan, and Derek Gottlieb.

Several people commented on draft versions of this book and encouraged me in pursuit of its goals. For this I would like to thank Alex Gil, Paul Harris, Rose Harris-Birtill, Ernesto Priego, and Ted Underwood. I would also like to thank the anonymous readers commissioned by Stanford University Press. As ever, I have profited from many conversations with Birkbeck colleagues about this book, including Joe Brooker and Caroline Edwards. I would like to thank Erik Ketzan for bringing specific legal issues to my attention. It is increasingly rare to be able to say it of university management in 2018, but I would like to thank the administration of Birkbeck for making our university such a pleasant place to work. Other friends, colleagues, and acquaintances have helped me—some face-to-face and some through social media—to write this work. Of those who spring to mind, conversations with Siân Adiseshiah, James Baker, Peter Boxall, Bryan Cheyette, Matt Kirschenbaum, Jenny Richards, and Jane Winters remain most clearly with me. Thanks to Simon Davies for helping to clean up some of my prose. My thanks to Yoshimichi Suematsu for helping me with the Japanese translation of *Cloud Atlas*. I would like, also, to thank David Mitchell, who is unfailingly generous in responding to queries from academics.

My (extended) family—Nan, Mum, Richard, and Alyce, as well as Helen's family of Susan, Sam, Juliet, Lisa, Carin, Anthony, and Julia—have all been supportive of my work in various ways, for which I am most grateful. Thanks also to Jane, Mary, Lucy, Heidi, and Mr. P.

Several prototype chapters of this work have appeared elsewhere, allowing me to test their viability with a range of critics. Part of Chapter 1 originally appeared as "'You Have to Keep Track of Your Changes': The Version Variants and Publishing History of David Mitchell's *Cloud Atlas*," *Open Library of Humanities* 2, no. 2 (2016). The version herein contains additional information about the splicing of the chapters of the novel and differences between versions, as well as further information on the Italian, Spanish, German, and Japanese translations. A section of Chapter 2 came from "Close Reading with Computers: Genre Signals, Parts of Speech, and David Mitchell's *Cloud Atlas*," *SubStance* 46, no. 3 (2018): 76–104. Reprinted by permission of the University of Wisconsin Press. © 2017 by the Board of Regents of the University of Wisconsin System. All rights reserved. An earlier version of Chapter 3 can be found in "The Historical Imaginary of Nineteenth-Century Style in David Mitchell's *Cloud Atlas*," *C21 Literature: Journal of 21st-Century Writings* 6, no. 3 (2018): 1–22. The version herein extends that work by additional comparison to the Corpus of Contemporary American English and provides extra evidence for the claims about the language Mitchell uses to construct his stylistic imaginary. I first experimented with the material on reading redaction in the conclusion here in my "On the Political Aesthetics of Metadata," *Alluvium* 5, no. 1 (2016): http://dx.doi.org/10.7766/alluvium.v5.1.04.

Finally, as always, I would like to thank my wife, Helen, with all my love. She is sharp and incisive, patient and kind, beautiful and loving. She even learned to appreciate this book, despite expressing skepticism when I first mentioned the idea and despite possessing little digital inclination. It is her support and love that has made this work possible.

All author royalties from this book are donated to Arthritis Research UK.

A NOTE ON CITATIONS AND EDITIONS

For reasons that will become clear in Chapter 1, citing *Cloud Atlas* poses numerous challenges. Citations within this book are, for the most part, both to David Mitchell, *Cloud Atlas* (London: Sceptre, 2004)—called the *P* edition—with ISBN 978-1-4447-1021-2, and to David Mitchell, *Cloud Atlas* (New York: Random House, 2008)—called the *E* edition—with ISBN 978-0-375-50725-0. Where the text differs among the UK, US, and Kindle editions, alternative sources are cited in each case with endnoted reference to the textual variance therein (in accordance with the *Chicago Manual of Style*, consecutive references to the same edition omit the edition details and refer to the last-cited version). References to the chapter "An Orison of Sonmi~451" are made through the Question and Response numbering system outlined in Chapter 1, allowing for verification across editions. References to translations of *Cloud Atlas* are given when under discussion and are to the specific editions listed in the bibliography.

Close Reading with Computers

Introduction

CLOSE READING, COMPUTERS, AND *CLOUD ATLAS*

> Reading literature with the aid of computational techniques is controversial. For some, despite the fact that almost all publishing and book dissemination in the twenty-first century depends on computational technology, digital approaches fetishize the curation of textual archives and are neoliberal in their pursuit of Silicon Valley–esque software-tool production.[1] For others, digitally amplifying reading-labor power might fulfill the notion of systematizing dreams advanced by early twentieth-century Russian formalism. For proponents this yields new, "distant" ways in which we can consider textual pattern-making.[2] For detractors there remain worthwhile questions about the quantifying processes of the digital humanities: should the humanities in reality always be qualitative in their approaches?[3] At the same time, though, the idea that the humanities hold a monopoly on aesthetics and its study is debatable. Mathematics, statistics, and computation certainly have a beauty and an intuition behind them, and they have also given us formulae, such as the "golden ratio," that add to our understanding of the intersections of aesthetics, nature, and perception.[4]

Despite the hostility from some quarters of literary criticism to computational methods, however, English studies has long been accustomed to using quantitative evidence in its reasoning; quantitative approaches are actually nothing new in the humanities. For just one example, consider that Dartmouth College offered a course entitled "Literary Analysis by Computer" as far back as 1969.[5] As Nicholas Dames has pointed out, Vernon Lee proposed a "statistical experiment"—a quantitative analysis—on literature in her 1923 *The Handling of Words*, itself prompted by a letter to *The Times* (London) from Emil Reich several years earlier.[6] Quantifications, repetition, and frequency are core components within the study of aesthetics, from Virgil's *Aeneid* to the present day.[7] While counting words is, alone, neither enough to denote linguistic significance nor sufficient to tell us much about literary sensibility, as some critics have forcefully argued, we are far more acclimatized to contextualized quantitative evidence than we might initially admit.[8] Certainly, if the use of computers to study literature contains within it a quantifying urge, it is not an urge that has been foisted on us solely *by* computers.

The usual way in which most scholars using computational methods in literary studies implicitly think of their practice is as akin to a telescope. "We have," it is pronounced, "these new tools, these telescope-like things that allow us to see many more texts than was possible before, just like the telescope allowed Galileo to see many more stars."[9] The methods are claimed to permit us, at a distance, to ingest, process, and perhaps understand texts within grand perspectives.[10] Literary history, we are told, can be seen unfolding over vast time periods, and we simply do not have the time in our lives to read that many novels.[11] This grand perspective is a noble goal, and scholars such as Stephen Ramsay and Ted Underwood (among many others too numerous to mention) have pointed both to the problems that such methods are supposed to assist with solving and the broad-scale study of, say, genre that becomes possible under such paradigms.[12] In other words, in such methods the computer becomes a tool that can "read" on our behalf. This is not "reading" as humans perform it. It is instead a mode under which we delegate repetitive labor to the machine and then expend our interpretative efforts on the resultant quantitative dataset. It is an environment in which we can "think along" with machines.[13] For, as Lisa Gitelman and others have rightly told us, there is no such thing as "raw data," and hermeneutics remain core.[14] Such methods are like a telescope, though, because, while we can see further, we also lose the resolution of close focus and must interpret the results. For some, such as Wai Chee Dimock, "the loss of the detail" in such activities "is almost always unwarranted" and can lead us only to an "overcommitment to general laws, to global postulates operating at some remove from the phenomenal world of particular texts."[15]

These computational practices must be situated within a universal, but often unspoken, bounding of mortality. Indeed, the reason for their development is that death cuts short every totalizing attempt to read everything. This is usually framed in the gentler terms of there being "too much to read within a human lifespan" and has led to various articulations of "critical not-reading," as Amy Hungerford's feminist take on "not reading David Foster Wallace" would have it.[16] For Hungerford, life is too short to read the (admittedly enormous) literary output of a man whose personal life seems saturated in misogyny.

Distant reading, then—and its related forms of cultural analytics, algorithmic criticism, various modeling techniques, and "writing machines"—is concerned with reductive but nonetheless labor-saving methods that use the untiring repeatability of computational tasks to garner statistically informed deductions about novels or other works that one has not read.[17] Predictably, this horrifies many who work in literary studies departments. But it is part of an acknowledgment of the fact that, for many years now, more contemporary fiction has been published every year than it is possible for a single person to read in a lifetime. (In 2015, according to Bowker data, almost three million new books were printed in English alone, of which 220,000 were novels. A good estimate for the number of days in a human lifespan is twenty-six thousand [approximately seventy-one years], using the World Health Organization's figures as of 2015, so one would need to read an average of ten novels per day, every day from age ten onward, to read all English fiction published in 2015.)[18] Again, reading avoidance is nothing new: "not reading," writes Lisa Marie Rhody, "is the dirty open secret of all literary critics."[19]

In one sense, then, telescopic distant reading is an antinecrotic practice, one that staves off the limiting effects of death. But it is also an antireading practice that substitutes for direct, human engagement with literature—at least, that is, once the methods and models have been developed.[20] It is nonetheless true and it should not be overlooked, as Richard Jean So notes, that the benefit of an "iterative [digital literary-modeling] process is that it pivots between distant and close reading. One can only understand error in a model by analyzing closely the specific texts that induce error; close reading here is inseparable from recursively improving one's model."[21] In this respect, distant and close reading practices perhaps diverge less than detractors sometimes imagine. That said, and put otherwise, there remains a death-avoidance-to-reading-avoidance trade-off ratio implicit beneath most broad-scale digital literary work. These techniques of scaling the wall of the "great unread" of literary history give us more labor power (an artificial life extension) at the expense of a sort of alienation from the literary text as traditionally conceived by literary studies ("not reading").[22] Perhaps, though, this underpinning limiting mortality is why so many critiques of digital humanities have framed it in terms of the "death" of traditional disciplinary practices.

CLOSE READING—WITH COMPUTERS

The processes of iteration, repetition, and quantitative analysis that are made possible by computational methods have an analogy not just in the telescope but also in another optical instrument: the microscope.[23] While both of these tools yield powers of amplification, it is the level of the minute, the unseen, that can be brought to vision beneath the microscope—a kind of newly angled hybrid text, as Geoffrey Rockwell has it, refocused under fresh optics.[24] For though Barbara Herrnstein Smith has objected to comparing traditional close reading to a microscope, there are textual elements that are too difficult in their minute scope for people to detect within novels without computational assistance.[25] What can the computer see, in its repetitive and unwavering attention, that was less (or even in-) visible to me as a human reader? What evidence might we gather for our understanding of texts at the *close* level through similar methods? Might such an effort rebalance the necroreading ratio and bring us back to the text?

Close reading, however, has come under fire in certain digital humanities circles.[26] For instance, it has been claimed that "if you want to look beyond the canon, close reading will not do it"; instead, what is sought is a "formalism without close reading."[27] In the new world of knowledge that such figures desire, knowledge "cannot mean the very close reading of very few texts," even while the definition of "distant reading" includes units that are "much larger" but also, crucially, "much smaller" than the novel.[28] Close reading has become, for a group of critical scholars, a form of theology that invests too heavily in the sacrosanct nature of a few texts, a fact that is not surprising given the historical links between, and cothinking about, literary and religious canons.[29] Shawna Ross provides an astute recapitulation of the various prominent digital humanities figures who have thought of computational techniques as opposed to close reading.[30] Lev Manovich, for instance, posits that "database and narrative are natural enemies," implying that "each claims an exclusive right to make meaning out of the world."[31] As another example, data that have been through machine learning processes are, for Rafael Alvarado and Paul Humphreys, possessed of "a representational opacity" that requires a second-order interpretative paradigm to be grafted on top, moving us ever further away from close attention to the object itself.[32] Finally, Matthew Wilkens also sees digital methods—albeit referring to specific types of geographic information systems (GIS)—as existing in tension with textual attention. If we deploy these methods, he claims, "we'll almost certainly become worse close readers."[33]

What does it mean, though, to be a good, bad, better, or worse close reader? What, for that matter, is "close reading"? As Peter Middleton notes, the phrase "close reading" refers to "a heterogeneous and largely unorganized set of practices and assumptions."[34] Indeed, just as "different versions of distant reading" are not really a "singular project," in Andrew Goldstone's words, there is no singular method that constitutes close reading.[35] Nevertheless, to many in the field of literary studies this question of what we mean by "close reading" might seem so obvious as to need no answer. We are used, in the present moment, to paying close attention to the language of writers and to using the fruits of this practice to make arguments. As Jonathan Culler puts it, "the practice of close reading, of examining closely the language of a literary work or a section of it, has been something we take for granted, as a sine qua non of literary study."[36] This was not always so. In Jessica Pressman's recent assessment, mirrored by others, close reading only "became a central activity of literary criticism" in the "modernist" period.[37] That said, although the discipline of "English language and literature" is relatively young, being founded in 1828 at University College London, it can feel surprising, from our contemporary vantage point, that it took until the modernist period for close reading to develop.[38]

Nonetheless, the Arnoldian conception of literary studies and *belles lettres*, or even the discipline's forebears in literary history and philology, gave way in the early twentieth century to the formalist New Criticism, pioneered by I. A. Richards. In *The Principles of Literary Criticism* (1924), before his influential *Practical Criticism* (1929), Richards introduced the notion that "unpredictable and miraculous differences" might come about "in the total responses" to a text from "slight changes in the arrangement of stimuli," and he noted that these are, therefore, worthy of study.[39] In another work, *How to Read a Page* (1942), Richards contrasts the biographer with the reader, the latter of whom is "not concerned with what as historical fact was going on in the author's mind when he penned the sentence, but with what the words . . . may mean."[40] Of note in Richards's turn to language and away from the authorial persona is the assertion that such an approach would allow the reader to go "deeper."

The spatial relationship between the metaphors of closeness and deepness, of proximity and profundity, in reading practices has never been entirely clear but has certainly been a subject of debate. As Nancy Armstrong and Warren Montag note, even the canonical figures of the digital field "won't let us construe the distance implied by distant reading in opposition to the closeness and polysemy of literary language."[41] Indeed, most post-1965 approaches to literature that posit a textual politics conceive implicitly of works of literature as ideological by-products of their time through a specific type of "knowledge effect." In a basic Marxist framework this claim to social binding is that the superstructure of art is conditioned by the economic base and, to a lesser extent, vice versa. But it is the Althusserian epistemology, as set out in *Reading Capital* (1965), that most strongly underpins contemporary ideas of "critical reading" or "literary critique" based on "close" and "deep" reading.[42] By examining textual presuppositions, it becomes possible, Louis Althusser claims, to see what a text *cannot say* as a condition of its ideological positioning within its own time. In this way, and although only an explicit articulation of a set of practices that had been building for some time, "symptomatic reading" was born—a mode of reading that conceives of texts as ideological artifacts with spoken and unspoken components—"sights and oversights"—that can be read critically and reflexively.[43] That is, texts exhibit symptoms—usually contradictions or conceptual difficulties—of the unspoken ideological environment in which they were written; these symptoms are the "*absence of a concept behind a word*," and they became the excavation site of most critical, nonsociological methodologies in literary studies.[44] As these two metaphors of space put it—a concept *behind* a word and a site of *buried* interpretative treasure to be *dug up*—symptomatic, critical reading poses a text-behind-the-text, a presupposition of "the existence of *two texts*" with a "*different text* present as a necessary absence in the first."[45] This epistemology, in other words, is one in which the effect of producing knowledge is conditioned by structures of ideology and empiricism, which can be detected *below* the surface of any writing—that is, at depth.[46] Such a reading method is core to critique, since it allows for the claim that texts might betray themselves and speak at depth in ways that are contrary to their surface readings.

Yet the seams of deep, close, symptomatic reading have begun to fray. Almost thirty years ago, Stewart Palmer asked what it might mean to perform "a critique of these critiques," and almost two decades later, Cathy N. Davidson and David Theo Goldberg suggested that it was time that we "critiqued the mantra of critique."[47] Five years after that, Stephen Best and Sharon Marcus pointed out that the politics of political reading are somewhat tenuous. For although it has "become common for literary scholars" in symptomatic traditions, they write, "to equate their work with political activism, the disasters and triumphs of the last decade have shown that literary criticism alone is not sufficient to effect change."[48] Likewise, N. Katherine Hayles has more recently noted that "after more than two decades of symptomatic reading . . . many scholars are not finding it a productive practice, perhaps because (like many deconstructive readings) its results have begun to seem formulaic."[49]

At the logical extreme of this growing suspicion of critique sits Rita Felski's 2015 tract *The Limits of Critique*, although this work has not received a universally warm welcome.[50] Felski's book places Althusserian symptomatic reading under the primacy of Paul Ricœur's phrase, the "hermeneutics of suspicion"—another term that implies a detective-like aspect in which hidden, deep, and unsuspected layers of truth are to be made manifest. This phrase is most commonly but erroneously traced to Ricœur's work on Freud, Marx, and Nietzsche, first published in French in 1965, five years after *Reading Capital* (but misdated by Felski to 1950).[51] Felski correctly acknowledges, however, that the phrase does not come from the *Freud and Philosophy* book, noting that "Ricoeur came up with the term at a later date while reflecting on the trajectory of his own work."[52] More specifically, as traced by Alison Scott-Baumann, the first use of this terminology is in Ricœur's preface to Don Ihde's *Hermeneutic Phenomenology: The Philosophy of Paul Ricœur*, in 1971.[53] The phrase also subsequently appears in "Biblical Hermeneutics" (1975) and *The Rule of Metaphor* (1975/1977). By 1982, however, Ricœur had abandoned the term, referring to "what [he] called in the past 'the hermeneutics of suspicion.'"[54] There is, notes Scott-Baumann, "more activity outside Ricœur's texts on the use of this term than within his texts."[55]

Despite the fact, then, that he really refers to a "school of suspicion" at one stage—rather than a "hermeneutics of suspicion" for any concerted period (and, in fact, abandons the phrase)—what is most apt about these Ricœurian words, for Felski, is that the "phrase throws fresh light on a diverse range of practices that are often grouped under the rubric of critique: symptomatic reading, ideology critique, Foucauldian historicism, various techniques of scanning texts for signs of transgression or resistance."[56] It is an attitude to close reading that combines "vigilance, detachment, and wariness (suspicion) with identifiable conventions of commentary (hermeneutics)—allowing us to see that critique is as much a matter of affect and rhetoric as of philosophy or politics."[57] The phrase "hermeneutics of suspicion" is a profitable description, Felski suggests, more as "a stimulus to thought" about contemporary close-reading practices than as a fully historicized phase within Ricœur's phenomenology.[58]

Amid Eve Kosofsky Sedgwick's "reparative reading," Best and Marcus's "surface reading," Althusserian "symptomatic" approaches, and Ricœur's "hermeneutics/schools of suspicion," it is clear that the phrase "close reading" carries with it a variety of orientations to depth and surface that are independent of closeness to language. As Culler puts it, however, even though "close reading need not involve detailed interpretation of literary passages (though there is plenty of that around in close reading, especially when the texts in question are difficult to understand)," it is about "attention to how meaning is produced or conveyed, to what sorts of literary and rhetorical strategies and techniques are deployed to achieve what the reader takes to be the effects of the work or passage."[59] Close reading seeks, in most cases, to press linguistic detail in the services of literary argument and interpretation.

Given the popular academic impression of digital and quantitative approaches to literature as concerned, then, with distance and scale, some readers might be surprised to hear that this question of close textual analysis has certainly occurred to many others in the digital space, although it is a less common way of operating. I do not in any way propose it as a novelty even while I aim here to invite a broader audience to the table.[60] It is not quite true, as Dimock puts it, that "unlike close reading, distant reading is meant to track [only] large-scale developments; it is not meant to capture the fine print."[61] For instance, as far back as 1987, John Burrows examined the novels of Jane Austen, in detail, through experimental quantitative methods.[62] In 1990 Eviatar Zerubavel graphed the "percentage of emotional content" in French poetry among poets born from 1790 until 1909 in twenty-year intervals, and Mark Olsen outlined the potential transformations that such studies could have (bridging the gap between the very specific/close in poetry and the broader/more general history).[63] Catherine Nicholson even traces the tension between the specific and close and the broad and general in reading practices as far back as 1598.[64] On the one hand, the esteemed journal *Literary and Linguistic Computing* (recently renamed *Digital Scholarship in the Humanities*) has featured, over the past three years, at least two papers that examine single texts in detail. On the other hand, the *Journal of Digital Humanities* has had none since 2015.[65] Other scholars, such as Miyuki Yamada, Yuichi Murai, and Ichiro Kumagai, have further focused on the visualization of linguistic features of single texts, in their case Charles Dickens's *A Christmas Carol* (1843).[66] The London-based artist

Stefanie Posavec also undertook a detailed visualization exercise with Jack Kerouac's *On the Road* (1957) in 2008, and the Novel Views project examined *Les Misérables*.[67] The list of close-yet-distant reading practices goes on. Notably, when such methods are used, they are usually framed as "textual analysis," which most often bears only a slight relationship to textual scholarship or traditional literary hermeneutics.

There is also a movement that seeks to read *digital* or electronic literature closely (which is not the same as close reading literature, *digitally*). For instance, Pressman has recently turned to the ways in which various contemporary works of e-literature remodel modernist texts into documents that provide "immanent critiques of their technocultural context."[68] Others, such as Hayles, have brought new-media approaches to the study of contemporary novels, such as Mark Z. Danielewski's *House of Leaves* (2000), over the course of several pieces, noting the emulation of digital technological artifacts within such works.[69] Zara Dinnen has recently shown how digital technologies have seeped into much contemporary fiction in a way that appears so normalized as to be almost banal, ways that make us feel as though digital media are nonmediating forms.[70] Such methods do not necessarily use digital or quantitative approaches to study conventional works of print literature but instead use conventional humanistic techniques to analyze works that take advantage of the digital medium or digital technologies and their representations.

Yet those works that do use digital methods to close read are for the most part distinctly *digital humanities* pieces or visualization art forms in their own right. This is not to denigrate, as some do, this area of digital humanities practice.[71] It is to point out that it can be difficult to reintegrate the two disciplinary spaces. This comes in part from the fact that, as Alan Liu has noted, those who value close reading have often sneered at activities in the virtual space, branding them the antithesis to their practices: "browsing, chatting, and affiliated modes of Net usage" are scorned as supposed "casual, quick act[s] of half-attention" and "easy consumption."[72] Furthermore, as David Hoover put it in 2007, there has been a consistent "marginalization of textual analysis and other text-centered approaches" that has pushed microlevel digital analyses of texts out of the mainstream.[73] Stephen Ramsay also laments that the "digital revolution, for all its wonders, has not penetrated the core activity of literary studies."[74] Ted Underwood points out that people have not really "tuned in very much yet" to such approaches, "beyond superficial controversies about close reading—distant reading."[75] Indeed, Andrew Jewell and Brian L. Pytlik Zillig write that they are aware "of only a handful of scholars who use text analysis in their literary criticism."[76] Perhaps, they write mournfully, someday "scholars will publish wide-ranging articles on broad themes and close readings using textual analysis."[77] I agree, for the results that can be obtained would, I contend, often be of interest to literary scholars; however, the disciplinary structures of the digital humanities make it difficult to reintegrate such work with mainstream literary criticism. Although I do not intend to rehash the many debates about digital humanities' bounded autonomy, what I aim to achieve in this book is a series of close-reading exercises that use computational techniques but that, in so doing, alienate neither the reader from the text nor the findings from mainstream literary criticism.[78]

In other words, through computational reading and following the calls of Alan Liu and Tanya E. Clement, this book goes "back to the text."[79] I here deploy a move away from identity thinking between texts and historical trends in order to recover the specific and the unique. For, as Theodor W. Adorno writes on a point to which I will return, "objects do not go into their concepts without leaving a remainder."[80] The same is true for literature, and this book seeks to recover for computational methods those textual remainders, those overspills that may be anomalies in terms of broad-scale history but that lend literary works their singularity.[81] This book uses digital methods where they are helpful and appropriate for close textual attention but abandons such approaches when they become overly forced; I aim to avoid everything looking like a technological nail, just because I have a digital hammer, as Alison Booth has recently put it.[82]

In particular, this book interrogates one specific text that I have chosen as an exemplar for the methods deployed herein: the popular, award-winning, and genre-bending contemporary novel by David Mitchell, *Cloud Atlas* (2004).[83] Mitchell is the author of eight novels at the time of this writing (one of which, *From Me Flows What You Call Time*, will not be published until the year 2114 as part of the Future Library project).[84]

But his third novel, *Cloud Atlas*—which Kristian Shaw labels the second in a global trilogy including *Ghostwritten* (1999) and *The Bone Clocks* (2014)—deals with a vast and (aptly) telescopic history.[85] This novel is divided into six generically distinct registers with a pyramid-style cascade toward the future in which each section breaks halfway only to move to the next chapter, providing an innovative formal mechanism. Certainly, others have also recognized Mitchell's text as a historico-generic work. Casey Shoop and Dermot Ryan, for instance, locate the novel within the space of "Big History," a mode that aims to survey the whole of human time.[86] Fredric Jameson, likewise, refers to the generic divisions of the novel in terms of a massive-scale imagined elevator that stops on "disparate floors on its way to the far future."[87] This is a text concerned with the ideas of time compression and the finitude of humanity in relation to the scale of history of which I have already spoken; Rose Harris-Birtill has even cited Mitchell's own use of the metaphor of the telescope to describe his fictional macroverse.[88] *Cloud Atlas* is, in a sense, a novel that performs a distant reading of world history and its future projection.

Many critics of the novel have remarked on its linguistic play and on Mitchell's seemingly protean ability to shift between generic moods at will.[89] In this sense Mitchell's novel contains multitudes; it is a case study for genre-shifting and multiple styles within a single novel even as it is templated and based on "recurring pattern[s]."[90] Critics have also noted the novel's incursion into digital space, with its imitations of new-media ecologies that John Shanahan has called the text's "digital transcendentalism."[91] It is, then, the way in which *Cloud Atlas* mediates a colossal philosophical historiography through minute and detailed attention to linguistic morphology within a new-media frame that attracted me to adopt the novel for a study of what might be possible for digital close reading. *Cloud Atlas* seems to effect the very compression of reading-labor time that is desired from computational approaches to big literary history through its language games and condensed world-historical progression.

For those unfamiliar with this novel it is worth a brief detour to explain its narrative progression. *Cloud Atlas* is composed of six distinct chapters: "The Pacific Journal of Adam Ewing," "Letters from Zedelghem,"

"Half-Lives: The First Luisa Rey Mystery," "The Ghastly Ordeal of Timothy Cavendish," "An Orison of Sonmi~451," and "Sloosha's Crossin' an' Ev'rythin' After." The text jumps, sometimes midsentence, from one chapter to the next, only to resume that narrative strand at the corresponding opposite end of the novel. Historical time moves forward from the 1850s through the twentieth century and into two final speculative future time periods, before cascading back down through time to the 1850s. This crossover between narrative and historical time is shown in figure 1.

While this narrative structure is, on its own, quirky (although Mitchell rejects the "experimental" label), the linguistic profile of each chapter is also supposedly mimetic of the time period in which the section is set.[92] Hence, when a chapter is set in the 1850s, the narrative voice is altered to the language of the time.[93] When writing of a postapocalyptic future, Mitchell's language is degraded, regressing to a phonocentric transcriptive model. This language shift is akin to what Brian McHale has called "genre poaching" within a "mediated historiography"—an appropriation of linguistico-cultural mimesis for each time period (albeit that a text set in the future cannot "appropriate" the literary style of that future without speculation).[94]

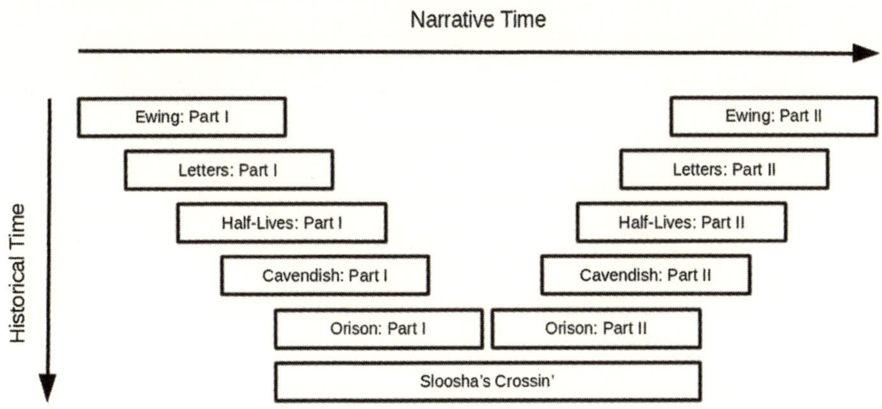

FIGURE 1. Narrative time, historical time, and chapter progression in *Cloud Atlas*.

It is also clear that Mitchell had particular literary sources in mind for each chapter when he wrote the novel, pulling these out in interviews and even embedding some clues within the text itself (see table 1).[95] Because Mitchell's chapters have certain literary lineages, it might be fairer to class this text less as a mediated historiography, although it certainly is that, than as a novel that, through its cultural appropriation, is *about* genre. This is a mode that I have elsewhere called "taxonomographic metafiction": "fiction about fiction that deals with the study/construction of genre/taxonomy."[96]

Chapter	Mitchell on Source	Other Sources	Source or Historical Time
Ewing	Jared Diamond, *Guns, Germs and Steel*; Melville, *The Encantadas* and *Moby-Dick*; Defoe		1997/~1855
Letters	Fenby, *Delius as I Knew Him*; Isherwood, *Lions and Shadows*		1936/1938
Half-Lives	*All the President's Men*; "any generic airport thriller"; James Ellroy	Hailey, *Airport* / postmodern detective	1976/~1968/ 1981–present
Cavendish	Kesey, *One Flew over the Cuckoo's Nest*; "Cavendish Is Cavendish"	1960/1970s farce	1962/~1970
Orison	"gossip magazines"	Post–golden age SF; Philip K. Dick	~1970
Sloosha's Crossin'	Russell Hoban, *Riddley Walker*		1980
Whole text	Calvino, *If on a Winter's Night a Traveller. . .*	SF of Ursula Le Guin	"Late 80s"

TABLE 1. The chapters of *Cloud Atlas*, their sources as named by Mitchell, other potential sources, and the historical time period and/or the source's date for each chapter.

This genre-construction, though, also has a unique applicability for the work to which I turn in Chapter 2, on reading genre computationally (I also address in that chapter the thorny question of what we actually *mean* by *genre*). For, in its heterogeneity, but nonetheless single authorship, *Cloud Atlas* gives us a way to ask what happens when authorship-attribution techniques are applied in adversarial settings against *generic* divergence. This novel further allows us to ask questions of historical fiction, linguistico-mimetic accuracy, and realist detail, as I do in Chapter 3. It is also a text with a curious publishing history that invites comment on textual variance and (the lack of) textual scholarship more broadly in the field of contemporary fiction. In its plurality *Cloud Atlas* is a fantastic playground in which to test a range of answers to many questions.

Of course, *Cloud Atlas* is hardly the only novel to adopt such an approach; John Mullan points to Michael Cunningham's *The Hours* (1998) and Iain Pears's *The Dream of Scipio* (2002) as precursors, even while he admits that he "cannot think of another novel that is so formally divided up between genres" as *Cloud Atlas*.[97] Dan Simmons's *Hyperion* (1989) also immediately springs to mind alongside the generic hybridity of Jonathan Lethem in novels such as *Gun, with Occasional Music* (1994). One could argue further that Jennifer Egan's *A Visit from the Goon Squad* (2010) moves toward this plurality, no matter how difficult it may be to classify that text as a "novel" as opposed to a "short-story cycle." Even a novel such as Roberto Bolaño's monumental *2666* (2004) distinctly changes in linguistic register among its constituent parts. Audre Lorde's *Zami: A New Spelling of My Name* (1982) and Josephine Tey's *The Daughter of Time* (1951) perform similar historico-generic leaps. In absolute terms Alan Moore's *Jerusalem* (2016) probably goes furthest toward a similar mode of generic hybridity, with its excessive overloading of voices.[98] Yet Mitchell's novel is emblematic precisely for its measured and neatly divided multigeneric mode; it is the example par excellence of such genre shifting. The novel is not one of genre crossing, in which new hyphenated genre identities are born, but one of multigenericity.

There are, however, important political challenges in writing a single-author (or, in fact, single-novel) study. In my undertaking to focus a set of computational practices back on the text, there is also a refocusing on a white, British, male, middle-class, heterosexual author.[99] While Mitchell's oeuvre certainly does not shy away from exploring issues of postcoloniality, racism, class and labor divisions, disability, gender, sexuality, and other identity forms, I am conscious of the ways in which this study closes in on one particular strand of authorial entity that has already been overprivileged in critical history. I am also acutely aware of the potential difficulties of writing about changes in *genre fiction* and its practice within a work of remarkably self-conscious *literary fiction*. For *Cloud Atlas* does not pass itself off as a work of genre fiction; it has high aspirations, albeit without snobbishness, gesturing toward postmodernism (explicitly mentioned in the novel) and other high-cultural reference points (such as Arnold Schoenberg). In addition to these challenges of authorial identity there is a distinct privileging in much of the critical scholarship of a "literary" work over "genre fiction" in which I neither believe nor wish to be invested. The novel, in fact, even mocks itself (to some extent) on this front in Adam Ewing's closing lines that interpellate the reader into a specific assumed social position: "You & I, the moneyed, the privileged, the fortunate."[100] Yet, for the formalist reasons of genre outlined above, it is *Cloud Atlas* to which I have turned, a work whose multigenericity acts as a near-perfect and unparalleled arena for the formalist trials to which I subject the text.

PREREQUISITES

Using a literary-computational microscope in the contemporary world involves a great deal of work. Indeed, just to study this one novel was much *more* work than any other literary-critical project I have ever undertaken. I began this project as a unified endeavor shortly after discovering the substantial textual variants between the editions that are detailed in Chapter 1. I quickly realized, though, that if I wanted to conduct further work on the novel, I would require a digital, plain-text version of the book.[101]

How to obtain this? The majority of literary works on which others conduct computational research are out of copyright and so can be freely circulated online. Many are on the excellent Project Gutenberg site. In my case I had an Amazon Kindle version of Mitchell's contemporary, in-copyright novel (complete with Digital Rights Management [DRM] protection) and a Sceptre paperback edition. The digital protections on the Kindle text, however, make the format unsuitable for the types of textual experiment with which I wished to engage. I needed a version that was unencumbered. The seemingly obvious solution was to remove these DRM protections. At around the same time, I began supervising a graduate student, Erik Ketzan, who also happens to be an accredited legal professional. In an informal capacity Erik brought a very specific legal problem to my attention.

In the UK, as of 2017, there is a provision in law that implements EU Directive 2001/29/EC.[102] This dry directive states that it is a criminal offense to break the DRM on digital files. In other words, it is illegal for me, even for personal or research purposes, to remove the DRM from an Amazon Kindle file. Neither author nor publisher nor any other rightsholder could, therefore, grant me permission to remove the DRM and absolve me of a criminal offense (which would contravene the research ethics procedures at my university). That said, there are supposed to be protections in the directive to allow personal use or research on such texts. Indeed, the act states:

> Notwithstanding the legal protection provided for in paragraph 1, in the absence of voluntary measures taken by rightsholders, including agreements between rightsholders and other parties concerned, Member States shall take appropriate measures to ensure that rightsholders make available to the beneficiary of an exception or limitation provided for in national law in accordance with Article 5(2)(a), (2)(c), (2)(d), (2)(e), (3)(a), (3)(b) or (3)(e) the means of benefiting from that exception or limitation, to the extent necessary to benefit from that exception or limitation and where that beneficiary has legal access to the protected work or subject-matter concerned.

In the UK this is implemented in Section S296ZE of the Copyright, Designs and Patents Act. Section S296ZE provides a way to contest situations wherein the rightsholder's Technological Protection Measures prevent an authorized exempted use, thereby implementing the EU directive. This involves a twofold process: (1) asking a publisher to voluntarily provide a copy that can be used in such a way and (2) contacting the secretary of state to ask for a directive to yield a way of benefiting from the exemption on Kindle format books for noncommercial academic research purposes. This process is very time-consuming and typically has little chance of providing the desired exemption.[103]

Because I wanted to get the work under way, rather than risking an unsuccessful and lengthy governmental appeal process, I had two options: (1) I could scan the text from the paperback, then run an Optical Character Recognition (OCR) process on the text, and then finally reread the novel and correct any errors alongside my digital version; or (2) I could manually retype the text from the Kindle or paperback editions. I eventually settled on the latter option, since I wanted to work on the Kindle variant of the work, knowing, as I do, that the UK paperback is substantially different but that the Kindle edition mirrors the US paperback. As a result, I spent many days retyping and then thoroughly checking a digital copy of *Cloud Atlas*. This was both a tiring and tiresome endeavor, and I hope that, at some point in an enlightened future, digital versions of in-copyright texts might be available to purchase in forms that will allow computational research to be conducted on them, as we have seen with recent moves in the HathiTrust archive. For now, though, suffice it to say that it remains an incredibly labor-intensive process even to get to the point where one has a research object on which to work.

This is why I refer, though, to the techniques conducted herein as a microscope rather than any kind of "distant reading" that might save me the work of actual reading. For it has saved me *no reading labor* using computational methods to study a single contemporary text that is under copyright. Indeed, in retyping the novel, I have read the text more closely than I have read any other novel. Yet, without the computational methods, I still *could not see*, as per my somewhat ironic epigraphic reference to Matthew B. Crawford's book on the value of manual labor. As Crawford puts it, it is as though the computational methods provided "the pertinent framework of meaning" that, previously, "I lacked the knowledge to see." Indeed, the methods that I use here—and that I have written the software to be able to use—perform a very old literary-critical function: through a type of deformative reconstruction, they make clear something that was directly under our noses but that still required elucidation.[104] In Crawford's phrasing, "the raw sensual data reaching my eye before and after are the same," but, prior to the retyping exercise and before I trained my computational methods on the text, "the features in question [were] invisible." Yet once such features "have been pointed out, it seems impossible that I should not have seen them before." The computational micro-, rather than macro-, scope can teach us things about texts that we could see with our own eyes were we infinitely patient and infinitely obsessive. But I am neither of these things, so I need the iterative microscope.

The techniques in this book that I call close-textual digital microscopy in some ways increase the possibilities in rebalancing the labor-death ratio. On the one hand, they still perform tasks that are too tedious for humans to undertake manually. On the other hand, at least for contemporary fiction, there is still an exceptionally lengthy, difficult, and time-consuming process to be undertaken before it is legally possible to use such techniques.

There are also some philosophical challenges with close-textual digital microscopy. What do we see through a microscope, and how can we be sure that the very ways of looking do not just mirror our own concerns? That is, how can we avoid the criticism that Adorno leveled at applied philosophy that such a method might read "out of works that it has invested with an air of concretion nothing but its own theses"?[105] Indeed, the epistemology of the microscope is an apt metaphor for the literary processes to which I turn here. Ian Hacking has comprehensively examined the ways of seeing *with* a microscope and concludes that while the microscope offers no insight on scientific realism—that is, whether what we see with a microscope is real—the instrument nonetheless provides a good "map of interactions between the specimen and the image of radiation."[106] Even if the "images" produced through the optic or literary-textual microscope contain artifacts of the invasive seeing epistemologies that we deploy, these can be dispelled, Hacking argues, through intersubjective confirmation.[107] For this reason, at the close of this book I offer up the underlying data from my microscopic experiments for others to scrutinize and reverify as they so choose. The source code for the programs that I have written—the blueprints for the microscopes—are also openly available online for inspection.

This is a book, then, in which I examine the publishing history, generic styling, and approaches to the interpretation of *Cloud Atlas* with the help of a range of computational methods. It is an attempt to drill down into the editorial changes that the novel underwent and to create a graphic stemma of textual variance and different editions. It is also an attempt to pinpoint more precisely the generic language tricks that Mitchell uses to create his shape-shifting novel, while isolating meaningful, distinguishing discriminators from consistent factors throughout his prose. It is also an effort to understand linguistic mimesis in historical fiction. To undertake these tasks, I use a range of techniques.

Although I work in this book on a single novel, for those who wish to think in larger terms, the computational methods I present herein can certainly be seen as exercises in methodological development and extrapolated to other texts. The methods that I develop vary in their mathematical and computational complexity, from the heights of Chapter 2 and authorship/genre attribution, down to the simpler, more repetitive techniques of Chapter 3. This book is not, however, a "how to" guide for text analysis. For that, I would recommend Jockers's *Text Analysis with R for Students of Literature*.[108]

As is customary—for I have not abandoned all tradition—I will close this introduction with an outline of the work's progression. This book is structured around a series of questions and answers that correlate roughly to the chapters. The questions pertain broadly to textual scholarship, to the syntax of genre, and to the language of historical fiction. The first of these questions is, What is the place of textual scholarship in contemporary fiction, and how might digital techniques aid us in understanding textual variance? Such matters have recently come to prominence in the field of contemporary literary studies. For instance, in his "Contemporary Fiction: Towards a Manifesto," published in *Textual Practice*, Robert Eaglestone laments that one understudied aspect of "contemporary fiction is what we might call the 'contemporary history of the book': the ways in which the business of publishing helps to shape and control contemporary fiction. There seems to be a dearth of research into this aspect of the field."[109]

In response to this rallying cry for greater engagement with literary sociology (the future of the history of the book, as Matthew Kirschenbaum termed it at his recent books.files event), it is on textual scholarship that I first train the digital microscope: the publishing history and version variants of *Cloud Atlas*. In 2003 David Mitchell's editorial contact at the US branch of Random House moved from the publisher, leaving the American edition of *Cloud Atlas* without an editor for approximately three months. Meanwhile, the UK edition of the manuscript was undergoing a series of editorial changes and rewrites that were never synchronized back into the US edition of the text. When the process was resumed at Random House under the editorial guidance of David Ebershoff, changes from New York were likewise not imported back into the UK edition. In the section entitled "An Orison of Sonmi~451," these desynchronized rewritings of UK and US paperbacks/electronic editions differ significantly—indeed, almost totally—at the level of linguistic expression, and there are a range of subepisodes that feature in only one or the other of the published editions.

The digital component that I here introduce is a novel method for the visualization of differences between texts. In fact, close focus on the variations between the versions of a novel is precisely the type of narrow depth for which I would say that computational methods can be most helpful. It is extremely difficult to succinctly explain, using conventional textual argument, precisely what has happened in the rewriting and editing of different editions. This is why complex, and to the layperson seemingly impenetrable, notations have been introduced into critical editions. The visualization that I deploy here, however, aids us greatly in understanding the ways in which the narrative is reflowed and ordered between the versions of the novel.

The second structuring question of this book pertains to the syntax and contexts of genre: What can a computational formalism tell us about genre? Answering this question requires a detailed discussion of the underlying assumptions and limitations of computational stylometry.

For instance, we might ask whether there really exists such a thing as a "stylistic naturalism" for every author or whether stylometry even actually measures subconsciously inscribed features of a text. That is to say, the linguistic and syntactic elements of most computational profiling are based on suppositions of authorship attribution, yet we too frequently overlook the implicit assumptions beneath such methods, which, I argue, actually give us a better insight into genre than into authorship.

I go on to show that authorship attribution techniques incorrectly cluster the chapters of *Cloud Atlas* as distinct "authors" using anything above the twenty most common words. This has implications for understandings of literary style and authorship since there is a consensus from what is usually used as an authorship attribution algorithm that Mitchell's generic segments are written by different authors. Instead, I conduct a context-free analysis of the syntax of genre using a part-of-speech (PoS) trigram visualization and analysis. This is a way of making visually clear part-of-speech formulations that appear only in one section of the text or another with a specific degree of additional frequency. Overall, this line of inquiry is designed to demonstrate the ways in which we can understand the microtectonic linguistic shifts in novels, through a set of computational methods. I here ask fundamental questions of what we mean by "literary style" and by what measures we can group different forms of writing. I use visualization-finding tools to locate points of interest, which are then resynthesized into close readings.

The last question that I ask in this book is, What does it mean to write as though in some bygone period? That is, how do issues of mimetic accuracy in historical fiction that purports to come from a particular time frame intersect with the formal elements of literary language and linguistics? Specifically, the first section of *Cloud Atlas* claims c. 1850 as its setting. Narrative clues date the intradiegetic diary object of this chapter to approximately the period between 1850 and 1910. This chapter argues, however, for the construction of a stylistic historical imaginary of this period's language that is not based on mimetic etymological accuracy. Using word-dating software that I developed, I appraise the etymological availability of Mitchell's terms for his characters and uncover substantial anachronism. I also show that racist and colonial terms occur with much greater frequency in *Cloud Atlas* than in a broader contemporary textual corpus, indicating that the construction of imagined historical style likely rests more on infrequent word use and thematic terms from (one would hope) outmoded discourses than on etymological mimesis. In closing, I argue that there are political implications to the "puncturing" of linguistic accuracy for our consideration of Ewing's journal and its colonial rhetorics.

The final argument that I make takes the preceding computational analyses and synthesizes the results into a close reading of *Cloud Atlas* that focuses on the idea of the object-mediated "archive" as central to the novel's depiction of alternation between the historically unique and the pattern-making efforts of historiography. In closing, I argue that this extends even further into a fragmentation and puncturing of history. While other critics—Caroline Edwards, Courtney Hopf, Patrick O'Donnell, and many others—have discussed the work of time and history in this novel, I argue for a most specific placement of the reader at the end of history, in a particular sense.[110] The mimetic cracks in the language of "The Pacific Journal of Adam Ewing" call for a reinterrogation of the "authenticity" of various performed-language contexts.

As a closing word: one early reader of this book remarked that my method herein is unusual, a mode in which I "pose questions, pursue and develop lines of analysis in response, which then lead to the next query, and the next analysis"—a mode of "writing narratives that tell stories." There is a certain amount of truth to this, although I am not sure that I can claim it to be such a distinguishing feature as the reviewer kindly asserted. In spite of this, it is correct that this book is not a sustained argument in the traditional literary-critical sense. I do not come, for the most part, with a preformed argument that I seek to validate through recourse to the text. (At one point in Chapter 3, for instance, I work through a method that proves not to work: a documentation of process for a null result.) Instead, I aim to chart the questions that the literary text prompted in me and to show how a series of computational methods at the microlevel allowed me to find some, albeit nondefinitive, answers to those questions. This could be called, as it was by this reader, a "critical or theoretical investigative reporting." In the last chapter I *do* resynthesize these undertakings within a more conventional literary-critical frame. But in documenting questions, processes, findings, failures, and interpretations in one volume—across the spaces of textual scholarship, genre and language, and historical fiction/mimesis—I take a more reflexive stance on the limitations of my various methods. After all, as one of my favorite-titled articles on the importance of modesty in one's digital claims puts it: it does not do to pitch too many hardballs, with so few going over the plate.[111]

Chapter 1

THE CONTEMPORARY HISTORY OF THE BOOK

> Among the many controversial statements made by Rita Felski in *The Limits of Critique*, there is at least one with which I agree. Felski notes that academics often undervalue many hidden types of publisher labor: "publishers, advertisers, critics, prize committees, reviews, word-of-mouth recommendations, syllabi, textbooks and anthologies, changing tastes and scholarly vocabularies."[1] Conversely, Robert Eaglestone laments in his "Contemporary Fiction: Towards a Manifesto" that these sites of publishing labor "do not see the point of" academics.

What has happened here, such that academics working on contemporary fiction are often underinvested in studying the labor practices of the publishing industry that condition the production and reception of literature, even while feeling undervalued for their own role in promoting such work? As Eaglestone puts it:

I think that every academic working in contemporary fiction has at least one bad story about trade publishers and agents. While some can be very helpful, in the main agents and trade publishers are very unhelpful and resistant to academics. They do not see the point of us, which is odd as we sell many, many thousands of copies of their books to our students (nearly a captive audience, in fact) and more importantly we create the intellectual and cultural infrastructure within which their

> business grows. ("I studied her in college so I downloaded the new one straight away.") Yet this, too, reveals that one issue in contemporary fiction is what we might call the "contemporary history of the book": the ways in which the business of publishing helps to shape and control contemporary fiction. There seems to be a dearth of research into this aspect of the field.[2]

While calling for a "contemporary history of the book," Eaglestone also claims that he wishes to be neither "a glorified journalist or modern antiquarian, nor simply a generic critic reproducing basic critical gestures."[3] Indeed, for Eaglestone, it is important that we remain "critics of contemporary fiction."[4] What, though, does the term *critic* mean in the study of contemporary fiction? How is it different from other periodizations?

What we talk about when we talk about "criticism" in the space of contemporary fiction is, by and large, the precise school of critical work at which Felski is taking aim. That is, it is the Althusserian and Ricœurian epistemologies, as set out in my introduction, that most strongly underpin contemporary ideas of "critical reading" or "literary critique."

The form of criticism that is *not* normally invoked when we say that we want to remain "critics" in the space of contemporary fiction is *textual* criticism. Textual studies or textual criticism refers to the philological study of the variants of a particular manuscript or printed book. Traditionally used when studying earlier literatures in which the production lineage is unknown or lost, there are a range of methods one can deploy to produce a critical edition from various witness documents and to re-approach the archetype document (although there are disputes around whether a reconstruction of an archetype document should even be the goal of textual criticism). This is ironic under the critical paradigms that Felski attacks, since such a mode would yield to us *direct* instances of unseen texts lurking behind the one in plain sight—that is, truly other versions of the text waiting to be unearthed. It would also be a study of the diverse labor forms that contribute to the existence of the text.

In the study of bygone periods such studies have clear merit. With multiple diverse variants claiming fidelity to an original copy-text,

Shakespearian scholars, for instance, were keen to understand the transmission histories of works. But the complicated legacy for the study of contemporary fiction is one within which the author is both central (interviewed, biographized, and scrutinized) and absent or "dead" (in a hermeneutic paradigm still derived from the high-theory era).[5] This led, in the 1980s, to Jerome McGann working against extant paradigms that sought to recover an ur-text and instead advocating for a collection of always-"corrupt" parallel texts that, in aggregate, constitute the social and historical event of a work.[6]

Yet in the contemporary era there are also version variants and textual differences. What does it mean for the close-reading practices of contemporary literary studies that texts in the contemporary age are *as prone* to variations in transmission and editing as they ever have been, even while there is no substantial effort devoted to textual criticism? Indeed, we actually have a *unique* opportunity in the study of contemporary fiction to examine these processes. Speaking with the authors and publishers themselves is not possible for many of our colleagues working in far-distant periods. Yet close readings and minute attention to novelistic language become laughable when critics do not realize that for some readers the text is a totally different experience.

This is not to say that textual criticism never happens around the contemporary novel. For instance, Tim Groenland studies the manuscript versions of David Foster Wallace's *The Pale King* (2011), a work that was unfinished at the time of the author's death and that was reassembled from fragments by his editor, Michael Pietsch.[7] Groenland argues that it is possible (indeed necessary) to close-read the genetics of a text within its own thematic bounds; that is, the multiple versions and permutations of textual histories can help us to build thematic close readings. This idea was spurred, however, by the incompleteness of the final work amid the blooming Wallace industry and is one of the only times that textual criticism seems to rear its head in the study of contemporary fiction.

Also now available, as just another example, are the papers of Toni Morrison, held at Princeton University Library. These include handwritten drafts of *Beloved* (1987) and other material that will undoubtedly supplement our understanding of Morrison's oeuvre. For Eaglestone, however, even though I disagree with his tongue-in-cheek periodization, the "'rule of thumb' is that the contemporary is the last ten years."[8] The eventual availability of manuscript drafts does not seem to fit easily within the study of *contemporary* fiction, whether or not one buys Eaglestone's definition of the "contemporary." It is also the case, as can be seen elsewhere, such as in Andy Weir's *The Martian* (2011), that editions are different from one another *at their moments of publication.*[9] For instance, I have discovered that Pulitzer Prize–winner Jennifer Egan's first collected work, *Emerald City*, was originally published in a 1993 edition rather than the more widely known 1996 version. This earlier version of the text, still available in UK national deposit libraries, contains a short story unknown to critics, as well as thousands of words of rewrites and line edits. Yet this type of comparative, close, textual study usually falls underneath the radar of the contemporary critic, despite *close reading* being the primary *modus operandi.*

Of course, to reiterate, and despite my warnings about the lack of textual scholarship in the field of *contemporary* fiction, there is a long history of the study of manuscript variance / textual scholarship, much of which, in the tradition of European genetic criticism, has focused on tracing the route from manuscript to published edition, while noting that the centers of textual authority in these routes are convoluted and difficult to pin down.[10] We have certainly also seen a good body of post–World War II scholarship that has focused on the variance between prepublication manuscript and final text, much of it in the US context arising from the collecting sprees of institutions such as the Harry Ransom Center.[11] There has also been, within the last decade, a special edition of *Variants* dedicated to the topic of textual criticism across multiple textual editions (version variance included).[12]

In the era of digital books the possibility of version variance—or even disappearance—through mutability becomes an especially important issue. For instance, in what must surely have been one of the least-well-thought-through corporate censorship moves in recent years, Amazon came under fire in 2009 for remotely removing a book from its users' Kindles. Citing copyright problems as the reason for removal, Amazon brought to the fore the issue of unstable textual variants in the digital age in a way that made many readers uncomfortable. The notion that the contents of one's library might vanish at the whim of a corporate giant caused great unease. Some wondered whether Amazon might change editions of digital texts even while their customers were reading them.[13] For, as John Lavagnino noted, as far back as 1993, it is a fundamental property of digital texts to be mutable: "as most have perceived, an electronic edition needn't ever stop growing and changing."[14] That Amazon targeted George Orwell's *Nineteen Eighty-Four* (1948) for this treatment—a novel famous for its critique of historical censorship and totalitarian interference with the rights of the individual—struck many readers as one irony too many.

This anxiety about Amazon changing texts and libraries is strange in another, related way. As I mentioned above, texts have always appeared in different versions, with relative corruption between editions. Perhaps, then, we might account for a slight technologico-positivist bias here; the assumption among readers seems to be that as technology improves, the risk of different editions emerging from the socioliterary production process will disappear.

Similarly, however, an examination of the North American digital edition of *Cloud Atlas* alongside its UK counterpart brings a fresh set of anxieties about literary production to light. For it quickly emerges that the texts are very different and that readers of *Cloud Atlas* based in the United States are likely to encounter a novel that stands starkly apart from that bearing the same title in the United Kingdom. Indeed, I have identified that there have been at least two English-language editions of *Cloud Atlas* in widespread circulation, from the very first day of its publication. As well as exhibiting many minor linguistic variations and copyedits throughout, these different editions also contain sections of narrative unique to each version that must change any close reading of the text. Given that so much literary criticism has now been produced on the subject of Mitchell's novel, these version variants are potentially problematic as they have not previously been noted. Using a combination of computational visualization, textual-scholarly, and more traditional hermeneutic methods, I lay out here the substantial differences among the editions of *Cloud Atlas* and point to the future work that must be done to understand the effects of the heavy rewritings that occur across the different versions of the text. I also outline the publishing history of the novel that resulted in these variations, as detailed to me by David Mitchell.

The main variations between versions of the text occur in the Sonmi~451 interview narrative and are different between the print and electronic editions of the novel (hence my salvo above on the theme of digital variance), but the texts also vary from region to region in print (US vs. UK). The "electronic" and US variants that I have identified are present in the edition with eISBN 978-0-307-48304-1 but also in other US editions, such as the Random House paperback with ISBN 978-0-375-50725-0.[15] The major and significant variations to Sonmi's narrative that I have been able to identify within this edition are presented in tabular form in Appendix A, although the first half of the text is substantially different even in matters of minor phrasing. Since the Sonmi~451 chapter is an interview that moves predictably between two partners in dialogue, the variant referents herein are structured by Question (Q) and Response (R) numbers as they occur within the UK paperback edition with ISBN 978-1-444-71021-2 and the US paperback edition with ISBN 978-0-375-50725-0. I refer to the UK paperback edition of the text as *Cloud Atlas P* (for paperback) and the US editions as *Cloud Atlas E* (for electronic, where I first noticed the variance, although I subsequently discovered that the US printed editions also vary from the UK paperback).[16] I here cover the major variations between the editions of the Sonmi~451 narrative as they relate to differences of *syuzhet*, theme, and linguistic expression, across the US, UK, and Kindle editions of the novel.

As an upfront note, it is also worth highlighting that textual scholarship dealing with electronic editions faces a *media* as well as a *textual* challenge. It is clear from much research that the embodied experience of reading a physical book differs from that of reading a digital version, either on a Visual Display Unit (VDU) or on an e-reading device such as the Amazon Kindle.[17] Further research is thus merited on the specific effects of reading Mitchell's novel in different media environments. In the particular case that I outline here, however, I am working less on the media form or distinctly digital side of Mitchell's text and more on the textual "version variants," as Burghard Dedner calls them, that represent "changes in different printings of the same work" and come about through the novel's publishing history.[18]

As highlighted in my introduction, textual scholarship on contemporary fiction is subject to the challenges posed by copyright legislation. Many of the conventional techniques of the critical edition that might be used to highlight textual genetics or version variants cannot apply without specific publisher and author permissions.[19] Furthermore, it is often difficult to understand the precise terms of the copyright, even on older works (the standard copyright term in most of the world is the life of the author plus fifty or seventy years, depending on jurisdiction). While the purpose of this chapter is to outline the version variants in Mitchell's novel, I have had to do so within the constraints of this copyright framework using minimal recourse to textual citation in the appendix within the bounds of fair dealing / fair use. Therefore, a great deal of this chapter presents paraphrased and abridged descriptions of the differences between versions that I nonetheless hope will prove useful. For pragmatic reasons, I have opted for such a method rather than taking either a more analytical/literary-critical approach or seeking permission from publishers to create a critical edition. That said, and as I will reiterate below, the way that I have mapped the versions of *Cloud Atlas* against one another is in itself a hermeneutic exercise that others may challenge. I outline my methodology for constructing this dataset in the next section and openly release this data for others to modify and build on. I also openly release the software for visualizing *syuzhet* modifications among version variants.

DIFFERENCES IN *SYUZHET*

The first of the changed elements in the text, *syuzhet*, is drawn conceptually from early twentieth-century Russian formalism (Propp and Šklovskij) and refers to the differences between the chronological content of the narrative (the *fabula*) and the way that a particular text organizes its presentation of that narrative (*syuzhet*).[20] (Note that I am not here referring to Matt Jockers's software of the name *Syuzhet*, which is a sentiment-analysis tool.) While such an approach of dividing texts between *fabula* and *syuzhet* can help us to understand a text's narrative flow, there are also several problems with thinking through this prism. For one, the *fabula*/*syuzhet* scheme privileges ideas of linear time and positivist progression through texts, even as we know that actual human experience of time is fragmentary and varied. For another, it assumes that the reader will mentally reconstruct the supposed ur-*fabula* out of any reading exercise, in which case we must ask what the actual purpose of the *syuzhet* is. Both of these ways of critiquing the *syuzhet*/*fabula* divide may be particularly problematic in the case of Mitchell's antipositivist novel, which works distinctly against ideas of linear time. But in the instance of variations across editions with respect to the Sonmi interview, the framing makes sense given that there are some significant reorderings in the presentation of the narrative.

Before turning specifically to the Sonmi chapter, I want to note that there is one other strange difference in where the chapters are cut between the editions.[21] In *P* the Ewing narrative breaks midway through the diary entry for December 2 with the line "Reading my entry for the 15th October, when first I met Rafael."[22] In *E* the break occurs in the entry for Sunday, December 8, closing with "*Sabbath* not being observed on the Prophetess, this morning Henry & I decided to conduct a short Bible Reading in his cabin in the 'low-church' style of Ocean Bay's congregation, 'astraddle' the forenoon & morning watches so both starboard & port shifts might."[23] This has the effect of rendering the first (analeptic) meeting of Rafael and Ewing in an uninterrupted passage in *E*, thereby more centrally foregrounding this character, who will later meet with disaster. Given the connection made in the text between Rafael and Ewing's son Jackson, to which I will return in my penultimate chapter, this is a significant change outside of the Sonmi section.

Turning now to the most modified portion of the novel, in all editions of *Cloud Atlas*, the *fabula* of the Sonmi interview remains broadly unchanged. The fabricant Sonmi~451 is being interviewed by an archivist shortly before her execution for writing a heretical tract known as the *Declarations*. She tells of her initial time working in Papa Song's dinery (clearly a parody of McDonald's, although this is more pronounced in one edition than the other) before her friend Yoona~939 becomes self-aware and rebels. The same "ascension" to self-consciousness/enlightenment then happens in

Sonmi, who is taken away to be the experimental subject of a cruel doctoral student who exposes her to psychological torture. After she is saved from this sadist, she is taken under the wing of a different student, who eventually reveals himself to be part of a rebel faction fighting the global corpocracy. Eventually, Sonmi is shown that the event of "xultation" promised to her kind while in slavery is actually a ritual of murder, where fabricants are killed and fed back to others in a cannibalistic scenario. Outraged, Sonmi writes her *Declarations*, a revolutionary pamphlet. As a final twist, however, she reveals to the archivist that she has known all along that the entire plot was a setup, a trick in which she will be presented as dangerous through a show trial so that the government can enact harsh laws on the population in order to fight terrorism and quash dissent. In the closing words of the interview Sonmi says that she has a longer endgame in spreading her *Declarations*. She then settles down, as her final request before execution, to finish watching "The Ghastly Ordeal of Timothy Cavendish," the next outer layer in Mitchell's novel.

Those reading either edition of *Cloud Atlas* would be able to summarize the narrative in this way and, to all intents and purposes in conversation, would probably not stumble across any differences that could not be attributed to a failure of memory. But there are substantial differences. In *Cloud Atlas P* (counting from the beginning of Sonmi's narrative), questions and responses 4, 5, 6, 8, 9, 11, 12, 21, 22, 23, 24, 32, 33, 37, 43, 44, 56, 60, 74, 128, 159, 172, 173, 189, 190, 207, and 208 have no correlative in *Cloud Atlas E*. Conversely, in *Cloud Atlas E*, questions and responses 10, 33, 34, 49, 61, 78, 116, 117, 118 (R only), and 176 have no matching component in *Cloud Atlas P*. While I will go on to deal with some of the thematic changes that these variances introduce, the other aspect worth noting is that the substantial additional volume of material in *P* causes a misalignment between editions in the Sonmi chapter. While part 1 of *E* consists of 108 questions and responses, *Cloud Atlas P* breaks after 131. Likewise, *P* contains a total of 210 questions, whereas *Cloud Atlas E* has only 194.

Although, as I will show, there is barely any precise, sustained, contiguous textual reuse between editions (the narrative has been almost totally rewritten in almost every sentence), the methodology through which I approached this comparative reading of the *syuzhet* was initially at a thematic level. If a question and answer contributed roughly the same overall meaning to the narrative, then I have called them functionally equivalent, even if there are linguistic differences that others may wish to explore. For instance, at one point in *P* we are given "How did you respond?" while in *E* the text reads "How did you respond to such blasphemous hubris?"[24] As these are functionally equivalent as prompts, I have treated them as synonymous. This approach led to a small number of borderline cases. For example, *P*8 concerns whether fabricants dream, while *E*6 asks whether fabricants have a sense of time. These are, in some ways, performing the same role within the narrative, namely to establish whether fabricants are sentient beings with the same categories of understanding and consciousness shifts as humans, thereby seeking to place them within a broad anthropocentric frame for moral consideration. In this case, though, the difficulty of correlation is compounded by the fact that *P*13 also asks about the fabricants' sense of time. I therefore opted to signal *P*8 as an isolated block that does not occur in *Cloud Atlas E* and to mark *P*13 and *E*6 as correlatives. Another way I could have done this would have been to split *E*6 as constituted by *P*8 and *P*13. In other words, I acknowledge that much of this parallel reading is hermeneutic in its data derivation and may be contested (*P*6 is one such instance). I do so nonetheless in the hope that others will refine this at a later date and use this work as a prompt for a set of more specific investigations.

In addition to the significant number of isolated, noncorrelated narrative blocks, it is also the case that in four instances the order of questions within the narrative is reversed across editions. *P*46 and *P*47 (equivalent to *E*31 and *E*32) are reversed, *P*191 and *P*192 (equivalent to *E*176 and *E*177) are switched, *P*58 moves to *E*40, and *P*55 is split into *E*43–44. These pertain respectively to media reports on the Yoona~939 deviancy or whether Yoona discussed the escape plan with Sonmi (*P*36/*P*47 and *E*32/*E*31), and the video evidence of xultation and the archivist's outrage at the suggestion of enforced cannibalism (*P*191/*P*192 and *E*177/*E*176). *P*58, however, moves up to *E*40 and concerns the memory capacity of fabricants. The final switch concerns the split of *P*55 into *E*43–44, which discusses Sonmi's comet birthmark. These are the points where the *syuzhet* of the story is changed.

To dig down into the differences between Mitchell's variant editions, and as it is fairly complex to discuss these elements in abstract question-and-response numbers between texts, I have schematized the overall comparison and flow between *Cloud Atlas P* and *Cloud Atlas E* in figure 2. This figure was produced by encoding the information that I had produced and interpreted in Appendix A into a JavaScript Object Notation (JSON) file that contains my correlation data (presented as a supplementary data file—"Digital Appendix 1"—with a note on the JSON dictionary structures available in Appendix B). I then modified Mike Bostock's implementation of Sankey diagrams for the software d3.js to allow unlinked weighted nodes (in order to represent sections of the text that did not have correlates in the other edition).[25] A high-resolution version of this image is also available in Digital Appendix 1.

The diagram should be read from top to bottom as a narrative chronology, with *Cloud Atlas P* represented in the left-hand column and *Cloud Atlas E* in the right. Instances of whitespace between links highlight areas where one edition contains questions and responses that are not present in the other. Points where the link lines cross represent the four instances of reordering of questions. Where a block-link splits, this represents cases where one question was broken into several in the other edition. As Jerome McGann noted as far back as 1987 that a "good textual-critical picture of any work will . . . highlight the various authorities and their relations with each other," it is also important to state that there is no authority relation in the ordering of *P* on the left and *E* on the right, as will become apparent when we arrive at the publishing history of the novel.[26] In other words, *Cloud Atlas P* should not be considered definitive over *Cloud Atlas E* or vice versa. Finally, the width (or "weight") of the link signals the relative number of questions and responses in a contiguous block. If there were five questions and responses that matched between editions, then the line width is ten (one for each question and one for each response). In this way we can visualize the displacement and reordering that has happened between the *P* and *E* editions of the novel. *PQ* represents "*Cloud Atlas P*-edition Question" while *PR* represents "*Cloud Atlas P*-edition Response." *EQ* and *ER* stand for the *E* edition's questions and responses. Where I refer to *P* or *E*, followed by a number (e.g., *P6*),

PQ4 -> PR6
PQ8 -> PR9
PQ11 -> PR12
PQ21 -> PR24
PQ32 -> PR33
PQ37 -> PR37
PQ43 -> PR44
PQ56 -> PR56
PQ60 -> PR60
PQ74 -> PR74
E-EDITION BREAK
PQ128 -> PQ129
PQ159 -> PR159
PQ172 -> PR173
PQ189 -> PR190
E-EDITION END
PQ207 -> PR208
EQ10 -> ER10
EQ33 -> ER34
EQ49 -> ER49
EQ61 -> ER61
EQ78 -> ER78
EQ116 -> ER117
EQ118
P-EDITION BREAK
EQ176 -> ER176
P-EDITION END

as above, I mean to encapsulate both the question and response for that number in either the *P* or *E* edition.

DIFFERENCES OF THEME

The visualization in figure 2 shows that these versions of the text differ substantially both in what they each do or do not contain and in the reordering of material. What, though, do these extra sections add to or subtract from the thematic concerns of each edition? It is, of course, beyond the scope of the textual-descriptive analysis in this chapter to conduct a comprehensive new literary reading; this must be conducted elsewhere, and the permutations are extensive. What I aim to do here is to point to the differences between editions as a touchstone for any future work that wishes to engage in detail with a specific version of the text. I will suggest various paths for ongoing interpretation that occur to me, but I will not have space to work these through in any but the most cursory ways until we reach the final chapter of this book.

Let us first turn systematically to the *P* text to identify aspects that appear there that are not present in the *E* edition. To begin with, *P*4–*P*6 provide far greater background about Papa Song's diner and the assembled cast of fabricants therein. Specifically, in *Cloud Atlas P* we are told that the diner is staffed by approximately "fourteen" fabricants and that "four hundred consumers could be seated," details of scale that are absent from *Cloud Atlas E.*[27] In *P*8 and *P*9, as before, we have a discussion about whether fabricants can dream that is not present in *E* (which could be important for thinking about the diegetic layering of the novel, with respect to dreams), and in *P*11 there is a comparison to a child's incomprehension of the labor of "work" compared to anything else that happens outside of a home. *P*12 provides detail of the elevator at Papa Song's, specifically the fact that it cannot function without a "soul" on board, an aspect that is reported in a different context in *E*32.[28] *P*21–24 give an interesting case of a narrative that does not occur at all in *Cloud Atlas E.* In this section of *P*, Yoona~939's initial deviancy is to "address a diner uninvited," whereas

FIGURE 2 (OPPOSITE). Visualization of the syuzhet reordering between *Cloud Atlas P* (left) and *Cloud Atlas E* (right). Available at http://www.sup.org/closereading/.

in *E* the first sign of trouble is instead a "dinery server behaving like a pureblood" (*E*21), primarily through enhanced eloquence.[29] *P*32–33 give additional background material on Seer Rhee's wife's glamour that is not in *Cloud Atlas E*; this is significant because his wife is, we are told, key to understanding this character. *P*37 asks whether Yoona~939 can read like a pureblood, whereas in *E*23 this question is dodged by signaling from the outset that the book is a picture book (and therefore that Yoona would not need to read).[30] *P*42, although in many ways functionally equivalent to *E*29, gives much more material on the bullying that Yoona~939 endured at the hands of Seer Rhee than does *Cloud Atlas E*. Indeed, in *P*42 Yoona is made to recite the Papa Song welcome ninety-five times before talking back to the Seer.[31] *E*29, by contrast, simply says in a single line that mental illness was a factor in triggering Yoona~939's deviancy.[32]

Meanwhile, *P*43–44 provide another subnarrative that does not occur in *Cloud Atlas E*. In this section of *P* Yoona confesses to Seer Rhee's face that she thinks he is a "roach," and he proceeds to beat her to a pulp, ripping out her acquired stars. In *P*44 it is made clear that while the Seer can do this and has the "right" to damage "property" (i.e., fabricants) with impunity, it will lower his standing, while in *E*21 we are told instead only that "Seer Rhee was thenceforth unable to discipline Yoona without implying criticism of a senior corp medic."[33] *P*56 gives details of a medical examination of Sonmi that does not feature in *E*. In *P*60 Mitchell provides more information about the difficulties Sonmi had in passing herself off as an unascended fabricant as well as the initial hint that there was a conspiracy under way, aspects that do not appear at all in *E*, at least not this early. *P*74 is an edge-case that can be correlated to *E*61 but is significantly different enough that I have here deemed it to be an isolated question and response. On the one hand, *Cloud Atlas P* opens with a paragraph on Sonmi's sleep patterns that does not appear in *E*. On the other hand, both *P*74 and *E*61 introduce Wing~027 and speak of natural awakening, free of stimulin, including some very similar, albeit imprecise, textual similitude ("Wing told me that any randomly thrown together pureblood" / "Wing said if a randomly assembled pureblood").[34] The final instance of additional material before the midway break in the *P* edition is in *P*128 and the question-only portion of *P*129. This concerns Sonmi's opinion of "The Ghastly Ordeal of

Timothy Cavendish" but also contains the foreshadowing line for both "An Orison of Sonmi~451" and for the following section, "Sloosha's Crossin' an' Ev'rythin' After": "It all sounds grimly dystopian."[35]

After the break in *Cloud Atlas P* there are fewer unique sections. That said, *P*159 gives information on the supposed scope of Unanimity's knowledge of the conspiracy, which is later contradicted by Sonmi's claim that the entire situation is an entrapment. *P*172 and *P*173 contain some additional information on the Abbess and her particular sympathies with the rebels, perhaps of interest to those studying the role of remote monasteries and their leaders in Mitchell's other works that feature similar characters and settings, *The Thousand Autumns of Jacob de Zoet* (2010) and *The Bone Clocks*. Moving toward the end of the text, *P*188–90 contains another assertion by Sonmi that the trial was all a show and also disbelief from the archivist at the horror of the feeding/execution ship. Finally, *P*207–8 concern whether Sonmi has regretted her life to date (she replies that she cannot, since "free will plays no part in [her] story") but also as to whether she loved Hae-Joo Im, none of which is present in *Cloud Atlas E*.[36]

Reversing the texts and now studying the chunks of *E* that are unique yields a somewhat different picture. In this variant *E*10 asks whether fabricants have personalities, which Sonmi confirms. *E*33 gives a straightforward opportunity for Sonmi to assert that her experience of subsequent events validates her future experience, a deductive logic that is found in only a few species. *E*34, however, is one of the hardest edge-cases to classify. This episode is roughly an amalgamation of *P*45 and *P*47, but these also feed into *E*31–32. But *E*34 presents the narrative of the kidnapping in a very different way from, say, *P*45, because *Cloud Atlas P* has to account for the previous beating and Yoona's degraded physical condition, which does not occur in the *E* text. *E*49 is again a brief question and answer, asking Sonmi whether she envied the naive ignorance/innocence of the other servers, to which she responds that envying this is still not equivalent to wishing to be among the ignorant. This is an interesting isolated segment since it foreshadows the questions about innocence that recur later aboard the execution ship but that do not occur this early in *P*. For information on *E*61 see the preceding discussion of *P*74. *E*78 notes that

Sonmi's description of the snow means that she "speaks like an aesthete," to which she poetically replies, "Perhaps those deprived of beauty perceive it most instinctively."[37]

Of *Cloud Atlas E*'s additional textual segments, however, *E*116 and *E*117 are perhaps the most important, for these pertain to the archivist and metahistorical statements, thereby implying that they are about *Cloud Atlas* as a novel but also gesturing to the idea that Sonmi's narrative will itself be archived and stored. In *E*116 the archivist notes that the existence of the archive is kept secret from the masses ("downstrata"), to which Sonmi replies, "Xcept from those condemned to the Litehouse"—her present situation.[38] In other words, in *E*116 the archive is revealed most fully to be a political function of the state, manipulated publicly at times of a sovereign power exercising its right of execution over its denizens. Such a line of thinking about state power is, indeed, more generally prevalent throughout the *E* text and is linked not just to the function of the archive's manipulation but also to the state's own perpetuation, which here yields a pre-Marxian or post-Fukuyamaian dystopian account of corpocracy (the capitalist consumer state) as a timeless, supposedly natural, phenomenon: "future ages," *E*117 tells us, "will still be corpocratic ones."[39] In this fixing of historical time as capitalist time, capitalism can be seen either as natural—that is, pre-Marxian, in the sense that Marx historicized and relativized capital, thereby disenchanting it of its "natural"-ness—or as the supposed victor among all other possible permutations of social relations (the "end of history" thesis to which I will return later, in which capitalism conjoined with liberal democracy is the final and unchanging form on which social production and relations supposedly come to rest, as outlined by Fukuyama).[40] By choosing which elements of the archive to make publicly visible, the implication of *E*116 and *E*117 is that while public history remains a narrative, it is here spun through state control.[41] Hence, although many works of historiographic metafiction appear to claim a liberatory function in their pluralization and reclaiming of dominant (white, straight, male, able) narratives (from Thomas Pynchon to John Fowles and Jean Rhys), it is difficult in Mitchell's text to fully conceive of such political potential, since the underlying archive itself has been subject to interference and blockage. This is not to say that real, extrafictional archives are not also subject to state control and selectivity. It is to note, instead, that in this case the situation is doubly complex since the pluralization of the novel itself gives us multiple, sometimes conflicting, chronologies around which to base our own interpretations. As the novel puts it in *E*Q19 and *P*Q30: "a duplicitous archivist wouldn't be much use to future historians" / "a duplicitous archivist wouldn't be much use to anyone."[42]

Furthermore, on this note, *E*117 contains several metahistorical elements that are crucial not only for the text as a whole (metafictional statements about *Cloud Atlas*'s time span and the interrelatedness of various histories: "The past is a world both indescribably different from and yet subtly similar to Nea So Copros") but also for the work's declarations on class in capitalist America, based on racism: "corpocracy was emerging and social strata was demarked, based on dollars and, curiously, the quantity of melanin in one's skin."[43] This politically and historically inflected line does not occur in *Cloud Atlas P*, although, as seen above, there are many elements of labor and brutality linked to slavery that are present in *P* and absent in *E*.

Finally, these remarks on race reach their peak when *E*176 provides an additional space for the archivist to express outrage at the murders of fabricants that intensifies his horror but also directly links the execution ship to the Holocaust, describing it as "industrialized evil," to which Sonmi replies that the archivist has underestimated "humanity's ability to bring such evil into being," with echoes of Hannah Arendt's account of a banal evil.[44] Indeed, if ordinary/banal evil is demonstrated by giving Seer Rhee an external existence in *Cloud Atlas P*, the Holocaust—to which this language of "humanity's ability to bring such evil into being" most often pertains—is far more explicitly articulated in the *E* edition. Certainly, both versions of the novel contain imagery that summons the Holocaust metonym of the gas chambers through the "slaughterhouse production line" in which "drains hoovered the blood." In the *P* text, though, much of the archivist's horror lies in his perception of the economic unfairness of fabricants being executed, instead of being taken to a retirement home, where they will be fairly "paid" for their lifetime of forced servitude. In *Cloud Atlas E*, by contrast, the *P* version's mere "nitemarish" becomes "industrialized evil," a historical enframement, as Christopher Sims puts it, of mechanized and routinized death, most frequently associated with the Holocaust.[45] The genocidal factory system is here hidden by a state that wishes to preserve its own existence, through overt political storytelling, based on covert manipulation of a hidden archive.

Such a comparison to the Holocaust is an important part of Mitchell's fabricant chapter, but it is also politically dangerous. For many years animal-rights activists and those who seek an end to "speciesism" have problematically compared the plight of slaughtered and experimented-on animals to the Nazi's "final solution."[46] Joanna Bourke has accurately summarized how this is in most cases a "lazy, inappropriate and probably counter-productive" analogy, even when the motive may be "honourable."[47] In *Cloud Atlas* the humanity of fabricants is denied in a way that is similar to the Nazi treatment of its Jewish victims. Yet the slaughter of Mitchell's fabricants is not predicated on a systemic anti-Semitism or racism; it is based on the economics of his corpocratic scene. Such a comparison, then, can be seen as unhelpful in understanding the conditions that produced the Nazi atrocity. It is, of course, possible to read Mitchell's novel as depicting not the Holocaust but rather merely a factory slaughterhouse, the latter being what is actually happening. I contend, however, that by transposing humans (fabricants) into the latter situation, it is difficult for the contemporary reader not to summon the Holocaust as the defining evil of the twentieth century. Such analogy and relativization of the Holocaust is deeply problematic.[48]

DIFFERENCES OF LANGUAGE

If these preceding elements form the unique thematic concerns of both *P* and *E*, which alter how the text can be read, it is also the case that almost all of the correlated sections have undergone extensive modification between editions. As just one example, consider *P*1:

> "Historians still unborn will appreciate your cooperation in the future, Sonmi~451. We archivists thank you in the present. . . . Once we're finished, the orison will be archived at the Ministry of Testaments. . . . Your version of the truth is what matters."

> "No other version of the truth has ever mattered to me."[49]

As opposed to *E*1:

> "On behalf of my ministry, thank you for agreeing to this final interview. Please remember, this isn't an interrogation, or a trial. Your version of the truth is the only one that matters."
>
> "Truth is singular. Its 'versions' are mistruths."[50]

Even though it is clear, within the progression of the interview, that these sections fulfill roughly the same narrative function across editions, it is also the case that a close reading here could yield very different interpretations. For those considering Mitchell's text within a frame of historiographic metafiction, there is a substantial difference between "No other version of the truth has ever mattered to me" and "Truth is singular. Its 'versions' are mistruths."[51] Indeed, the former contains a social-constructivist view of truth while the latter renounces such a stance. It is also the case that the reference to "historians still unborn" immediately places the entire section of *P* in the context of a future archive, preserved for history, whereas in *Cloud Atlas E* this context is less pronounced.

Likewise, the responses to *P*2 and *E*2, although only subtly different, can result in wildly different interpretations of the significance of particular responses. Take *P*R2:

> "I have no earliest memories, Archivist. Every day of my life in Papa Song's was as uniform as the fries we vended."[52]

And then compare this to *E*R2:

> "Fabricants have no earliest memories, Archivist. One twenty-four-hour *cycle* in Papa Song's is indistinguishable from any other."[53]

In *P*R1 there is a subtle jab at McDonald's (and other generic fast-food venues), along with a pun on *uniform* for the outfits of the servers. In

*ER*2, however, there is no such attack on corporate cultures, but there is an insertion of the italicized word *cycle*. The word *cycle* is, of course, key to *Cloud Atlas*. The text builds up through its layers, only to wind back down, traveling forward through history, only to return to the past. The central subnarrative of the novel is also a future civilization cyclically regressed to the iron age that draws inspiration from Russell Hoban's *Riddley Walker* (1980).[54] (That is: *Cloud Atlas* is in part a work of speculative fiction about a far-distant future that uses a literary precursor from the past as its structuring linguistic principle, a literary reference cycle.) In using the term *cycle* here to refer to life at Papa Song's, the *E* edition implies that the fabricants' daily existence can stand as a synecdoche for the grand cycles of history that run throughout the novel.

Indeed, the primary conclusion that I have been able to draw from this comparison is that with the extent of modifications in these variants—at levels of *syuzhet*, theme, and language—the different editions of *Cloud Atlas* are so distinct as to render close readings between editions almost incomparable. That said, sometimes critics do get away with using a single version. Patrick O'Donnell, for example, dedicates quite some space to the ratios of division of the Sonmi narrative, describing "An Orison of Sonmi~451" as split "5/8th to 3/8th."[55] O'Donnell is using the *E* text here, which can be seen when he gives a spaced version of "conurbdwellers" (*PR*167) as "conurb dwellers" (*ER*155).[56] In O'Donnell's favor, though, even in the *Cloud Atlas P* text the ratio of the two different variants remains approximately ⅝ to ⅜ since the *P* edition is longer but breaks later. And with apologies to the specific figures on whom I am picking here (I could have selected almost any previously published work that deals with the Sonmi section of the text), Nicholas Dunlop has argued that the fact that purebloods cannot distinguish between fabricants is "a matter of myopic hegemonic perception," based on the fact that Sonmi says, "Pureblood [naked] eyes cannot discern these differences, but they exist."[57] Yet this line does not exist in *Cloud Atlas E*, only in *P*. This would weaken such an argument in the *E* text by connecting the myopia to the eyesight reference.[58] Elsewhere, whole theories of the postmodern intertextuality of *Cloud Atlas* have been composed that neither know of nor mention the different editions and how they interact.[59] (Perhaps such variance would better be termed *intra*textuality.) There is,

I would therefore nonetheless venture, no "*Cloud Atlas*." With echoes of Louis Hay, there are at least two *Cloud Atlases*.[60]

THE TRANSMISSION AND PUBLISHING HISTORY OF THE VARIANTS

The differences between the published editions of *Cloud Atlas* are not the resultant errors of any technical process. We are often lulled into a false sense of security in the study of contemporary fiction, believing that a perfection of production techniques would mean that editions must be identical. It is true that the processes for creating print and digital are by now largely the same and should not result in substantially different editions.[61] But these are not the only ways in which discrepancies and variants can enter circulation; literary production is social and coproductive, not merely technical. As Matthew G. Kirschenbaum has put it: we should acknowledge not only "the highly complex scene of writing," in which "text morphs and twists through multiple media at nearly every stage of the composition and production process," but also "the hybrid, heterogeneous nature of both individual persons and their personalities."[62] Indeed, in the case of *Cloud Atlas*, when I first encountered these variations, I hypothesized two possibilities for how this differentiation could have arisen: (1) that Mitchell deliberately submitted different versions for different editions, with or without the knowledge of or at the request of the publisher; or (2) that the publisher accidentally used a prerevision version and failed to implement subsequent changes. Either of these possibilities, however, complicates a widespread belief that textual variance is a phenomenon unique to archival research into texts from past eras.

It turns out that the truth of the lineage lies somewhere between these two hypotheses. In January of 2016 David Mitchell replied to my query on how these variants had been introduced:

> The differences between the two editions came about by a combination of chance and my inexperience. The chance element was that in spring 2003 my American editor left my publisher Random House to take up a job elsewhere. I think 3 or 4 months passed before David

> Ebershoff, who would be my US editor until the end of 2015, took me and my weird and risky new novel under his professional wing. During this interregnum the manuscript for CLOUD ATLAS was "orphaned." I interacted with my UK editor and copy-editor on the manuscript, but there was no-one in New York "synch-ing up" the changes I made with the US side to form a definite master manuscript, as has happened with all my subsequent novels.
>
> In late summer (I think) David Ebershoff took me over, and gave the MS to the Random House copy-editor plus, I think, an external copy-editor, and presented me with a substantial list of line edits which the UK team had not highlighted (as is normal, and it goes both ways).
>
> Due to my inexperience at that stage in my uh three-book "career" it hadn't occurred to me that having two versions of the same novel appearing on either side of the Atlantic raises thorny questions over which is definitive, so I didn't go to the trouble of making sure that the American changes were applied to the British version (which was entering production by that point probably) and vice versa. It's a lot of faff—you have to keep track of your changes and send them along to whichever side is currently behind—and as I have a low faff-tolerance threshold, I'm still not very conscientious about it, which is why my US and UK editors now have their assistants liaise closely.
>
> These days when I ask one side to make a change to the MS or proof, the other applies the same amendment, and all is well. Back in 2003 this wasn't the case, hence the two versions. Though to be fair to me I really never dreamed back then that anyone would ever notice or care enough to email me about it, or that the book would still be in print 13 years later, let alone sell a couple of million copies and be studied or thought about by academics.[63]

Without regressing to a naive conflation of authorial intention and copy-text, it is, nonetheless, of note that the textual variations and relative corruption between editions result from social editorial and authorial processes: a transmission history.[64] There was no one single point at which a different edition was submitted by Mitchell; rather, the interaction between author and editors/publishing houses separated by geographical distance caused the editions to fall out of sync. We can also accurately say of the textual stemma here that the two versions of *Cloud Atlas* are cogenetic and do not fall into a neat consecutive historical lineage. That said, *Cloud Atlas E* is, on the whole, a later version because of the editorial delay on the US side, even though its genetic root lies in the same submitted manuscript as *P*.

It is also notable, in this instance, how much we can glean about the editorial processes that went into the production of this text. While we do not have access to the original manuscript that was submitted—and Mitchell's "low faff-tolerance threshold" makes it unlikely that we will get hold of it in any near future—we can infer, from the extensive differences between the texts, that at least one of the publishers asked for substantial rewrites.[65] It could be, of course, that one of these editions is closer to the original submitted manuscript than the other. It could also be the case that both went through extensive rewrites from their shared ancestral manuscript. What is clear is that there were different house styles and copyediting standards applied at each publishing house. *Cloud Atlas P*'s house style, as below, allows ordinal numbers in the text, for instance (3rd, etc.), while *E* prefers these to be spelled out (third). There certainly seems to be potential evidence here against Mark Crispin Miller's notorious attack on Random House as a corporate publisher two decades ago, in which he excoriates their editing procedures.[66]

It is important also to reflect on how *Cloud Atlas* has been disseminated in its translations and to identify the specific source editions from which the translators have worked, which I have begun in figure 3. For, as Claire Larsonneur has pointed out, translation is a key theme across Mitchell's corpus.[67] My own initial work on the Editions de l'Olivier French version of the text, *Cartographie des Nuages* (2007) (ISBN 978-2-87929-485-8)—translated by Manuel Berri (who is thanked in an acknowledgment in the English *P* and *E* editions)—indicates that the work was done from *Cloud Atlas E*. This can be seen in the first response of the Sonmi interview section, where Berri has clearly translated from *E*R1: "La vérité s'écrit au singulier. Ses « versions » sont des contrevérités" (roughly: truth is written in the singular, its versions are untruths).[68] The film version of *Cloud Atlas*, for what it is worth, also seems to have derived its script from the

E edition (which tallies with its Hollywood/US location). Indeed, the opening words of the Archivist (*E*Q1) are only slightly different from the film text here ("on behalf of my ministry, thank you for agreeing to this final interview" (*E*) against "on behalf of my ministry and the future of Unanimity, I would like to thank you for this final interview").[69]

The German version of the novel—*Der Wolkenatlas* (2007) (ISBN 978-34-9924-036-2), translated by Volker Oldenburg—gives for the first answer: "Eine andere Wahrheit für mich nie gezählt" (again, loosely translated: "no other truth ever counted for me," roughly corresponding with *P*R1's "no other version of the truth has ever mattered to me"). The Italian edition, *L'Atlante delle nuvole* (2014) (ISBN: 978-88-6836-137-2), translated by Luca Scarlini and Lorenzo Borgotallo, gives "nessun'altra versione ha mai contato per me" (roughly: "no other version ever counted for me"); again, a *Cloud Atlas P* translation despite the cover image featuring the *E*-derived film poster.[70] The Japanese edition, translated by Chiho Nakagawa, is also a *P*-text version (note that the Japanese edition is published across two books, with the first book containing the first half and the second the other; ISBNs 978-4309206110 and 978-4309206127). The edition can be verified either through the opening of the interview in the first volume or in the second volume when the final questions of the Sonmi chapter end with reference to the Chairman of Narcissism and his need to consult future historians.[71]

These diverse outsourcings of translation rights indicate that licenses have come from both the *P* and *E* edition rightsholders, and translators have worked from different versions, leading to an extremely messy worldwide dissemination pattern. There is not even a coherence of European translations, as evidenced by the German, Italian, and French editions coming from different paths on the tree, as shown in figure 3.

DEATH AND THE ARCHIVE

It is true that many other parts of the novel are different in more minor ways than in the Sonmi narrative, and I have not produced a detailed line-by-line concordance of the whole text. Indeed, such a move would undoubtedly violate copyright law. As two randomly selected examples of the ways in which the *P* and *E* texts differ elsewhere, though, see: "Isn't

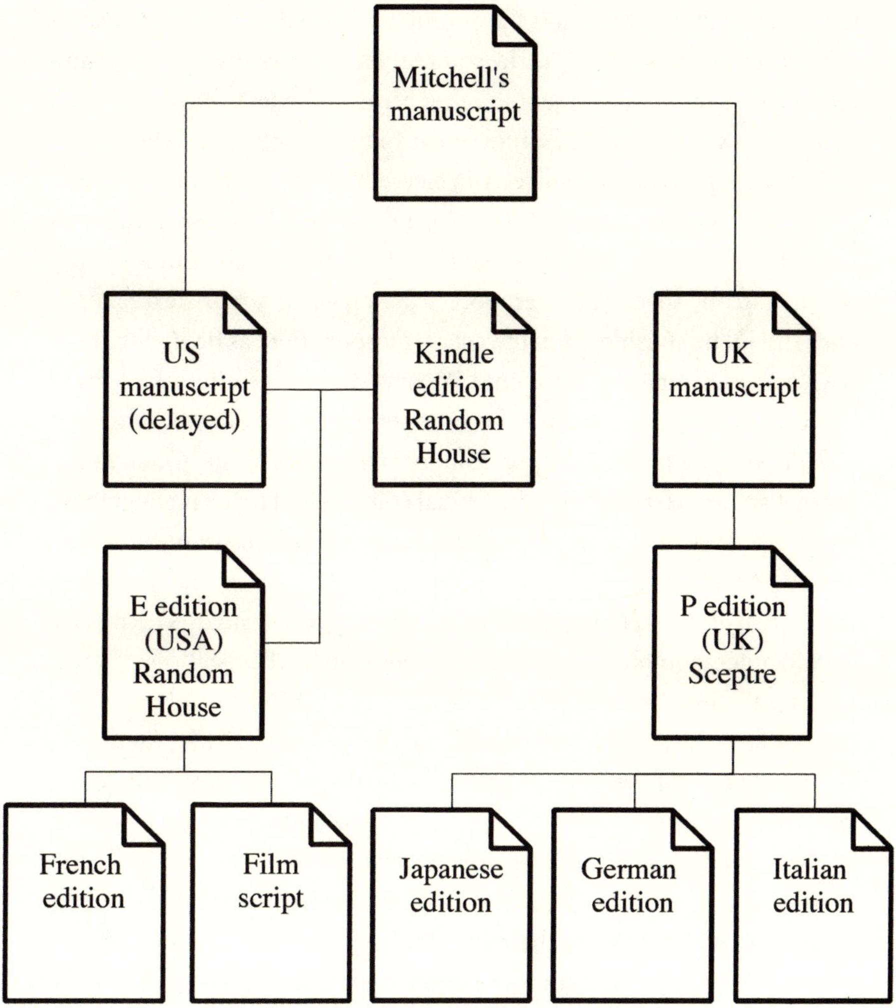

FIGURE 3. Production flowchart for the versions of *Cloud Atlas*.

that what all dumped women do?" (*P*) / "Don't all dumped women?" (*E*); and "3rd Avenue" (*P*) / "Third Avenue" (*E*).[72] Also, one of Robert Frobisher's letters is dated differently: "3rd—vii—1931" (*P*) / 6TH—VII—1931" (*E*).[73] Certainly, however, it is the Sonmi narrative that bears the greatest differences between editions. The comprehensive rewritings of the Sonmi section are simply not present in other areas of the text, although much of it bears the hallmarks of editorial copyediting for house style.

Taking this textual variance as an element of *Cloud Atlas* that can and should be *read*, the suggestion that this raises—for those teaching *Cloud Atlas*, for those studying other texts by David Mitchell, and for those working in any space of contemporary fiction—is that transtextual variance should be considered in the act of interpretation, as textual scholars have suggested for quite some time. We have unique identifiers for texts in the form of ISBNs, but we have become complacent about assuming that all editions are equal on first publication. When we write of "*Cloud Atlas*," to what are we referring? Is it the textual edition cited in the bibliography? Nominally, yes, but more often the assumption is that we mean this to refer to the ur-structure, the named entity of texthood that is "the novel."

There is also a set of implications from this type of textual-genetic work for other demographic groups. *Cloud Atlas* won the British Book Awards Literary Fiction Award and the Richard and Judy Book Club Book of the Year Award. The novel was shortlisted for the Arthur C. Clarke Award, the Booker Prize, and the Nebula Award.[74] In order for the work—and every other work on the shortlist—to be compared and discussed by judges in these circumstances, one must hope that the process at each of these prizes was one where the panel were sent the precise, same editions of the texts.[75] But which editions they were, we may never know. It may also be impossible to ever ascertain whether different prize panels evaluated the same edition, rendering comparison of the prizes more difficult. Likewise, *Cloud Atlas* and other works that take off on the prize circuit often find their way into amateur reading groups. While, in my anecdotal experience, the degree of close reading at such gatherings differs wildly from group to group, in the age of the internet, where transnational online groupings take place, there is a very real possibility of coreaders encountering the textual difference in this volume and others like it within their cadre.[76]

The case that I have presented here, however, is that we should be more careful and meticulous in the reading of editions and the verification of identity across versions of contemporary fiction, even when these works have only just been published.[77] This should also pertain to our thinking about the labor structures of the production of contemporary fiction, which it seems can be heavier at the editorial house than is often acknowledged until much later in a text's afterlife. Clearly, Mitchell cannot be the only author within the past decade-and-a-half to have considered the synchronization process between presses to be more "faff" than a definitive edition was worth. It is also apparent to me that, as Jerome McGann highlighted some years ago, the locus of authority in the text of *Cloud Atlas* is hardly just the author; it includes a variety of labor, editorial, and reception points.[78] This socialized mode of literary production is an element that tended "to become obscured in criticism" of the 1980s and is still occluded today, I would argue, when it comes to contemporary fiction.[79] Computational/digital visualization of the differences between novels can also help us to understand the rearrangement of forms and to overcome the *media challenge* of communicating such textual modification in the world of contemporary copyright.

It seems clear, then, that the name of the novel, if we are to write in such terms, must refer to the sum of all variants and the degree of deviations if it is to have traction, even on the very first publication. It is certainly true that our contemporary novels are not so bounded by their covers as we might like to think. Such texts must be treated, as N. Katherine Hayles has put it, as "distributed media systems," spread across diverse forms and traced through genetic roots, contributed to and built by multiple modes of editorial and authorial labors.[80] For, at least in the case of David Mitchell's *Cloud Atlas*, the pluralized texts speak like the character Hae-Joo Im, for once in both editions: "I am not xactly who I said I am."[81]

Yet, as I began to suggest above, there is a clearer interpretative paradigm that begins to emerge from the version variants of this novel that pertains to the distributed media system that we call "the archive." The term *archive* has been hotly contested. Jacques Derrida has claimed, with a degree of hyperbole, that "nothing is less clear today than the word 'archive.'"[82] There are, indeed, many definitions of what we mean by an "archive." For Michel Foucault, the "archive" is the sum of material traces from an *épistémè*, the term used in his early work to designate a bounded unit of history in which specific ways of thinking were made possible.[83] Other postmodern historiographers, such as Dominick LaCapra, have warned of believing that an archive can ever substitute for the truth, eschewing the "archive as fetish."[84] Furthermore, as Gayatri Chakravorty Spivak, Thomas Richards, and Suzanne Keen have all highlighted in different ways, structures of power and colonialism shape and mediate the archive.[85] Despite the proliferation of discourses about the archive and the many contexts within which the term is situated, however, there is some truth in Derrida's take on history: "archivization produces as much as it records the event."[86]

In accordance with the textual scholarship and visualization that I have conducted above, the main argument that I seek to make at this point is that the technologies and forces that produce history—that is, *the archive*, wrapped in narrative—are central to *Cloud Atlas*. Indeed, in the sequence of the penultimate narrative—"An Orison of Sonmi~451"—it is clear that the archive is of great import. Sonmi, facing a death sentence, is questioned by an "archivist," who intends to file her final testimony, all encoded within a novel that transforms each of its own narrative sequences into a recorded history, with almost every narrative section appearing as an object in a subsequent section. Most importantly, however, Mitchell's novel even plays with these archival concepts at the level of the edition, yielding textual variants across electronic and print media, an aspect unacknowledged by any existing criticism. The cumulative effect of these elements is to transform *Cloud Atlas* itself into a metatextual work that queries the stability of any archive, even while linking the technologies of history to power.

This is not to say that Mitchell intended this effect. Indeed, I suggested to Mitchell that he might be toying with the reader here and playing with the "archival" interview format. Archiving something for safekeeping, as the archivist is doing with the unrepeatable words of the death-penalty convict, implies that the archival object is stable, unique, and preserved. To present such a process in a text where the different variations obviate stability, uniqueness, and singular preservation would, I thought, make for a tidy transtextual ironic statement, an aspect that I read more thoroughly in my final chapter. Mitchell, however, in his typically self-deprecating fashion, noted that while such a reading gives "a new heft to the archivist's words," he believes "the discrepancies could not really be called a transtextual statement" but were instead born, in his words, from "sloth and authorial innocence."[87]

Yet, as I argued in my introduction, *Cloud Atlas* is a novel that is concerned in equal parts with history and genre (among many other elements), an aspect mirrored in the approaches between which I swing in this book. The text's broad temporal span and self-referential prose make it inevitable that it will be read as a work that is about history itself.[88] Indeed, elements of postmodern historiography are explicitly referenced in the novel, with Mitchell writing of "flashbacks" to the "1980s with MAs in Postmodernism and Chaos Theory."[89] This element of viewing history as an imperfect narration and documentation of events is emphasized in the novel, however, since all of its representations are narrated, even those within the text. Consider that three of *Cloud Atlas*'s narratives are written and read as texts by other characters within the novel, while three are respectively viewed as a film, seen in a holographic device, and related through the oral storytelling tradition. For instance, the seafaring voyage of Ewing is a story read by Frobisher and related in his letters to Sixsmith. In turn, Luisa Rey reads the Frobisher letters after Sixsmith is murdered by Bill Smoke. Likewise, Timothy Cavendish reads the manuscript for "Half-Lives: The First Luisa Rey Mystery" while on his ill-fated train journey, himself later appearing as a film in Sonmi~451's narrative. All of these stories are contained within the book's central tale, "Sloosha's Crossin' an' Ev'rythin' After," but this is, itself, finally nested within a coda that is narrated by Zachry's son. With this final blip of a coda, *Cloud Atlas* makes it perfectly clear that the reader will find no representation of a "real" world in this novel, only stories representing stories representing stories—a *One Thousand and One Nights* or a *Manuscript Found in Saragossa* (c. 1847).[90]

Yet, although *Cloud Atlas* takes various time periods from the nineteenth century through the apocalypse as its settings, these textual eras are not just historical epochs; they are also genres derived from source texts (see table 1 in the introduction). In fact, a parallel chronology of *Cloud Atlas* can be seen not as nineteenth-century colonialism through postapocalypse but rather, more precisely, c. 1855 to 1980. This can be explained when Mitchell's own statements on the sources for the narratives are juxtaposed with additional likely references.[91]

In this way *Cloud Atlas* can be read as a text that is about both the nature of history and the nature of *literary* or cultural history, through an encapsulation in a quasi-archival form. As each narrative is embedded in a filed object and read or seen by characters in a subsequent time, the aspect of mediation through an archive becomes central. As Courtney Hopf has pointed out, in the case of each of its sections, Mitchell's novel encrypts the previous narrative in order to archivally preserve the historical events and generic codification within the form of a fileable object (a book, a video, etc.).[92] The historical narrative itself is contained within the intra-actions between these intradiegetic objects. The generic form, however, is often contextually encoded. For instance, that Luisa Rey's narrative is a generic thriller is encoded in the paperback, pulp, series-bound airport-fiction-style publication of "Half-Lives: The First Luisa Rey Mystery." Indeed, it is the metadata of the *title* of this publication, combined with the technology of the codex, that encodes the generic history here, as though the narrative were an archive to be filed. *Mystery* gives a key to the kind of reader that will enjoy the work, while the "First Luisa Rey" clause indicates the serialized nature of this imagined volume and its conformance to the dynamic, protagonist-centered spy thriller. The term *half-lives* is a ploy by Mitchell to acknowledge the "halving" that occurs throughout the metatext's (*Cloud Atlas*'s) splicing technique.

The Luisa Rey subnarrative, then, along with all the narratives of *Cloud Atlas*, is produced as a discrete text by variegated techniques of archivization, including a focus on metadata and semantic contexts, alongside a set of linguistic techniques to which I will turn shortly. In the first place the history is presented to the reader as though it might be unmediated, so far as such a thing is possible: a quasi-realist thriller narrative. The text then moves to bind this "historical" element within a bounded book manuscript that can be read by Timothy Cavendish in a later narrative. Importantly, though, Mitchell encodes the generic formulation of the preceding narrative through the metadata of that "book" (primarily its title) but also from the broader intertextual resonances that this title can trigger and its proposed/assumed publication format. Finally, Mitchell inverts this structure and, through the play on "half-lives," changes this intradiegetic book object into a type of structural metadata for *Cloud Atlas* itself. As a description of *Cloud Atlas*'s narrative technique, "Half-Lives: The First Luisa Rey Mystery" details the novel's own structure. Metafictive aspects can also be signaled through objects' metadata.

But this focus on notions of the archive runs more deeply and more explicitly throughout Mitchell's novel. One of the most striking of *Cloud Atlas*'s narratives is the unusual SF take on a bildungsroman on which I have here focused, where Sonmi goes from her slave-like existence to consciousness of the horrors of her race's existence. This finds its apex in the scene where Sonmi is shown her fellow fabricants being murdered and fed back to the rest of the slave population—a kind of grim fusion of *The Matrix* (1999) and *Soylent Green* (1973).

For the purposes of this chapter and my initial focus here on archives, the most important aspect of the Sonmi chapter is its interview format. Crucially, the entire tale is told through analepsis from an interview with the archivist. The archivist poses questions to which Sonmi responds. Although Mitchell has stated that this format is based on "gossip magazines" (see above), it is a curiously morbid type of gossip that would preserve the last words of a condemned prisoner. Instead, the section reads more like a journalistic witnessing or formal preservation of a being whose death has already happened but who just so happens not to have yet been executed. This is, in many ways, akin to what Roland Barthes sees in the *punctum* of a photograph: the way in which the time of life can leap out even after the instance of death, causing strange perturbations in the viewer's chronological perception.[93]

Mitchell's archivist, though, is doubly complicit in producing the event as much as recording it. In the first instance the framing and posing of questions in a specific way is designed to preshape Sonmi's narrative. By directing the conversation that will be recorded, the archivist has great power in mediating the past. In the second, more powerful sense in Mitchell's text, however, the archivist is also literally responsible for producing the event. For, as a member of Nea So Copros's ruling Unanimity faction, the archivist's interview is part of a conspiracy to try and then to execute Sonmi~451. The archival "footage" stored in Mitchell's invented medium of an orison is actually part of the unfolding reality and will be used as documentary evidence against the fabricant in the passage of future laws. And, of course, this approach has been seen in actual history. Totalitarian regimes, such as that which existed under Joseph Stalin, are notorious for manipulation of the media archive for political purposes in the present. Among the most famous of these, besides the removal of Trotsky from several well-known photographs that also feature Lenin, is the doctored image of Nikolai Yezhov (see figure 4), former head of the NKVD (the body that housed the precursor to the KGB). Indeed, it was central to Stalin's authority and future plan of action that those executed in the purges were never seen, on the record, to have had a central role in government. This precept, of course, was also well encapsulated in Orwell's seminal dystopian narrative to which I turned earlier, *Nineteen Eighty-Four*: "who controls the past controls the future; who controls the present controls the past."[94] As with Mitchell's future dystopia, manipulation of the official archival record can lead to a cementing of power in the present.

The data of Sonmi's interview must be put into a structured retrieval format if it is to be of any use. Metadata are needed for any archive: "structured information that describes, explains, locates, or otherwise makes it easier to retrieve, use, or manage an information resource."[95] But the metadata surrounding objects requires persistence of the referent if this function is to be fulfilled. If two different photographs are both archived under the same metadata, then the result will not be the ease of use of the information resource but confusion when different external resources refer to the metadata but have different objects beneath them. While many of Stalin's photographs were doubtlessly successfully altered and all traces of the preceding versions erased, the fact that the replacement versions did not, in all cases, manage to obliterate their antecedents invalidates the metadata around the photograph of Kliment Voroshilov, Vyacheslav Molotov, and Joseph Stalin.

FIGURE 4. Nikolai Yezhov is erased from history after his execution during the Great Purge. Public domain image under article 1281 of book 4 of the Civil Code of the Russian Federation No. 230-FZ of December 18, 2006, and article 6 of Law No. 231-FZ of the Russian Federation of December 18, 2006.

The same can be said of Mitchell's text. For the reader, the political neutrality of the implied metadata around Sonmi's interview is compromised. The reader knows that the interview will be filed under a record that labels Sonmi a traitor and a dangerous insurgent, even though the entire "insurrection" was engineered by the city's ruling party. Furthermore, the reader also knows that the metadata will be lost and all original contexts obliterated. This is because, in the book's most futuristic (but also, as with Hoban's *Riddley Walker*, technologically regressed) narrative, Sonmi is worshipped as a god. In other words, while the preservation of a stable object is crucial for the moral and functional integrity of metadata, the preservation of metadata is also vital for the semantic richness of objects—a function that must otherwise be deferred to socially contingent hermeneutics (a close reading, perhaps).

This would be all well and good as an intradiegetic literary critical analysis of Mitchell's novel and the "Orison of Sonmi~451" subplot. There is an archivist, complicit in the manufacture of a stored and cataloged reality whose metadata degrades over time and which can legitimize thinking about the text in terms of archives: so far, so straightforward. Mitchell's text becomes more interesting, however, when we turn back to the textual variants differentiating editions of *Cloud Atlas*. For, deliberate or not, the archive of Mitchell's text is unstable. Indeed, between versions of Mitchell's novel there are significant textual differences, specifically in the Sonmi~451 section of the work. This yields an interesting set of interpretative possibilities, given the archival context of this section, and despite Mitchell's disavowal of the differences as mere "sloth and authorial innocence." Which version of the myth—*P* or *E*—is known to the characters in "Sloosha's Crossin'" who worship Sonmi as a god? The novel is, after all, about the failed transmissions of cultural artifacts—films, books, orisons—that contribute to fresh mythogenesis. Yet *Cloud Atlas* itself causes such proliferation among its own readers. Mitchell's own mythopoesis is plural from the outset.

Taking this textual variance that I have outlined and computationally visualized in this chapter, then, as an element of *Cloud Atlas* that should be *read*, signaled through the heaviest modifications occurring around the narrative pertaining to the archive, the first thing we might say is that the archive—the versions of Mitchell's novel and as with the case of Yezhov under Stalin—has been manipulated in order to present multiple "versions of the truth." It has done so in the context of the death penalty, in which the sovereign state has exercised its "right" to torture and execute for the reinstatement of its own legitimate power.[96] In truth, the archive here, in the form of the holographic recording device (the "orison"), *is* the public display of the defendant's body. That this is explicit in the text through the rhetoric of a "show trial" (linking it to Stalinist Russia but also to sovereign power's display of the condemned's body) only strengthens the centrality of the pluralized and unstable archive as an instrument of state repression. What is perhaps curious is that Mitchell's future world should be so dependent on the forms of political rationality and legitimacy—sovereign powers and executions—that the principal theorist of such modes, Michel Foucault, believed were already waning. It is not only the "Sloosha's Crossin'" narrative that bears the hallmarks of a future time that holds within it the past but also "An Orison of Sonmi~451." I contend that it is not possible to read the intradiegetic context of Mitchell's novel, which focuses heavily on notions of archival storage and representation in different media, without a consideration of the transmedia ecologies of the editions of his own book.[97]

The second aspect that is of interest here is the way in which the Sonmi narrative, so different between editions, clusters notions of "deviancy." Both editions refer to the Yoona incident as a "deviancy," and aberration that is to be punished in the highly regulated and hierarchical world of Nea So Copros. The archivist, for example, is also bound by hierarchy and is an extremely junior figure ("An eighthstratum archivist can't dream of getting such security clearance!" / "An eighth-stratum archivist wouldn't get such security clearance in his wildest dreams!").[98] When two textual editions containing this narrative are vying for legitimacy, we are faced with the prospect of relativism and normalization: which text is deviant? Deviancy requires a dominant center, a hegemonic norm, from which to deviate. By removing this center and norm across editions, Mitchell metatextually (quite literally from "beyond" [meta] any single text) erodes the legitimacy of the future state of Nea So Copros, as "deviancy" is revealed to be a phenomenon that can only be relative to another core. Given that this future state (and clear reflection on our present) is based on slavery, this reading of textual variance is in keeping with the text's ethics.

So from the initial comparison of the version variants and the computational visualization of the rearrangements therein, I come here to a single conclusion, to which I will later return: a central point of Mitchell's novel that has received entirely insufficient critical attention is the role of the archive. *Cloud Atlas* is a novel that is *about* archives, and it is a book that is about fiction as an archival encoding process. In its textual materiality it is also a novel that *reveals*, rather than simply speaks of, the dangers but also opportunities of multiple encodings. It does so within the context of the authority of the state and the death penalty, which I have here argued have a parallel to *authorial* authority. This is, I believe, how we should begin to close-read the variant versions of *Cloud Atlas* and its microliterary history.

Chapter 2

READING GENRE COMPUTATIONALLY

> Genre is as tricky to define as is the "archive." It is a cliché to note that nobody seems able to agree precisely on what we mean by *genre*. Is it, as Jacques Derrida once characteristically teased, the case that "genres are not to be mixed" and that "as soon as genre announces itself, one must respect a norm, one must not cross a line of demarcation, one must not risk impurity, anomaly, or monstrosity"?[1] Are genres part of rule-following practices conducted by writers, in which various conventions are internalized and reproduced according to shared Wittgensteinian communal undertakings?[2] Does the study of genre succumb to Robert Stam's critiques of extension, normativism, homogeneic definitions, and biologism?[3] Are our analyses of genre always ones of cyclicality and endless regression, seeking an origin for a practice that is defined by sorting into already-existent categories?[4] (Yet, if so: whence these categories?) Do texts that play with genre in metafictional ways ask us to consider the structure of genre, as they once asked us to consider the study of history?[5] Or is genre actually something more akin to what Lauren Berlant proposes in *Cruel Optimism* (2011), where she writes of conceiving of a moment from within that moment itself as "a temporal genre whose conventions emerge from the personal and public filtering of the situations and events that are happening in an extended now

whose very parameters . . . are also always there for debate," an emerging social arrangement that provides "an affective expectation of the experience of watching something unfold"?[6]

Many questions and no consensus. For scholarly writing about genre is a genre of its own, particularly within fields such as speculative/science fiction into which I have not here even delved. I have written, thus far in this book, of Mitchell's multigenericity in *Cloud Atlas* and the ways in which theme and language begin to intersect to create a generic tapestry, all without defining *genre*. I do not and cannot here define *genre* in an adequate way to address its decades of study. We can, though, ask a smaller-scale question: what does it mean to "write as David Mitchell does in *Cloud Atlas*"? What distinctive traits might computational microscopy identify within Mitchell's writing and style that are invisible to the naked eye? What could such an analysis tell us about genre? As Ted Underwood has put it, computational methods can turn the lack of definition of genre to their advantage: "We can dispense with fixed definitions, and base the study of genre only on the shifting practices of particular historical actors—but still produce models of genre substantive enough to compare and contrast."[7]

One of the most basic things that we can do with computational techniques is to conduct an analysis of the most frequently used words in a text. That doesn't sound very exciting on its own, and such an approach has been the subject of critique and even ridicule, but it turns out that the subconscious ways in which authors use seemingly insignificant words is an extremely effective marker for authorship attribution.[8] That is, most texts by the same author can be accurately clustered by comparing the distance between word frequencies within each work (on which, more below). I wondered, though, what would happen if I undertook such an analysis on each section of Mitchell's novel. Would the underlying—and presumed subconscious—elements of language change between sections? Or would we, in fact, end up with Mitchell's persona inscribed within these texts? A set of stylometric techniques can help us to answer some of these questions.

As the name implies, computational stylometry is the use of computers to measure (*-metry*) the stylistic properties of texts (*stylo-*). Stylometry, as a quantifying activity, has a long and varied history, from legal court cases where the accused was acquitted on the basis of stylometric evidence, such as that of Steve Raymond, through to authorship attribution.[9] In the latter case, as charted by Anthony Kenny, the discipline dates back to approximately 1851, when Augustus de Morgan suggested that a dispute over the attribution of certain biblical epistles could be settled by measuring average word lengths and correlating them with known writings of St. Paul.[10] From this humble beginning we are now at the point where it is claimed that computational forensic stylometry can "identify individuals in sets of 50 authors with better than 90% accuracy, and [can] even [be] scaled to more than 100,000 authors."[11]

In terms of a background to stylometry, a significant breakthrough, or at least a key moment of success, took place around 1964 with the publication of Mosteller and Wallace's work on the set of pseudonymously published *Federalist* papers of 1787–88, which were pushing for the adoption of the proposed Constitution for the United States. Mosteller and Wallace analyzed the distribution of thirty function words (articles, pronouns, etc.) throughout the *Federalist* papers and managed to come to the same conclusion of authorship as other historians, based in this case on statistically inferred probabilities and Bayesian analysis.[12] As Patrick Juola frames it, there are several reasons why this corpus formed an important test-bed for stylometry: "First, the documents themselves are widely available . . . , including over the Internet through sources such as Project Gutenberg. Second, the candidate set for authorship is well-defined; the author of the disputed papers is known to be either Hamilton or Madison. Third, the undisputed papers provide excellent samples of undisputed text written by the same authors, at the same time, on the same topic, in the same genre, for publication via the same media." In Juola's words, "a more representative training set would be hard to imagine."[13]

If the *Federalist* papers represent a significant success for stylometric authorship attribution, there have also been some disastrous failures. In the early 1990s a series of criminal court cases turned to forensic stylometry to identify authorship of documents (for example, Thomas McCrossen's appeal in London in July of 1991; the prosecution of Frank Beck in Leicester in 1992; the Dublin trial of Vincent Connell in December of 1991; Nicky Kelly's pardon by the Irish government in April of

1992; the case of Joseph Nelson-Wilson in London in 1992; and the Carl Bridgewater murder case).[14] Indeed, it is frequently the case that court trials turn on the authorship of specific documents, be they suicide notes, sent emails, or written letters.[15] These specific cases, however, all relied on a particular technique known as "qsum" or "cusum"—for "cumulative sum" of the deviations from the mean—which is designed to measure the stability of a measured feature of a text.[16] The only problem here was that, almost immediately, the cusum technique came under intense scrutiny and theoretical criticism, ending in a live-television broadcast failure of an authorship attribution test using this method.[17] Despite this failing, specific stylometric techniques remain available as evidence in courts of law depending on their academic credibility and the jurisdiction's specific laws on admissibility.[18]

The other most well-known case of failure in the field of stylometry occurred in the late 1990s, when Don Foster attributed the poem "A Funeral Elegy" to William Shakespeare using a raft of stylometric approaches.[19] The attendant press coverage landed this claim on the front page of the *New York Times*, and the community of traditional Shakespeare scholars reacted in disbelief. When Foster refused to accept traditional historicist arguments against his attribution, stylometric work by multiple groups of scholars pointed to the seventeenth-century playwright and poet John Ford as the far more likely author of the poem, which Foster eventually accepted.[20] While, as Juola points out, "this cut-and-thrust debate can be regarded as a good (if somewhat bitter) result of the standard scholarly process of criticism," for many scholars it marked the sole interaction that they have ever had with stylometry, and the result could only be a perception of notoriety, braggadocio, and inaccuracy.[21]

That said, in recent years there have also been some extremely successful algorithmic developments for detecting authorship. Perhaps the best known of these is the 1992 "Burrows's delta."[22] With apologies for a brief mathematical explanation over the next page or so, Burrows's delta (the word here meaning the mathematical symbol for "difference": Δ) consists of two steps to conduct a multivariate statistical authorship attribution. First of all, one measures the most frequent words that occur in a text and then relativizes these using a "z-score" measure. A z-score measurement is basically asking, "By how much does a word's frequency differ from the average deviation of the other words?" The first thing that we would calculate here is the "standard deviation" of the entire word set. A standard deviation means the square root of the average of the squared deviations of the values from the average. Or, in other words: work out the average frequency with which words occur in a text; then work out (for each word) how many more or less times that word occurs relative to the average; square this and add up all such deviations; then divide this by the number of words; then square root the result. To get the z-score, we next take an individual word's frequency, subtract the average (mean) frequency, and divide this result by the standard deviation of the whole set. This is conventionally written as score (*X*) minus mean (mu: μ) divided by sigma (standard deviation: σ):

$$\frac{X - \mu}{\sigma}$$

Once we have a ranked series of z-scores for each term, the second operation in Burrows's delta is to calculate the difference between the words in both texts. This means taking the z-score of, say, the word *the* in text A and subtracting the z-score of the word *the* in text B. Once we have done this for every word that we wish to take into account, we add all of these differences together, a move that is the mathematical equivalent of taking the "Manhattan distance" (named because it moves across the multidimensional grid in right-angled blocks like the streets in the borough of Manhattan, rather than going "as the crow flies") between the multidimensional space plots of these terms.[23] That is, if you plot each of the word frequencies on a multidimensional graph, with one axis for each text and one for frequency, the Manhattan distance is the route you have to take, in 90 degree turns, to get from the term in one text to the same term in the other. In Burrows's delta, the smaller this total addition of differences is, the more likely it is that the two texts were written by the same author.

Burrows's delta has been seen as a successful algorithm for many years, as validated in several studies.[24] It is, mathematically speaking, relatively easy to calculate and seems to produce good results. But it is not entirely known *why* the delta method is so good at clustering texts written by the same author, although recent work has suggested that such a "text distance measure is particularly successful in authorship attribution if emphasizing structural differences of author style profiles without being too much influenced by actual amplitudes," as does Burrows's delta.[25]

Burrows's delta is also a somewhat outdated way of thinking in computational terms for authorship attribution. As of 2019, if one wanted to classify a text as written by one author or another, one would usually construct a model of authors and texts using machine learning methods for identification rather than using a mathematical algorithmic process.[26] This would typically involve profiling a range of features and balancing them against one another within the model that one creates.[27] This is the type of "model thinking" toward which Caroline Levine has recently gestured: ways of thinking that are compatible with humanistic scholarly practice but that move "across scales and media."[28]

But Burrows himself was always cautious about what he was doing. When writing of "authorial fingerprints," for example, he noted that "we do not yet have either proof or promise" of the "very existence" of such a phenomenon.[29] Burrows also points out that, "not unexpectedly," his method "works least well with texts of a genre uncharacteristic of their author and, in one case, with texts far separated in time across a long literary career."[30] So why use the delta method at all? Why not use a better, newer machine learning approach to text classification? In this chapter I am not actually interested in identifying authorship. We know from Chapter 1 that with the exception of Ebershoff's edits to the Sonmi~451 chapter in *E*, David Mitchell is the author of all the diverging segments of *Cloud Atlas*. A machine learning approach might confirm this or get it wrong. But machine learning approaches are also notoriously difficult to inspect. The reasons why a machine learning algorithm has made a specific classification are hard to determine. By contrast, I seek to examine the different linguistic properties of texts written in a variety of linguistic genres by the same author; that is, I wish to look at the *process* of classification rather than the end result. Algorithmic failure, in such cases, becomes intensely productive as it reveals the fault lines of difference within a text. Burrows's delta is a much better method for this type of work. It is an algorithm with a strong track record, backed by mathematics that can be understood by humans, even when operationalized, unlike many newer unsupervised or partly supervised machine learning approaches such as topic modeling, word embedding, or sentiment analysis.[31] This trajectory also brings us to a point where it is worth delving deeper into the underlying assumptions of many stylometric methods.

ASSUMPTIONS ABOUT WRITING STYLE

There are a number of supposed premises on which most stylometric methods rest, and these pertain to their uses as means of identifying authorship. Before moving to work on *Cloud Atlas*, I want briefly to cover these since they bear more broadly on how we conceive of literary style. These assumptions are (1) that authors have a "stylistic naturalism," (2) that stylometry measures subconsciously inscribed features of a text, and (3) that authorship is the underlying textual feature that can be ascertained by the study of quantified formal aesthetics.

The first of these assumptions, that there is a "stylistic naturalism" to an author's works, is premised on the idea that most of us, when writing, do not consider how our works will be read by computers. As Brennan and Greenstadt put it: "In many historical matters, authorship has been unintentially [*sic*] lost to time and it can be assumed that the authors did not have the knowledge or inclination to attempt to hide their linguistic style. However, this may not be the case for modern authors who wish to hide their identity."[32] Language is a tool of communication among people, designed to convey or cause specific effects or affects. The stylistic features of texts are usually considered a contributor to the overarching impact of the communication. Indeed, the scansion and rhythm of a work of prose, for instance, is an important feature of well-written texts, the three-part list being a good example of this in persuasive rhetoric. Yet the selection and prioritization of specific stylistic features (rhythm, cadence, word length, repetition) has consequential effects on the other elements of language that are deployed.

In other words, and to put it bluntly: there are hundreds of stylistic traits of texts that we can measure and determine. It is not possible for an author to hold all of these in working memory while writing; instead, authors write for intended readerly outcomes. The presumption that an imagined reader will react in various ways to one's writing is, or at least should be, the overarching concern when writing. It is this that leads to an idea of what I call a stylistic naturalism: the conceit that authors write in ways that are somehow blind to the processes of the measurement of stylometry.

I would instead seek to couch this slightly differently. Any good author is aware that his or her writing is to be "measured"—so to speak—by a reader. But there is a constant play of balance at work here. In prioritizing one set of measurements—for instance, one could notice as a reader the long, rambling sentences of David Foster Wallace's *Infinite Jest* (1998)—others must inevitably be ignored. Authors are aware that they are being measured; they just must choose which measures are of most significance for their literary purposes. This is a type of "natural" writing, then, that can only be called natural in that it is social and not individual. Anticipated readerly reactions condition the writing process. As Juola puts it, on the one hand, "the assumption of most researchers . . . is that people have a characteristic pattern of language use, a sort of 'authorial fingerprint' that can be detected in their writings. . . . On the other hand, there are also good practical reasons to believe that such fingerprints may be very complex, certainly more complex than simple univariate statistics such as average word length or vocabulary size."[33]

A subassumption underlying the "stylistic naturalism" claim is that authors behave in the same way when writing their various works—or, at least, that stylometric profiles do not substantially change even if authors deliberately try to alter their own styles. This also assumes that authors' own styles do not change naturally with time—a contentious claim.[34] Indeed, in 2014 Ariel Stolerman and colleagues identified shifting stylometric profiles of authors as a key failing in traditional "closed-world" settings.[35] (What Stolerman et al. mean by "closed-world" here is that there is a known list of probable authors, and a computational classifier is trained to correctly attribute unknown works based on known stylometric profiles rather than an environment where any author should be grouped apart from all others.) Yet what happens, in stylometric terms, when an author such as Sarah Waters moves from a neo-Victorian mode to writing about the Second World War? What happens when Hilary Mantel writes about Margaret Thatcher, as opposed to the Tudor setting of *Wolf Hall* (2009)? What happens when Sarah Hall shifts from the feminist utopian genre of *The Carhullan Army* (2007) to the more naturalistic and contemporaneous setting of *The Wolf Border* (2015)?

These questions bring us to the obverse, but somehow linked, counterpart of the assumption that there might be a stylistic naturalism—that is, that stylometry can measure subconsciously inscribed elements of texts. As David Holmes puts it, at the heart of stylometry "lies an assumption that authors have an unconscious aspect to their style, an aspect which cannot consciously be manipulated but which possesses features which are quantifiable and which may be distinctive."[36] This is a different type of stylistic naturalism claim, one that, instead of asserting that authors are behaving in ways that make them unaware of stylometric profiling, looks to an author's subconscious as a site of unchangeable linguistic practice. Indeed, Freudian psychoanalysis has long held that aspects of communication and language harbor revelations about a person over which that person has little or no control.

That said, as I will show shortly, all but one of the different narrative sections of *Cloud Atlas E* can be distinguished from one another through the relative frequencies of the terms *the*, *a*, *I*, *to*, *of*, and *in*. Yet who among us, when writing, is conscious of the relative frequency with which we ourselves use these terms? These seemingly unimportant articles, pronouns, and prepositions are used *when we need them*, not usually as a conscious stylistic choice. In other words, the internalized stylistic profile of our individual communications usually determines how, why, and how frequently these terms are used; they are thought to be beyond our control. Such features are, therefore, conceived of as subconsciously inscribed elements of a text that it is difficult for an author to modify, even if he or she knows that stylometric profiling will be conducted on that text. As I will go on to show, David Mitchell's novel, in its genre play, does manipulate such features.

All of this brings me to the final assumption that I identify in most work on stylometry—namely, that authorship is the underlying textual feature that can be ascertained by the study of quantified formal aesthetics. Of course, there are lengthy poststructuralist debates about what authorship actually means for the reception of texts.[37] There are also disputes in labor and publishing studies about how the individual work of "authorship" is prioritized above all others, when actually there are many forms of labor without which publishing would not be possible: typesetting/text encoding, copyediting, proofreading, programming, graphical design, format creation, digital preservation, platform maintenance, forward-migration of content, security design, marketing, social media promotion, implementation of semantic machine-readability, licensing and legal protocols, and the list goes on. The first challenge here for stylometry is to understand what impact these polyvalent labor practices have in the crafting of a single, authorial profile. As above, we know that David Ebershoff requested substantial line edits to the US edition of *Cloud Atlas*. What sense does it then make to say that the figure identified as "David Mitchell" would correlate to a stylistic profile of this text? At best, if the stylometry is working correctly as an attribution system centered on the author, it would identify this text as a harmonized fusion of Mitchell and Ebershoff.

The challenge that I actually want to pose to these three straw-figures that I have drawn up against many stylometric practices is one foreshadowed by Matt Jockers and others at the Stanford Literary Lab, namely that the author-signal is often neither the sole nor the most important signal that we can detect through stylometry.[38] Indeed, the first pamphlet of the Stanford Literary Lab found that, while the pull of the author-signal was strong and seemed to outweigh other signals, various quantitative signatures also corresponded to those features that we might call "genre."[39] Instead, especially in the case of Mitchell's rich and varied novel, one version of which was heavily edited by another person, and which deliberately employs mimicry and pastiche to achieve its proliferation of stylistic effects, it might be more appropriate to consider the *genre* signals that a text emits.

INVESTIGATING MITCHELL'S GENRES THROUGH COMPUTATIONAL FORMALISM

To investigate the distinctions between the chapters of Mitchell's novels, the first thing that I was keen to check was whether the most basic methods of Burrows's delta analysis of z-scored Manhattan distances could correctly segment and group the different sections of *Cloud Atlas E* within a hierarchical dendrogram. This would, I hoped, ascertain at the highest level whether Mitchell's writing is truly differentiated between chapters or whether there is an underlying authorial stylistic signature at work.[40] To do this, I used the "stylo" package in the statistical programming language R to ascertain the most frequent words (and then the most frequent bigrams for characters) in the whole novel, and then hierarchically to rank these and z-score them above the average for each section.[41] Computing the Manhattan distance on each of these (for words and two-character groupings) rendered the clusterings shown in figures 5 and 6.[42]

What this shows us is not particularly sophisticated or novel, but it does verify the most cursory of stylometric phenomena here. Mitchell's novel is strongly differentiated between sections in terms of the unique lexical content and the order in which the most frequent terms occur. This is the case whether we take the one thousand most frequent words or the one thousand most frequent bigrams. What is perhaps more curious is that the same holds true (although I haven't pictured it) when one computes this based solely on words in the top one thousand that occur in *all* of the narratives (of which there are 284, most of which are common words such as *the*). In other words, the frequency with which Mitchell uses common words varies enough between different sections of the text to enable the analyst to statistically distinguish them from one another.

In fact, we can actually be far more granular than this in a description of the novel and its specific segments. With the exception of "An Orison of Sonmi~451" (and excluding "Sloosha's Crossin'" for the obvious reasons of its total linguistic separation from the rest of the novel), the sections of *Cloud Atlas E* can be distinguished from one another and grouped purely by how frequently Mitchell does or doesn't use the six most frequent words: *the*, *a*, *I*, *to*, *of*, and *in*. When scored by the same classic delta paradigm as above, the only mistaken classifications are that Orison part 1 is billed as part of "The Ghastly Ordeal of Timothy Cavendish" while Orison part 2 is mistaken for a Luisa Rey Mystery segment. All other parts of the novel differ from each other by enough of a margin, by *only* the use of these six words, as to make the chapters distinguishable from each other, as seen in figure 7. To classify accurately

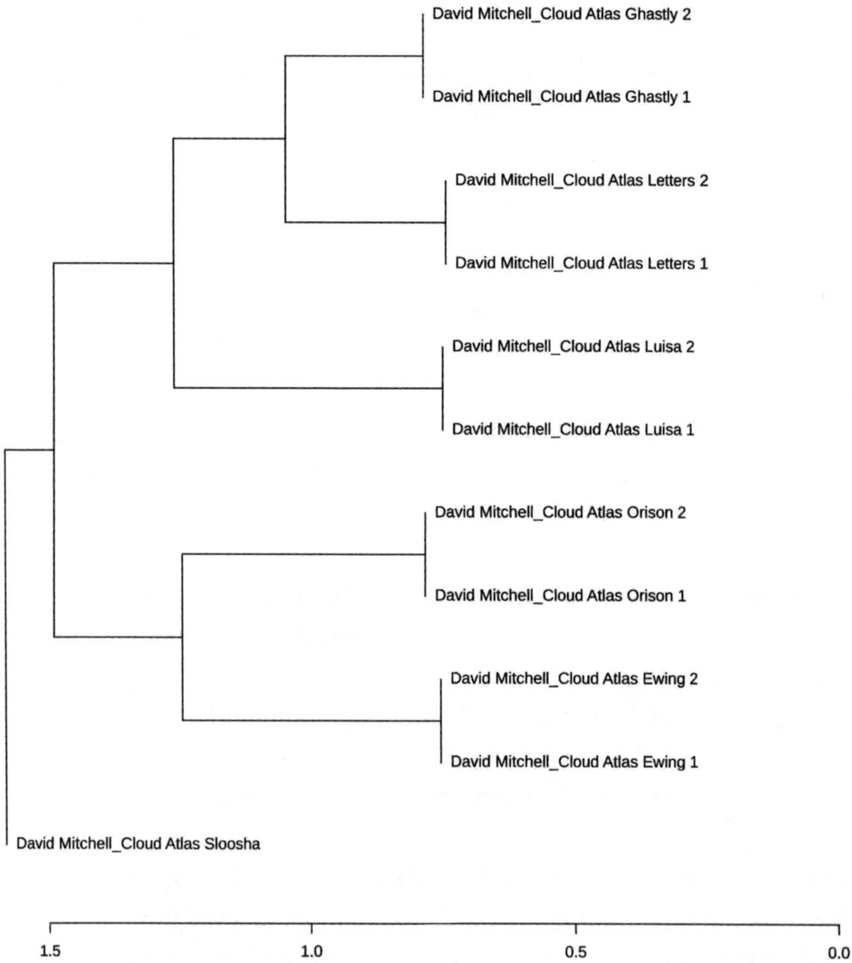

FIGURE 5. The sections of *Cloud Atlas E* grouped by classic delta (z-scored one thousand most frequent words differentiated by Manhattan distance).
Data Source: Digital Appendix 2: Figure 5.

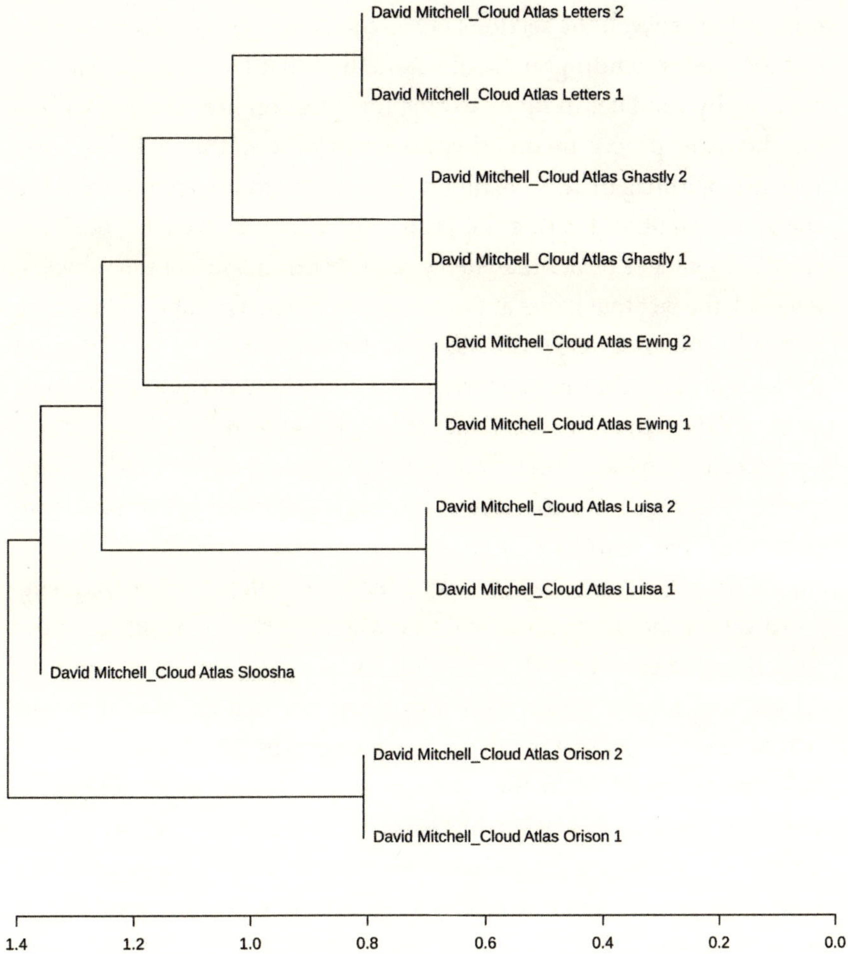

FIGURE 6. The sections of *Cloud Atlas E* grouped by classic delta (z-scored one thousand most frequent bigrams of characters differentiated by Manhattan distance).
Data Source: Digital Appendix 2: Figure 6.

"An Orison of Sonmi~451" with its counterpart requires an expansion to just the twenty most common words in the novel: *the, a, I, to, of, and, in, my, you, was, his, it, for, on, me, is, he, but, that, with.*

Such a low barrier of most-frequent-word counts as an accurate discriminator between the sections of Mitchell's novel is quite remarkable. But the cluster dendrogram analysis method that I am using is hard to statistically validate. In other words, the question here is whether, if I ran this same procedure on other novels that did not share the stylistic variance of Mitchell's text, we might see random groupings and what the statistical likelihood is that the groupings shown above have been arrived at by chance rather than being distinct feature-sets of the subtexts. After all, the fact that it was at the twenty-words mark that the clustering worked, while not below that, is arbitrary and based on my advanced knowledge of the dataset (the novel). This could lead to a type-three error, or HARKING: hypothesizing after results are known.[43]

According to Maciej Eder, validation of cluster-analysis dendrograms can be undertaken, to an extent, by using a technique called bootstrap consensus tree plotting.[44] Essentially, this technique reruns the clustering algorithm over multiple iterations for many different most-frequent-word values and produces a final tree when a certain percentage of the underlying trees agree with each other. Running this same procedure on *Cloud Atlas E*'s one hundred most frequent words at 93 percent and 94 percent confidence (that is, one percentage point higher or lower than the six-word threshold where the algorithm breaks down), we would expect, from the above investigation, to see the correct clustering of all but "An Orison of Sonmi~451" at the 93 percent mark. Indeed, figures 8 and 9 (one at 94 percent and one at 93 percent) seem to give some validation to the findings.

This validation technique and underlying clustering analysis tells us a few things about the initial, internal stylistic properties of Mitchell's novel. First, if one is only interested in the identification and distinction of the chapters of the novel using the most minimal feature-set possible, then, in fact, 92 percent of the distribution of words between the different sections of the text is irrelevant. This is not to say that they are not also different, just that they are more closely correlated than the 8 percent

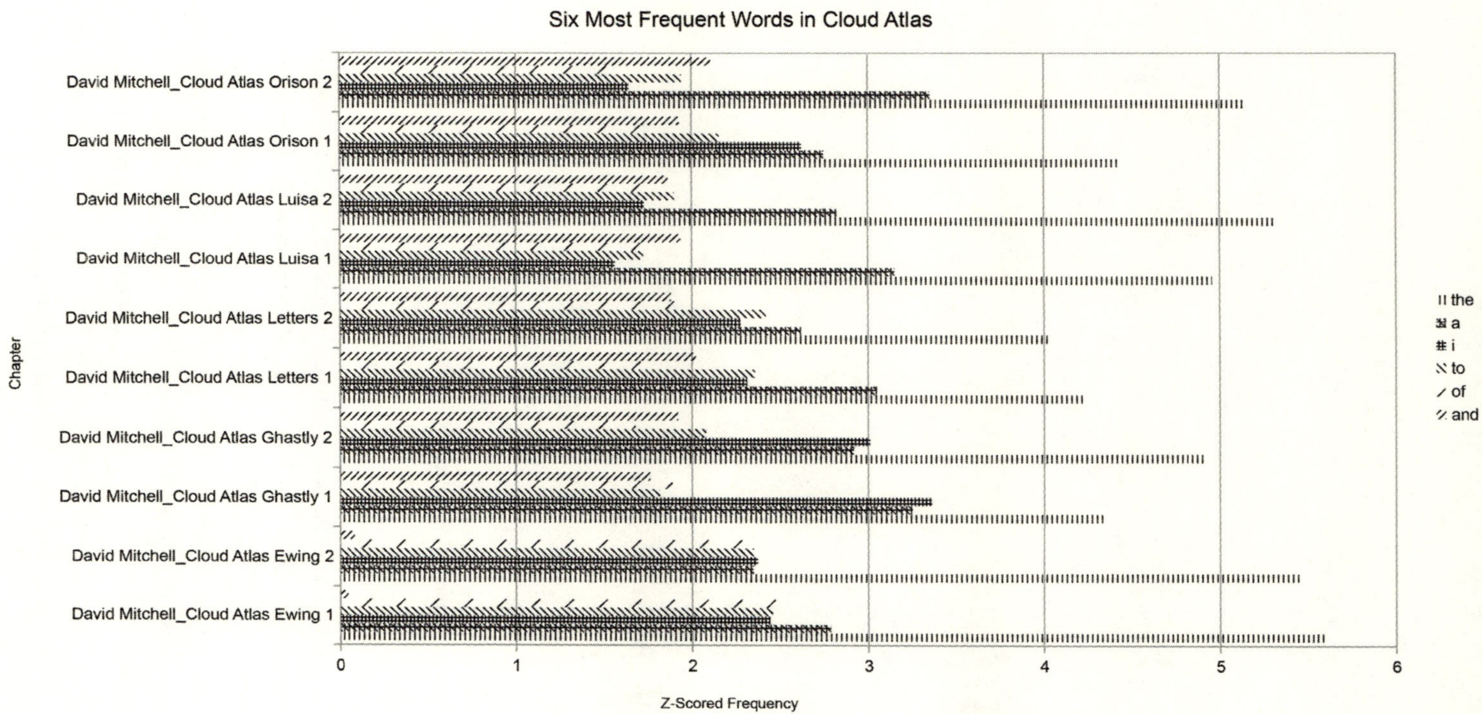

FIGURE 7. The z-scored frequency occurrence of the six most frequent words in *Cloud Atlas E* in all chapters except "Sloosha's Crossin."

Data Source: Digital Appendix 2: Figure 7.

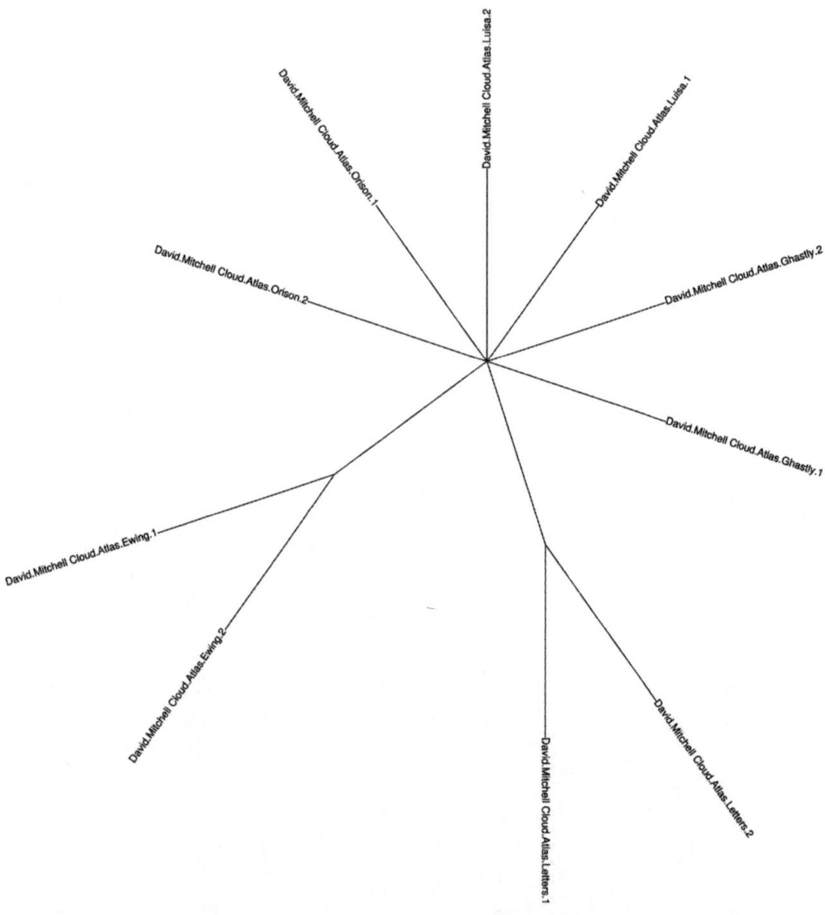

FIGURE 8. *Cloud Atlas E* classified using 2 to 101 most frequently used words in a bootstrap consensus tree with 94 percent consensus of underlying clusters.
Data Source: Digital Appendix 2: Figure 8.

that act as strongly discriminative markers of each section. Second, while a conventional reader might argue that it is the unique thematic and stylistic elements of each subtext that are important ("orisons," nuclear reactors, sea storms, retirement homes, etc.), the shifts in grammatical register that Mitchell deploys to distinguish his chapters from one another force perceptible microchanges among words that usually go unobserved.

Two other experiments are relevant here, and I will cover them quickly. The first that is worthwhile in the realm of authorship attribution

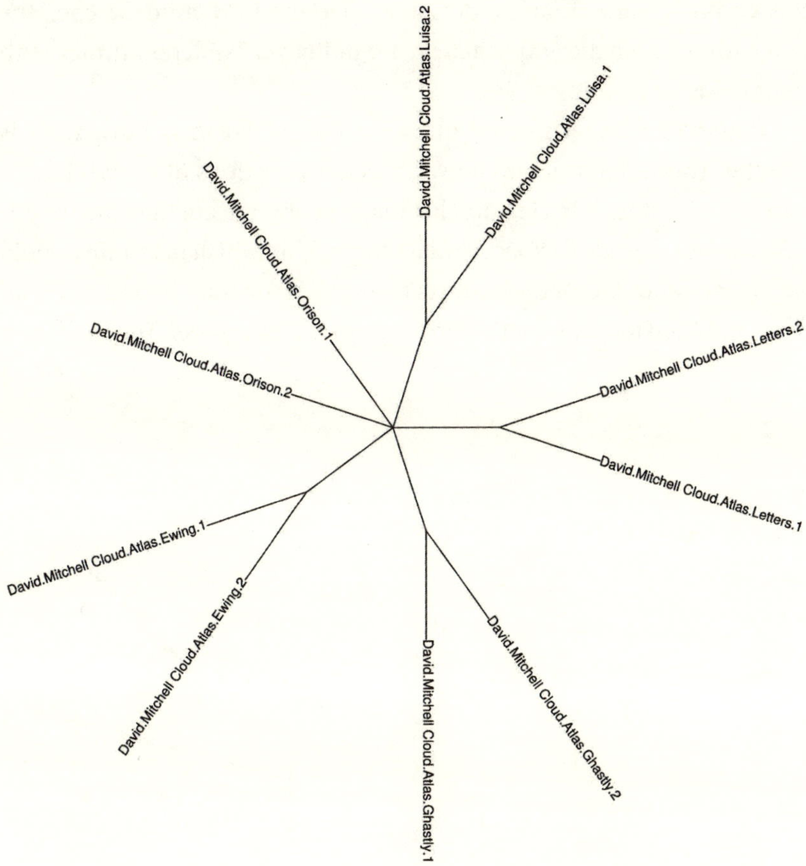

FIGURE 9. *Cloud Atlas E* classified using 2 to 101 most frequently used and shared words in a bootstrap consensus tree with 93 percent consensus of underlying clusters. All but "An Orison of Sonmi~451" are clustered correctly.
Data Source: Digital Appendix 2: Figure 9.

techniques is to validate the claim by a character in the novel that "Ewing puts me in mind of Melville's bumbler Cpt. Delano in 'Benito Cereno.' "[45] While the character may be put in mind of that text, conventional authorship attribution methods using Burrows's delta cluster Ewing neither with Melville's *Moby-Dick* nor with "Benito Cereno" (see figure 10). Indeed, even comparing just the top four words in the Ewing chapter alone against Melville's novels is enough to differentiate them—that is, using nothing except the frequency order of *the*, *of*, *and*, and *a*.[46] While this chapter may put a human reader in mind of Captain Delano in "Benito Cereno," the two authors, Melville and Mitchell, are doing very different things with their prose stylistics.

The second experimental question that is worth investigating is whether this differentiation between generic sections of *Cloud Atlas* is unique or whether it is a feature that may be common among other multivocal novels. The ideal experimental setup within which to test this would be to take other multigeneric texts from the same time period as *Cloud Atlas* and then to reconduct the modeling on these works. The challenge,

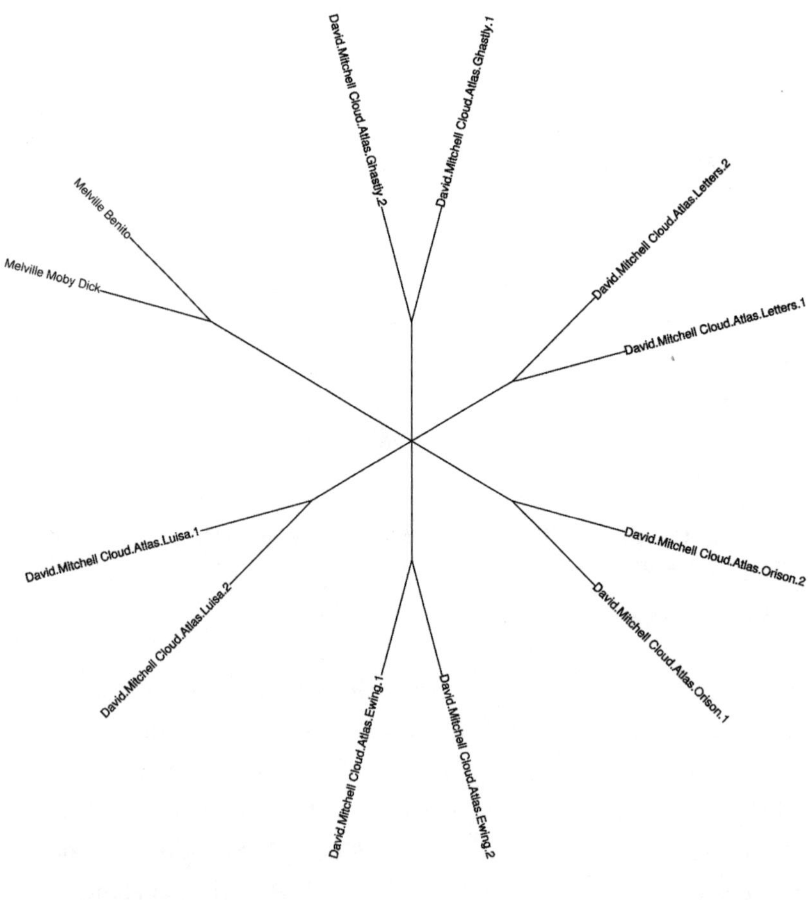

FIGURE 10. Melville and *Cloud Atlas E* compared by delta cluster bootstrap consensus tree at 0.8 consensus with twenty to one hundred most frequent words.
Data Source: Digital Appendix 2: Figure 10.

as above, is that the labor in preparing such a corpus for a minor correlative experiment is huge. For this reason it is far easier to turn to nineteenth-century novels that nonetheless also possess a multigenericity or multivocality. For the purpose of a small-scale test, I decided to use Bram Stoker's well-known 1897 novel *Dracula.* This text works well for such an exercise since its chapters are divided into different documentary registers within its epistolary mode. For instance, we have the diaries/journals of the characters Jonathan Harker, Mina Murray/Harker, and Dr. John Seward. I hypothesized that each of these diaries should, to some extent, present itself within a differentiated stylistic framework. After all, Stoker wishes the reader to believe that each could have been written by a figure with his or her own stylistic naturalism.

The comparison to *Cloud Atlas* here is hardly perfect. Whereas *Cloud Atlas* spans a wide range of subjects and ranges across epochs of time, with each section mediated through a known and recognizable generic form, *Dracula* is a far more confined novel. The various diaries in *Dracula* all revolve around the same central plot, for instance. They are all set within roughly the same time (or, at least, they are barely temporally separated compared to *Cloud Atlas*'s leaps into the far-distant future). Regardless, then, of the challenges of finding a suitable comparison text in *Dracula*, I nonetheless hoped that the novel might prove similar *enough* to give some initial confidence to either a positive finding (that *Dracula* exhibited the same differentiation) or a negative result (that *Dracula*'s sections do *not* differ in the same way as the chapters in *Cloud Atlas*). Put otherwise: I wanted to know whether the intradiegetic voicing of *Dracula* could fool Burrows's delta method into thinking that each diary was written by a separate author, as does *Cloud Atlas.*

To conduct the experiment, I took several diary sections from *Dracula*: Harker's diary from chapters 1 and 2; the Murray diary portions from chapters 4 and 8; and Seward's diary from chapters 12 and 13. The textual version that I used was the freely available Project Gutenberg edition produced by Chuck Greif and the Online Distributed Proofreading Team. In this way I had six segments purportedly written, in Stoker's fiction, by three different authors, with two sections each. Knowing that the chapters of *Cloud Atlas* can be differentiated from one another using just twenty words, I opted to begin my experiment on *Dracula*'s voicing by using the thirty most common terms (as a generous head start). At this level Stoker's novel shows a strong similarity between Harker's diary segments. These are clearly written in a similar and, to some extent distinctive, register. Chapters 1 and 2 are identified as written by the same author even using just thirty words (and, in fact, at the lower level of ten most frequent words). But that is where the similarities end. Murray and Seward are terribly confused at this point. Chapters 4 and 13 are classified on their own branches, while Chapters 7 and 12 are misclassified as by the same author at thirty most frequent words. Even at much higher levels of word usage, chapters are misclassified. At the five-hundred-word mark, for instance, Seward and Harker are both accurately clustered. Murray, however, remains misplaced as though authored by two different writers. In my experiments it took 566 most frequent words to accurately cluster all diary portions by the correct intradiegetic authors.

The extreme differentiation between the chapters of *Cloud Atlas* is not a feature shared by *Dracula*. That said, Harker's narrative does stand separately from the other sections, while Seward and Murray become confused and clustered together (in fact, correctly in an authorship attribution sense, given that both are really authored by Stoker). It could also be that temporal properties of the text's authorship are being reflected in this analysis. On the one hand, it seems clear that chapters 1 and 2 (Harker) are simply split in two from one initial run of writing; and these cluster closely together. On the other hand, I do not know when the Murray and Seward narratives were composed relative to one another, but it is possible that they were more intertwined than the initial Harker chapters. As Robert Eighteen-Bisang and Elizabeth Miller, commenting on Stoker's notes, point out, it is very difficult to determine the chronology of the novel's authorship.[47] As above, there are good reasons why this is an imperfect comparison, but it is my wager that the substantial stylistic, measurable differences between the chapters of *Cloud Atlas* are not shared by many other novels.

In some ways, though, using these methods is more of a performance stunt than a help with close reading. Certainly, the fact that we can distinguish between Mitchell's registers using only function words tells us something. Namely: these chapters differ from each other not just in the realm of theme but also in grammar. This is probably not surprising to a reader of Mitchell's novel. It does, however, open the way for a more detailed investigation of the linguistic differences between the text's sections.

There are differences of linguistic style that would be interesting to test with the above measures but that pose challenges, even within a computational environment. For instance, does Mitchell write his men and women in different ways? As I will discuss below, the "Luisa Rey" chapter, one of the few with a female protagonist, is among the most linguistically different from other sections of the novel. But binary tests for gender in language are both socially complicated (how is the gender identity determined and in what terms?) and linguistically frustrating (are comparative contexts for speakers identical?). In the latter realm, for instance, within the context of *Cloud Atlas*, it would be useful to be able to compare the language of the male archivist with that of the female Sonmi~451. But since the archivist's language is near-universally that of a question while Sonmi's is usually an answer, the linguistic structures that we might here measure and assign to a gender position are prewarped by their functional role. Question-words will appear with great frequency among the archivist's words, while they are barely present in Sonmi's. In short: there are too many variables in operation to be able to assign differences in speech pattern between Mitchell's characters to gender. Often this is the way when close reading with computers: one can be lulled into believing that one has measured one phenomenon when, in fact, the posited causal relationship between the words and the result in the narrative is, after all, only correlative.[48]

MICROTECTONICS

These microtectonic, subsurface shifts of linguistics that constitute changes to genre and register between the chapters of *Cloud Atlas* could also reasonably be expected to remanifest in part-of-speech (PoS) trigrams. A "trigram" refers to a set of three consecutive entities, while by "part-of-speech" I here mean a named word type (noun subject → verb → noun object, for example, is a part-of-speech trigram). After all, the reconfiguration of the frequency of basic blocks of speech, such as determiners (articles), seems likely to affect the grammatical composition of each one of the texts.

To investigate what might happen to Mitchell's prose within the linguistic variations of his chapters, I used the feature-rich part-of-speech tagging software known as the "Stanford tagger," which uses a cyclic dependency network to assign a set of symbols to each part of speech.[49] Tagging parts of speech, however, is not an easy computational problem.[50] Many words have multiple functions and are highly dependent on the context. This method of PoS tagging uses a set of trained models (on a broader English corpus) to look for similarities in linguistic structure and demonstrates a 97 percent accuracy in test runs, although I have here again ignored "Sloosha's Crossin'" in my determination of accuracy. It is not likely that the tagger would work well against Mitchell's mutilated fictional language of that central chapter. The 97 percent accuracy benchmark, remember, means that for every one hundred words of the novel, three will be misclassified.

As an example of how this tagger works, let us take the sentence "We make sail with the morning tide," which comes from the first chapter of Ewing's narrative.[51] The Stanford tagger transforms this sentence into a symbolic dictionary of parts of speech. In this case the output reads: "PRP VBP VB IN DT NN NN." A full lookup of these abbreviations is given in table 2. Translated back into English, this means: "we [personal pronoun] make [verb, non-third-person singular present] sail [verb, base form] with [preposition or subordinating conjunction] the [determiner] morning [noun, singular or mass] tide [noun, singular or mass]." Note here that we can see an erroneous transformation: *morning* is actually being used as an adjective, but it is misclassified as a noun. *Sail* is also misclassified as a verb when, in reality, it is the direct object of *make*. Using the Stanford tagger, I converted each chapter of *Cloud Atlas E* into its corresponding PoS version, yielding largely unreadable text files of the underlying linguistic structure of the novel, as determined by a 97 percent–accurate machine reading approach (the results are available in Appendix B: Digital Appendix 2: Part-of-Speech Tagging).

Tag	Description
CC	Coordinating conjunction
CD	Cardinal number
DT	Determiner
EX	Existential *there*
FW	Foreign word
IN	Preposition or subordinating conjunction
JJ	Adjective
JJR	Adjective, comparative
JJS	Adjective, superlative
LS	List item marker
MD	Modal
NN	Noun, singular or mass
NNS	Noun, plural
NNP	Proper noun, singular
NNPS	Proper noun, plural
PDT	Predeterminer
POS	Possessive ending
PRP	Personal pronoun
PRP$	Possessive pronoun
RB	Adverb
RBR	Adverb, comparative
RBS	Adverb, superlative
RP	Particle
SYM	Symbol
UH	Interjection
VB	Verb, base form
VBD	Verb, past tense
VBG	Verb, gerund or present participle
VBN	Verb, past participle
VBP	Verb, non-third-person singular present
VBZ	Verb, third-person singular present
WDT	Wh-determiner
WP	Wh-pronoun
WP$	Possessive wh-pronoun
WRB	Wh-adverb

TABLE 2. Parts of speech produced by the Stanford tagger, derived here from the Penn Treebank classification.

The first aspect that I wanted to know was whether PoS tagging provided another way by which we might group the chapters of *Cloud Atlas E* as distinct from one another. To achieve this, I began by running bootstrap consensus tree imaging (see above) of the top one thousand PoS components that occur throughout the novel, insisting that 90 percent of them agreed with one another in how the texts were clustered. Indeed, as shown in figure 11, it does appear that in nine hundred of the one thousand iterations on which I performed the cluster analysis, it is possible to group the texts by the PoS trigrams.

That said, the sensitivity of differentiation between the chapters is here far less than when using word frequency. In fact, we cannot use the twenty

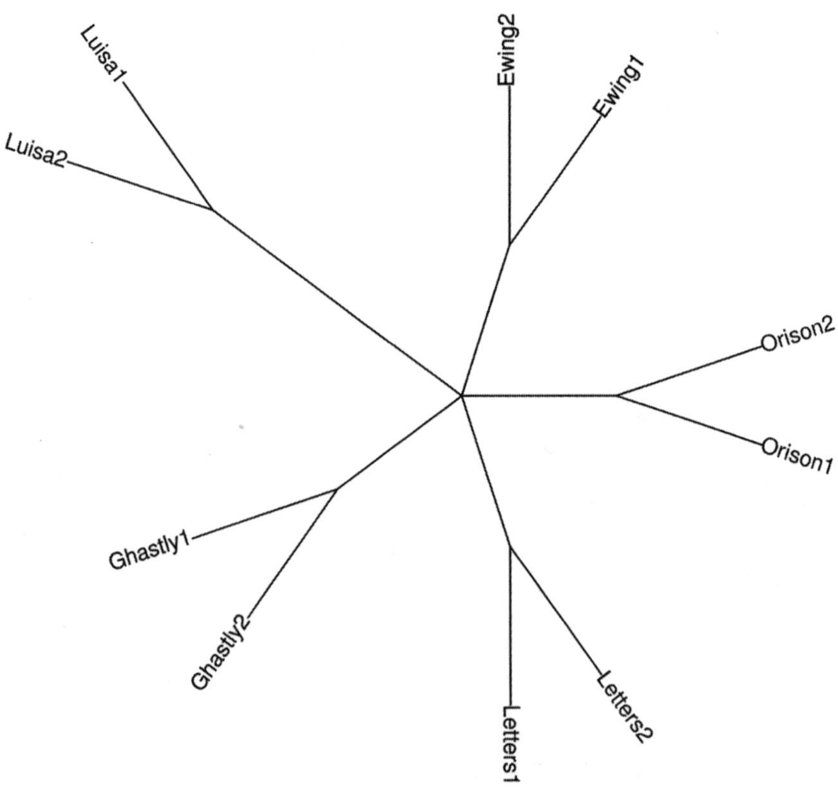

FIGURE 11. Bootstrap consensus tree of part-of-speech tagged version of *Cloud Atlas E* including all unique PoS constructs of one thousand most common PoS trigrams.
Data Source: Digital Appendix 2: Figure 11.

most common parts of speech because there is too much overlap. There is also an insufficiently strong signal if we use only the PoS trigrams that are shared between the sections of the novel. Where the text becomes interesting is when we see standout deviations of linguistic patterns that occur in certain of Mitchell's chapters and not in others.

Consider figure 12, for example. This shows the one thousand most-to-least common PoS trigrams throughout the text, sorted by an average across each portion of the text. It also provides a useful visual index of where the texts vary from one another in terms of their unique linguistic features. If one looks approximately 1⁄15 of the way into the graph, there is one isolated point that juts out well above the others in height. This marker turns out to represent the fact that the Luisa Rey portion of *Cloud Atlas* uses the figuration NNP NNP VBZ (proper noun singular → proper noun singular → verb, third-person singular present) to a far higher extent than any of the other chapters.

This NNP NNP VBZ formula comes about because of the Luisa Rey section's unique tendency to reuse the full name of its characters before any present-tense verb. To take but the first few instances, we can clearly see "Rufus Sixsmith leans," "Luisa Rey hears," "Maharaj Aja says," "Javier Moses leafs" (*P*) / "Javier Gomez leafs" (*E*), "Nancy O'Hagan has," "Jerry Nussbaum wipes," "Dom Grelsch breaks," "Joe Napier watches," "Albert Grimaldi scans" (*P*) / "Alberto Grimaldi scans" (*E*), "Isaac Sachs closes," "Roland Jakes drips," and "Bill Smoke watches," among many, many other instances.[52] (Note also here the renaming of Javier Moses / Javier Gomez between editions; this affects whether we can read Javier as the son of the threatened "Dr. Moses" at the Seaboard plant.)[53] While this trigram is present at around the 0.1 percent mark in all other chapters of *Cloud Atlas E*, the Luisa Rey portion is distinct in having almost ten times as many relative occurrences.

That said, although figure 12 is helpful in determining which linguistic features are of interest and are unique to each section, a better way to achieve this is to calculate the standard deviation from the average frequency and to note outlier points by comparing them to this. For instance, in the example I was just using, the average frequency of occurrence of the NNP NNP VBZ is 0.30. The standard deviation (that is, the average amount by which every chapter frequency for NNP NNP VBZ varies

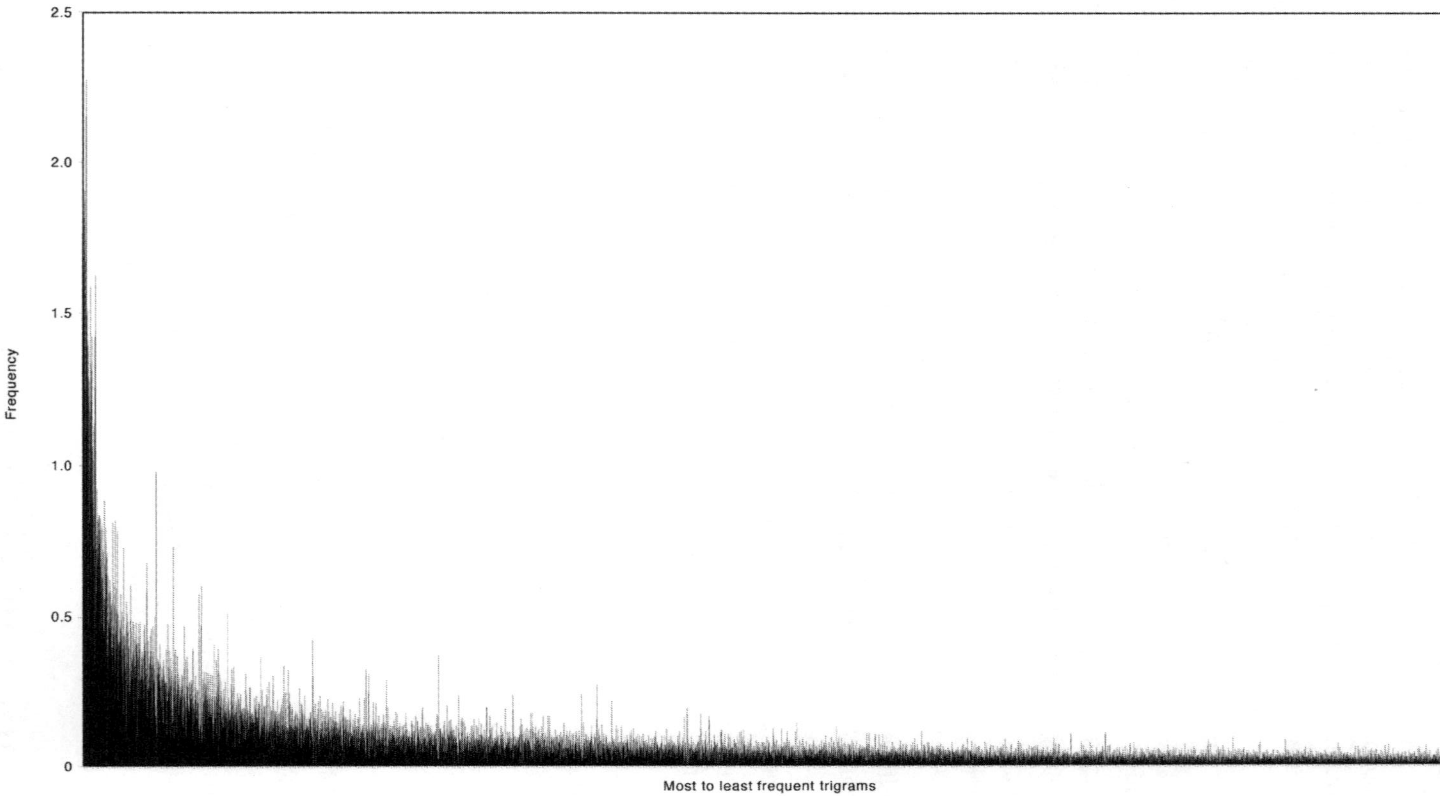

FIGURE 12. The one thousand most common PoS trigrams in *Cloud Atlas E* across all sections except “Sloosha’s Crossin.”
Data Source: Digital Appendix 2: Figure 12.

from this average) of this line is 0.33. The Luisa Rey chapter, at 0.97, is 1.98 standard deviations above the mean, which, assuming a normal distribution of PoS trigrams across the whole text, is in the top 5 percent of anomalous results. If we plot the standard deviations and remove all entries from the table where no single text reaches a 1.9 standard deviation, we can create a stacked percentage chart (figure 13) that can serve as a strong visual index of unique part-of-speech formulations.

In this chart the vertical width of each striated band represents the relative use of the 123 trigrams that score at a standard deviation of 1.9 as though the sum of each column were 100 percent. This allows us to visualize the difference between sections for each trigram without the actual frequency values between each trigram masking internal differences. In other words, columns cannot be compared to each other on an absolute basis. The fact that one column is taller than another does *not* mean that the trigrams on the right that are wider than those on the left actually occur more frequently. What it does mean is that, in relative terms, the taller the bar, the more frequently a section uses a trigram *compared to the other sections within its column*. Indeed, the results toward the right of the graph are often the difference of only a single greater occurrence of a trigram between sections (and given that we have a 3 percent error rate, we should be wary here). In this sense such results are both more *and* less reliable: they are more reliable as markers of distinction, since they occur precisely a single unit more or less than counterpart chapters, error rate notwithstanding; they are less reliable because the variance is far more likely to have been introduced by utter chance rather than any aesthetic/stylistic control on Mitchell's part.

Indeed, on this type of calculation and visualization, the Luisa Rey portion of the narrative differs the most from all others, with seventy-four out of one thousand trigrams occurring at the 1.9 standard deviation mark. For example, another formulation that is uncommon among the other parts of the novel except for the Luisa Rey section is VBZ DT NN (verb, third-person singular present → determiner → noun, singular or mass). This is partly a result of the novel's present-tense setting and consists of formulations such as "hits the sidewalk," "slams the balcony," "hears a clunk," "shows the world," and so on.[54] Indeed, the present-tense narration of the Luisa

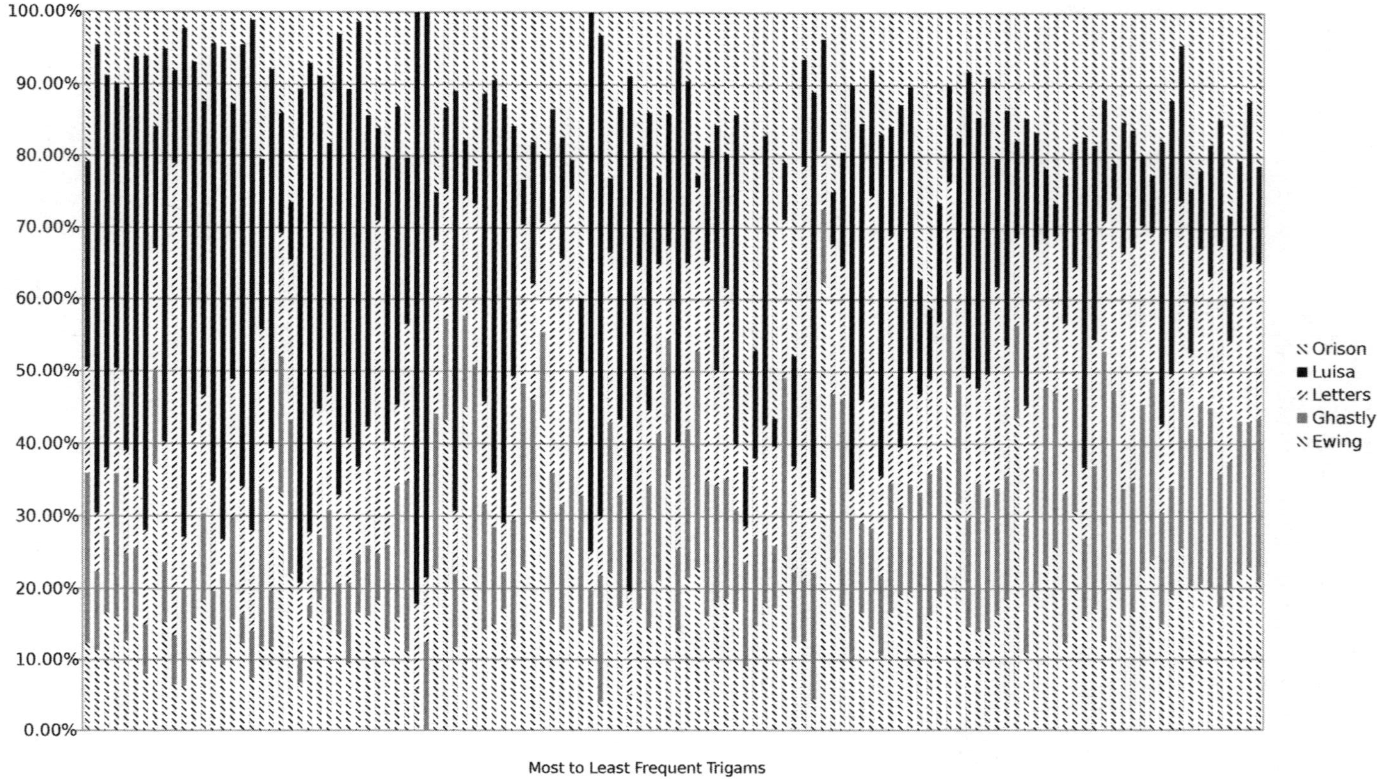

FIGURE 13. PoS trigrams at 1.9 standard deviations in *Cloud Atlas E* as a stacked percentage chart.
Data Source: Digital Appendix 2: Figure 13.

Rey chapter gives it a unique flavor, and there are many instances of VBZ-type formulations that do not exist elsewhere in the novel. For instance, we also see NNP VBZ DT (proper noun, singular → verb third-person singular present → determiner) with a much greater frequency in this chapter than elsewhere ("Luisa inspects the," "Luisa manages a," "Javier attaches the," etc.).[55] In fact, as a general rule the Luisa Rey segment can be said to differ characteristically from the other sections of *Cloud Atlas* in its use of present-tense narration that includes VBZ formulations occurring with 1.9 standard-deviations more frequently than the average of other portions of the text. As one would expect as a correlative, many VBD (verb, past tense) formulations occur at significantly lower levels in the Luisa Rey narrative. This is clearly part of the generic distinction of the thriller formation of this portion of the novel. The chapter is lent a fast pace by the present-tense trot of the text. The reuse of full names at the start of each chapter serves to seemingly relocate the action in a slamming fashion, a total and distinct replacement of the reader through full-name appellation.

That said, the use of present-tense narration for crime thrillers is not necessarily as common as might be believed when reading the Luisa Rey chapter. Dan Brown's Robert Langdon novels are written in the past tense, and sampling recent thrillers shows a set of novels that move between tenses. For instance, Robert Harris, in thrillers such as *An Officer and a Spy* (2013), alternates between present-tense and past-tense narration to build a projected frame diary around the central historical plot. Likewise, John le Carré's *A Delicate Truth* (2013) also segues between tenses. Ian Rankin deploys this shifting technique in his crime fiction. While narration of his protagonist, Rebus, sticks largely to the past tense, in works such as *Tooth and Nail* (1992; originally titled *Wolfman*), the interior monologue of the antagonist murderer is lent an urgency through an abrupt move to the present. As a final example, Elly Griffiths's Ruth Galloway crime-fiction novels are written in the present tense, her Stephens and Mephisto series in the past. While it is possible that a formal quantitative study of contemporary crime-thriller fiction might reveal a prevalence for one narrative perspective, my anecdotal survey here leads to the hypothesis that such novels—or at least authorial oeuvres of those producing such work—are usually of hybrid tensing.

Of course, in the case of Luisa Rey, the present tense is the logical choice to *differentiate* the crime section from the other portions of the novel. This is not an unusual way of writing for a crime thriller; far from it. But the rationale for the selection of tense must be seen in contrast to the remainder of the novel and the desire to firmly delineate the stylistic profile of this chapter.

The next most linguistically distinct portion of *Cloud Atlas E* is "The Pacific Journal of Adam Ewing," which contains fifteen trigrams that occur at over or under 1.9 standard deviations from the mean (albeit not all of which seem to distinguish the chapter from others in a reliable fashion; see above). Indeed, Ewing's narrative can be categorized as overusing IN DT NNS (preposition or subordinating conjunction → determiner → noun, plural), represented in formulations such as "on the stairs," "than the digits," "through the paths" (italicized in *E*), "inside the coils"; DT NNS IN (determiner → noun, plural → preposition or subordinating conjunction), seen in "the fangs of," "the pearls of," "the works of"; and NNP CC PRP (proper noun, singular → coordinating conjunction → personal pronoun), which are mostly instances of "Henry & I."[56] Put otherwise, the Ewing narrative is linguistically distinct in order to achieve two features of its generic register and thematic concerns that are important for the text. The first is that, in the use of DT NNS IN and NNP CC PRP, the Pacific Journal chapter gives many more comparative and locative descriptions of characters and artifacts than do other portions of the text. This lends a degree of formal pedantry to the voice here that is not present elsewhere. In the second case the NNP CC PRP formulation is integral to establishing the supposed friendship with Henry Goose that leads to Ewing's near-downfall. But the tight usage of "Henry & I" here, consistently with no slippage, contributes to the historical imaginary of the 1850s writing style, as from an era where grammar was "correct" and people wrote in a formal register. This is an aspect to which I will return in Chapter 3.

By contrast, Ewing's narrative is short on JJ JJ NN (adjective → adjective → noun, singular or mass) and RB JJ NN (adverb → adjective → noun, singular or mass). While Luisa Rey's narrative contains a "hopelessly uneven gunfight," a "mostly empty wine" bottle, and "very little traffic," such formulations are rare in the "Ewing" diary.[57] This lends a specificity or qualifying nuance to the Luisa Rey narrative. It is also, though, clearly a trope of hackneyed, overwritten airport thrillers to modify every term that is used in this way.

The other sections of the novel are not so clearly differentiated from one another by part-of-speech formation. The "Letters from Zedelghem," "The Ghastly Ordeal of Timothy Cavendish," and "An Orison of Sonmi~451" chapters are possessed of far fewer statistically significant linguistic outliers than the other sections of the novel. For instance, one of only two outliers in "The Ghastly Ordeal" is the underused RB DT JJ trigram (adverb → determiner → adjective). An example of such a formulation from the Pacific Journal is Te Whanga being described as "nearly an inland" sea.[58] What it might mean that "The Ghastly Ordeal of Timothy Cavendish" does not use such a formulation as frequently as the other chapters, however, is unclear to me. This is where various computational techniques break down without some imaginative thinking; the mechanistic description itself is insufficient. It is undoubtedly *true* that the language in this section of the novel is behaving differently at this point as a knock-on consequence of thematic and genre stylistics. But why the RB DT JJ configuration should be significant—and what this linguistic formation (a premodifier) denotes/does—is not obvious, at least to me.[59] This is not, for instance, a known trait of gender-specific communication, at least in professional legal writing (i.e., the formulation RB DT JJ is not known to occur specifically in relation to any gender characteristic of author or subject).[60] Certainly, Cavendish is a bombastic character, overly sure of himself, so perhaps the qualifying nature of such adverbial statements would be contrary to his nature. Such a reading, though, is a bit of a leap, since the character is also fond of overwriting his narrative. Nonetheless, these linguistic formations—just some of the many that the amplifying visualization technique allows us to see—are the substrate on which Mitchell's genre effects are built, whether or not we can understand why.

SEEING THE OCEAN FOR THE DROPS

I have attempted in this chapter to provide a demonstration of the ways in which computational methodologies can be used to garner new linguistic empirical evidence that can then be fed back into traditional close-reading and theoretical approaches. There are many more techniques to be explored here, particularly in the realm of machine learning for authorship attribution. What I have tried to show, though, is that digital methodologies need not be utilitarian in the way that they approach literature. We can use these approaches in symbiosis with more conventional literary interpretation. Indeed, I have given significant thought to what we mean by "literary style" through a questioning of the conditions under which, I contend, we frequently assume that writers work. This theorizing was made possible through the digital approaches of stylometry. I then moved to examine how we might use a computational approach to pull out significantly more common part-of-speech patterns among portions of a novel. This, in turn, opened the possibility of a more informed linguistic understanding of Mitchell's genre techniques.

The benefits of such an approach are reciprocal: literary theory can be enriched through a new set of methodologies and the cracks in our thinking that they expose, while literary criticism is armed with a fresh set of formal observations that are difficult to spot by eye but that can be extracted using computational techniques. In many ways the methods I use here and that I have described as a microscope can also be understood through a different, imperfect, somewhat mixed, metaphor: filtration. As the ocean of the text is sifted for material that we might use, its drop-like composition at the linguistic level that causes the macro-oceanic effects can be better discerned. Such a forced metaphor is apt for thinking about *Cloud Atlas*. For as Mitchell's Ewing closes the novel, he asks of the reader: what is any ocean but a multitude of drops?

Where to from here? In Chapter 1 I argued that the transtextual variance of *Cloud Atlas* refocused the novel on the central importance of the *archive* to the work's own textual-historical world-building. From the linguistic analysis in this chapter I want finally to draw attention to a specific feature of the novel's microtectonics, as I have called them. Specifically: *Cloud Atlas* is a novel about power structures and the interrelations of wholes to parts.

Such a view is also reflective of Mitchell's broader corpus. For instance, in *David Mitchell's Post-Secular World: Buddhism, Belief and the Urgency of Compassion*, Rose Harris-Birtill—who perhaps knows more about the whole body of David Mitchell's writings than any other living critic—argues that the interrelatedness of Mitchell's grand "macro-novel" or "uber-book" is best represented through the cartographic metaphor of the Buddhist mandala. In Harris-Birtill's view, formed from extensive interviews with the author, Mitchell is crafting an epic-scale world across his books and short stories, over a gigantic historical period. Yet Harris-Birtill also notes that this macronovel is constructed from differently denominated units: "the smaller scale of the short narrative unit, the larger scale of the novel, and the macro-scale of the fictional universe." For Harris-Birtill it is "the 'smaller' narrative unit" that "is unquestionably prioritised in [Mitchell's] writing process";[61] a focus on the minute—the drops of the ocean—builds toward the total of the macrowork.

Against Claire Larsonneur, Paul Harris, and Robin Visel, Harris-Birtill shuns the metaphor of the "fractal" in understanding Mitchell's novelistic worldview.[62] Yet, whether we use the image of a fractal or a kaleidoscope of differentiated repetition, *Cloud Atlas* nonetheless iteratively and structurally repeats its own macrolevel power relations at the level of the subunit.[63] The clearest incarnation of this is the less-than-subtle birthmarks that the characters from the novel's different time periods almost all share. By physically inscribing identical marks on his characters' bodies, Mitchell asks the reader to look for structural and thematic similarities in narrative. It is also clear that the narratives are *not* the same; each has a specificity even while it possesses commonalities with and overlaps the others.

This focus on the relationship between the part and the whole has a lengthy and hearty philosophical pedigree. It is most pronounced in the dialogue between Hegelian idealism and the Frankfurt School thought of Theodor W. Adorno.[64] In Hegelian ontotheology it is only in totality that truth is found: "Das Wahre ist das Ganze" (the whole is the true).[65] By contrast, while Adorno retains some vestige of theology, his is a reworked materialism that, as Robert Hullot-Kentor puts it, shines "the image of divine light not to behold the deity as its source above, but to illuminate a damaged nature below."[66]

Adorno recognizes that wholes and totalities can possess a sort of truth, particularly with respect to the dialectical method: "the dialectical method as a whole is an attempt to cope with this demand by freeing thought from the spell of the instant and developing it in far-reaching conceptual structures."[67] In his well-known *Minima Moralia* (1951), however, Adorno famously states that "the whole is the untrue."[68]

Adorno expands on this statement in his later "The Experiential Content of Hegel's Philosophy": "'The whole is the untrue,' not merely because the thesis of totality is itself untruth, being the principle of domination inflated to the absolute; the idea of a positivity that can master everything that opposes it through the superior power of a comprehending spirit is the mirror image of the experience of the superior coercive force inherent in everything that exists by virtue of its consolidation under domination."[69] For Adorno, the dialectical model of knowledge is one saturated with domination. At the moment that an object becomes classified, its specificity is absorbed and lost in the name of understanding: "to think is to identify."[70] In Hegelian logic this falls under the heading of "determinate negation": "the negation of [the concrete object's] particular content" in order to achieve synthesis.[71] For a trivial instance, at what point does a dog become a "dog" rather than one specific unidentified hairy organic mass? At what point do we recognize or ignore the specificities of the objects that we classify? For "objects do not go into their concepts without leaving a remainder."[72]

Such a "remainder" is the specificity of objects that defies their aggregation into untrue wholes. To give primacy to the specificity of the object is the aim of Adorno's project of negative dialectics, against Hegel's assertion that thinking inheres in the identity (synthesis) between identity and nonidentity (contradiction). In many ways there is also a *utopian* impulse in this focus on the specific, the one-time, the unique. It lies in the insistence that we do not simply aggregate upward to classes and assumed knowledge but instead focus on the differentiated that will never happen again. It is not necessarily an anticollectivist drive—Adorno's work is, after all, situated within a Marxist lineage—but it is also a celebration of difference and individual qualities.

When appraising the relationship connecting David Mitchell's short stories, novels, and his macroworld, it is easy to erase this relationship between the specific and the whole. Finding connections in order to link and aggregate is a satisfying literary-critical activity. Yet it is also the case that Mitchell's component stories, chapters, and novels have their own unique features that cannot just be minimized for the sake of forging connections.

The unique language of the chapters of *Cloud Atlas* that I have examined here is one such feature that demonstrates a drive toward uniqueness and, at the same time, to connection. In this chapter I have shown a variety of ways in which we *can* delineate the literary language of the chapters of *Cloud Atlas E*. This is a move toward specificity, a questioning of the unique content of each chapter and how it differs from the others. At the same time, these chapters all sit within literary-generic forms; they are constituted by their direct and sometimes explicit comparison with other literary works. This is the second point that I wish to draw out for the argument to which I will return in Chapter 4: *Cloud Atlas* is a novel about the interplay among the one-time, the specific, and the unique and a broader context of synthesis, comparison, and interlinkage.

Chapter 3

HISTORICAL FICTION AND LINGUISTIC MIMESIS

> Perhaps the chapter that must perform the most work in *Cloud Atlas* is "The Pacific Journal of Adam Ewing." Certainly, one could argue that the final, distant-future section, "Sloosha's Crossin'," has chronological priority, looking back on the other chapters of the text from a historical vantage point. One might also assert that the "Letters from Zedelghem" are central to the text, for it is there that the synechdochal "*Cloud Atlas Sextet*" is composed.[1] Ewing begins and ends the novel, however, thus placing its language and themes under more intense literary-critical scrutiny.[2] The chapter must not only introduce this strange book but, owing to *Cloud Atlas*'s unusual narrative structure, also convey that sense-making function of an ending toward which Frank Kermode gestured.[3] This diary object that is later read by Robert Frobisher certainly has an important role in this novel.

Adam Ewing's diary itself is written in the supposed style of a seafaring narrative of the mid-nineteenth century. As I remarked in the previous chapter, Frobisher notes in both editions of the text that "Ewing puts me in mind of Melville's bumbler Cpt. Delano in 'Benito Cereno.'" Yet, despite this being a metatextual setup maneuver by the novel that undoubtedly "expos[es] its concerted effort to 'forge' the form of a historical journal," the work in the preceding chapter showed that authorship attribution of the Ewing narrative using common stylometric properties of bigram or trigram frequencies (through Burrows's delta method) correlates the text neither with Melville's *Moby-Dick* nor with "Benito Cereno."[4] By at least one stylistic measure, the text fails in its attempt to condition its readership into a specific generic mode through authorial affiliation.

The novel also gives its own internal dating for the Ewing narrative. The reader is told, by Frobisher, that "mention is made of the gold rush, so I suppose we are in 1849 or 1850."[5] If we take the diary at face value, then Frobisher is almost right. In fact, the year must be precisely 1850, since this is the only year in the 1850s range that has November 7 (the first dated entry in the diary) falling on a Thursday. Hence, also, by the internal chronology, when Ewing notes that "today is [his] thirty-fourth birthday" on Sunday, January 12, 1851, he reveals that his precise birthday is January 12, 1817.[6] In its tight internal chronology that *does* match the historical record, the text even manages here to parody the act of literary interpretation; Frobisher is akin to the paranoid critic who would seek out such information.

Indeed, it is worth noting that this type of fact-finding, undertaken by Frobisher, can be called "paranoid." For it confuses the fact that, during the historical development of the novel, "the quality of being history-like [had to] become separable from the fact of being a history and acquire a validity of its own," as Michael McKeon has it.[7] Frobisher is the paranoid critical reader who seeks to uncover the truth of a deceptive diary object with which he is presented. His paranoia is also rewarded in this instance, since it is important to note that we cannot take the date of the diary at face value. As Frobisher again puts it, in what is perhaps a defensive authorial move by Mitchell, there is "something shifty about the journal's authenticity—seems too structured for a genuine diary, and its language doesn't ring quite true."[8] Frobisher clearly suspects, through his questioning of the aesthetic, that the entire thing is a literary forgery—which, of course, it is.[9] Mitchell is the ultimate forger here (although it is by license of the reader), but in the intradiegetic setup of the text, Jackson Ewing looks likely to have doctored the diary.

The reader knows, from the final pages of the diary, that Jackson Ewing, the son who has "edited" this published diary, was born before Ewing set sail in 1850. But we are also told that Jackson Ewing is the same age as the first hazing victim aboard the ship: "Rafael was Jackson's age."[10] Rafael is described as having "boyish spirits" and is a "virgin" with respect to this being his first seafaring expedition, but he is also bearded, and the once "sprite lad" has become a "sullen youth," perhaps indicating that he is in his late teens.[11] Assuming, then, an earliest birthdate of January 1, 1835, for Jackson Ewing, it seems likely that the furthest date within the text's internal chronology for editing and publication of the diary, taking an optimistic human lifespan average of sixty years for the time, might reasonably be 1895. The diary would also have to have been edited after Ewing's return at a later date. If one wanted to be generous, one could extend this by fifteen years to 1910, so as to also chime approximately with the date of the diary's "discovery" by Frobisher in the "Letters from Zedelghem" section of the novel, a few years later.

The date range that this yields for Mitchell's Ewing chapter is, then, 1851 to 1910. But the chapter is not a traditional "historical fiction." Certainly, it possesses some of the tropes that we traditionally ascribe to historical fiction: a sense of "heft and authenticity" and a time frame beyond the knowledge of present-day human readers.[12] It is also clearly the case that the chapter required intricate research to write, in accordance with the rules of the Walter Scott Prize for historical fiction. Yet where Mitchell's text differs from other works of contemporary historical fiction—such as Mantel's *Wolf Hall*—is that the *linguistic style* purports to be of the time. That is, Mitchell aims to write as though the diary was actually produced in the 1850 to 1910 time frame.

There are other works of historical fiction that also attempt such historico-linguistic mimesis. Thomas Pynchon's *Mason & Dixon* (1997) springs to mind among these as a text littered with mock-archaic typographic features (ampersands are liberally scattered within that novel, and certain, though by no means all, nouns are capitalized). This novel uses parodic voicing and stylistic features to make its serious points about the Enlightenment and colonial cartography.[13] Likewise, for a futuristic setting, Russell Hoban's *Riddley Walker*—which formed the basis for Mitchell's mutated future language of "Sloosha's Crossin'," already mentioned several times in this book—deploys a mutilated narrative style throughout, the language bearing but a phonetic similarity to our own: "On my naming day when I come 12 I gone front spear and kilt a wyld boar he parbly ben the las wyld pig on the Bundel Downs any how there hadnt ben none for a long time befor him nor I aint looking to see none agen."[14]

By most accounts, Mitchell's novel is successful at imitating the linguistic style of the period in which it purports to be set. But the questions that I want to ask here are, How does Mitchell achieve this? What are the limits of linguistic mimesis in *Cloud Atlas*? And what kind of historical imaginary could function as a model against which we could measure Mitchell's prose?

Asking these types of question pushes this inquiry into the realm of encyclopedism and encyclopedic narrative. Certainly, *Cloud Atlas* contains some of the urge toward totalization that critics since Edward Mendelson have thought of as crucial to encyclopedic works.[15] The encyclopedic author, writes Mendelson, "attends to . . . the whole social and linguistic range of his nation," an aspect that can be applied to Mitchell's novel when the word *nation* is replaced by *planet*.[16] Yet, in recent days, what we mean by *encyclopedic* has begun to change. For Mendelson, encyclopedic narratives "are products of an era in which the world's knowledge is vastly greater than any one person can encompass," and, as a result, he claims, such narratives turn to synecdoche.[17] David Letzler amplifies this point for the information era, noting that, in fact, the "real problems of encyclopedism" are "limited resources" such as a "mortal lifespan." Encyclopedism then becomes, for Letzler, concerned less with "epistemology or mastery" than with "organizing, searching, and filtering an unmanageably vast amount of data into a form wherein it can be used."[18]

In asking questions of the underlying linguistics of novels—when their words number in the hundreds of thousands—we quickly find ourselves in this realm. The labor becomes, even at the microlevel, too extensive for mastery without techniques for marshaling the linguistic data. We need a tool that can repetitively check words against source data and ways in which we can understand frequencies among broad linguistic corpora. This is where the computational techniques of this chapter can help. In the previous chapter this data wrangling was still present; it was not possible to interrogate style at the close, microlevel without such work. But the mathematical complexity of authorship attribution techniques may have led to the false impression that computational methods are difficult and that they must always involve an understanding of statistics. In this chapter I instead show how even simple acts of brute, repetitive searching and reference, facilitated by software, can furnish us with textual evidence that was otherwise inaccessible. In turn, this leads to further questions about mimesis and historical fiction.

ETYMOLOGICAL MIMESIS

Assuming that Mitchell's diary object attempts an accurate depiction of language from the time of its purported authorship, an obvious first question to which we can turn a computational method is, Are there words in the diary whose first usage falls later than the date of the Ewing section of *Cloud Atlas*? To gauge the "authenticity" of the diary through the appropriateness of its linguistic register, I conducted two initial acts of text parsing on *Cloud Atlas E*'s first section, "The Pacific Journal of Adam Ewing," the portion to which Frobisher refers. The first pass that I made was to split all words within the text into their own lines and then to eradicate any words that appeared in the Project Gutenberg version of Herman Melville's *Moby-Dick*. Using this text as a filter enabled me to remove words that were clearly in use in 1851, the first publication date for Melville's novel. The second step was to produce a piece of software that would "scrape" sets of open-access dictionary sites for claimed "first usages" of words and to run the remaining words through that software.[19] The idea behind this was that it should give an indication of any obvious outlier words, which I would then be able to check more thoroughly.

It is worth making a brief digression at this point to outline some of the difficulties of trusting etymological source data. I used two dictionary sources for this project: one was Dictionary.com, and the other was the experimental Oxford Dictionaries API (that is, the *Oxford English Dictionary*). In the case of Dictionary.com the sources on which this site draws for its etymological data are not entirely clear. That said, a sampled check of their etymologies compared to other dictionaries—such as the *OED* and Merriam-Webster's—indicates a close correlation. Yet, of course, etymological research is a historical process like any other, prone to flaws, revision, bias, and the perils of document destruction. The science of etymology is far from precise. Furthermore, the science of data-mining such sources, as used here, is even less precise. There were many words that I was unable to automatically classify and that were simply marked as having an unknown etymological start date. That said, because I was specifically looking for words that fall *outside* those accessible to Jackson Ewing in the novel, this presents less of a challenge. Indeed, so long as there were some anachronistic results, there would be something happening in the novel's style that would have a knock-on effect on its interpretation. In other words, this type of approach is good for answering a simple, well-defined (but nonetheless limited) query that I would phrase as "return as many as possible, but not necessarily all, words in a text that have etymological first-usage dates after 1910."

To militate against the above challenges of etymological research data, I decided to reduce further the terminologies studied (in addition to deduplication and the *Moby-Dick* filter) to words that appear in Ewing part 1 that have etymological data in both the *OED* and Dictionary.com. At the time of authorship, the *OED* had just released an experimental API that allows for word lookup. This includes a date-range parameter. But since there are multiple senses for many lemmas, with different first-use dates, after an initial computational filter, I had to check manually the majority of the remaining terms. Nonetheless, this resulted in a final unique vocabulary of 896 words out of an original 13,246 terms for which I then had two sets of etymological first-use dates. As can be seen in figure 14, there is generally a close correlation between the two dictionary sites for the distribution curves. The words that fall after the 1900 cutoff point, however, are different between the two sources.

Taking, then, a latest in-text "publication date" of 1910 for the first section of the "Pacific Journal" yields, in my search of Dictionary.com, just six anachronistic words that would definitively not have been available to either Adam or Jackson Ewing and that occur in both editions of the text: *home-town* (*P*) / *hometown* (*E*) [1910–15],[20] *spillage* [1920–25],[21] *lazy-eye* [1935–40],[22] *returnees* [1940–45],[23] *Latinos* [1945–50],[24] and *A-frame* [1960–65].[25] The *Oxford English Dictionary* disagrees, however. For *hometown*, it tells us, was coined in 1851, *returnee* in 1870, and *A-frame* as early as 1827. The *OED* also yields a number of terms from the

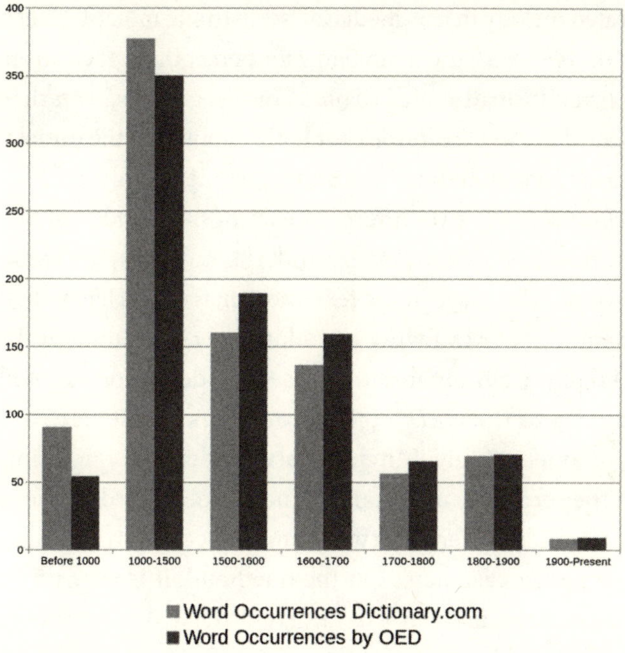

FIGURE 14. Word distributions in part 1 of "The Pacific Journal of Adam Ewing" in *Cloud Atlas E* by first usage according to Dictionary.com and the *OED*.
Data Source: Digital Appendix 3: Figure 14.

novel as being after our cutoff date that Dictionary.com does not. In the *OED*, through the automatic approach, we are given *bizarreness* (1920),[26] *spillage* (1934), *slumped* (1937),[27] *pulsed* (1942),[28] *colour* (*P*) / *color* (*E*) (1944),[29] and *scuttlebutt* (1945).[30] There are some strange things going on here that are worth briefly unpacking.

In the case of *bizarreness*, *slumped*, and *pulsed*, the *OED* API simply disagrees with Dictionary.com, claiming that the specific forms of these words, deriving from older ancestors, were not used until these later points. This is probably because my software is pulling out the incorrect part-of-speech definitions for first usage within the specific contexts. Two words have more interesting stories behind them, though.

Color seems an unlikely candidate to have been coined, even in its American spelling, in 1944. Indeed, this is the case. What has actually happened here is that the *OED* API has taken *color* in the sense of "any of various musical devices or techniques used to enhance the performance of a piece, esp. a repeated melody in late-medieval isorhythmic motets"; a very specific definition of *color*, with the main entry for perceptions of electromagnetic radiation listed instead under *colour*. This usage of *color* in the musical sense appears later in *Cloud Atlas* but hardly applies to the initial use here: "a Bonapartist general hiding here under assumed colo[u]rs."[31]

Scuttlebutt also has two different meanings. The older, given by Dictionary.com as first occurring around 1800, means "an open cask of drinking water." The usage in the text, though, is that "Henry shall inform the 'scuttlebutt' that Mr. Ewing has a low fever," meaning in this case a person who puts a rumor about. This second definition as a colloquialism, according to the *OED*, comes from 1945, while Dictionary.com yields 1905. Interestingly, Mitchell puts this term in quotation marks, as though the speaker is using an informal or new word. Although there is disagreement between my two etymological sources, *scuttlebutt* is definitely an edge-case here. On the one hand, it is very unlikely that it would have been used in the informal sense during the period of purported authorship of the document. On the other hand, Dictionary.com does put such a use at 1905, so it makes sense to exclude this from the final definitive list.

This leaves, then, just three terms that I believe can be said with certainty to have been absolutely inaccessible either to Mitchell's historic author or to the intradiegetic editor: *spillage*, from 1934; *Latino*, from 1946; and *lazy-eye*, from 1960. In the case of *spillage*, the text is recounting the debate between the Moriori elders as to whether "the spillage of Maori blood" will "also destroy one's *mana*." Interestingly, a third source, the Online Etymology Dictionary, disputes this entry, claiming it for the nineteenth century.[32] Mitchell could have avoided this slip through reverting to the verb form, *spilling*. The term *Latino*, however, is definitely a twentieth-century construction: "'Passionate Latinos,' observed Henry, bidding me a second good-night." While this term did not actually come to prominence until after the Second World War, the use, here, of a racial epithet has an important different effect for the construction of a stylistic imaginary of the nineteenth century, to which I will turn shortly. Finally, Mitchell gives us a "parlo[u]r . . . inhabited by a monstrous hog's head (afflicted with droop-jaw and lazy-eye), killed by the twins on their sixteenth birthday."[33] The sources that I consulted give this slang term for amblyopia as appearing in the middle of the twentieth century.

The first thing to note is that this is a very good attempt at linguistic mimesis within a work of purported historical fiction. Despite Mitchell's disclaimer through Frobisher about the accuracy of the diary, to have used only thirty-three terms in total from after 1850 (the earliest date of composition) is a substantial achievement. At the same time, the admission that "the language doesn't quite ring true" is either a tacit defense or an outright confession of linguistic inaccuracies.

The second important aspect that this language use changes, however, is our understanding of the text's metaleptic slippage. In fact, the precise datings of first usage here alter the slippage twofold. The use of words that entered the language after 1850 but before 1910 (as a generous estimate) validates Frobisher's assessment that the diary has been subsequently edited within the narrative (in the *OED* these words are *moniker*, *hometown*, *wide-eyed*, *boredom*, *play-act*, *despoiling*, *cartography*, *loin-cloth*, *far-flung*, *maturer*, *bronco*, *returnee*, *primed*, *prodded*, *windjammer*, *commandeer*, *wiped*, *marooned*, *excoriating*, *transliterated*, *intuited*, *slowing*, *unlocked*, and *empathy*). But our knowledge, also, that three of the linguistic terms in the portion of narrative that Frobisher reads were not coined until *after* the time of that section introduces a far stranger violation of diegetic layers. For, just as Adam Ewing's narrative is told by Jackson Ewing, and "Sloosha's Crossin'" is told by Zachry's son, this linguistic dating gives an authorial intrusion by Mitchell at this moment—the type of authorial self-inscription seen in much metafiction, here played out in a more subtle, undoubtedly unwitting, linguistic fashion.

The third notable aspect, though, is that there are remarks to be made on the linguistic styling of pastiche, parody, and historical fiction in their attempts to become believable. It is clear that readers are very poor at both identifying terms that are anachronistic and dating the first use of words. I had no idea that *spillage* came from the 1920s. Indeed, I am unsure that, if asked, readers would be able to point to these words as the markers of the language seeming not to "ring true." How, then, does one create a linguistic styling that *appears* mimetic of 1850 when working under the assumption that readers will not know when words are coined? For if readers do not know the truth of the language and the dating of words, then they cannot be capable of spotting when the text veers away from linguistic reality.

These questions of historical accuracy at the microlevel bring to the fore a problem that has vexed historical fiction and its study for many years: to what extent is mimesis to the historical record *important* for historical *fiction*? For instance, Harry E. Shaw notes that there are two types of representational phenomena at play in historical fiction. A work "may represent societies, modes of speech, or events that in very fact existed in the past," or it may "promote some sort of historical effect within the work."[34]

This "historical effect" can be seen in many contemporary takes on fantasy. In Kazuo Ishiguro's remarkable (though not universally well-received) fantasy novel *The Buried Giant* (2015), for instance, the inhabitants live in a hybrid ancient Saxon world of Arthurian knights, ogres, and dragons.[35] Although the trait is hardly exclusive to *The Buried Giant*, I call the world "hybrid" because it contains elements that seem historical even while introducing mythical, fantastical aspects. The novel engages, clearly, in a mode of mythopoesis: sowing its otherworld within a reader's own past reality, cross-fertilizing between a Tolkienesque universe and ancient Britain. Among the most interesting facets of this novel, however, is the mist of forgetting that covers Ishiguro's land. Indeed, the inhabitants of his story have only the weakest sense of history, a poor historical consciousness, and are unable to remember even recent events that were nonetheless, by all accounts, central to the characters' lives. As the warrior Wistan puts it, "Who knows what went on here in ancient days?"[36]

The Buried Giant is clearly not simply a fantasy tale but is also a rumination on history. In fact, it is a rather pessimistic meditation on the ability of fiction to reconstruct a past. Like Wistan, the reader may hope that "by travelling beside" Ishiguro's characters, "the memories would awaken." Like Wistan they may too find, though, that "they've not yet done so."[37] Ishiguro's novel closes with an ambiguous warning. As the memory fog lifts, the infidelities and betrayals of the journeying couple, Axl and Beatrice, are revealed, in parallel to a warning of ancient nationalistic grudges. At the end of the novel it remains unclear whether Axl and Beatrice are allowed to journey together to the heavenlike island or whether these past grudges cause them to fail the ferryman's potentially unpassable test. What is clear is that *The Buried Giant* warns of recovering history, unless one is prepared to forgive its wrongs in the present.

It is also clear that *The Buried Giant* and Mitchell's "Pacific Journal" are not intended to be taken as truly historical, even while they carry within them a "historical effect." The question then becomes, To what extent does it matter whether or not historical details are correct? For Hilary Mantel's Tudor fictions, the detail of the past matters intensely. In one journalistic interview she professed that "although she 'would make up a man's inner torments' she would never invent the colour of his drawing-room wallpaper," yielding a dedicated archival approach to the facticity of her fictional past eras. At the same time, Mantel acknowledges the historiography of her enterprise, noting that "history is not the past" but instead "the method we've evolved of organising our ignorance of the past."[38]

Other authors in recent days have expressed greater skepticism regarding the degree to which their fictions must, or even *can*, be historically "accurate." For Ferrie in Don DeLillo's *Libra* (1988), the interconnections in narrative are what cut across otherwise independent variables and create the binding force that we call "history": "Think of two parallel lines. . . . One is the life of Lee H. Oswald. One is the conspiracy to kill the President. What bridges the space between them? What makes a connection inevitable? There is a third line. It comes out of dreams, visions, intuitions, prayers, out of the deepest levels of the self. It's not generated by cause and effect like the other two lines. It's a line that cuts across causality, cuts across time."[39]

Thomas Pynchon also recognizes that there is a negotiation involved in the accuracy of historical fiction. When defending Ian McEwan against charges of plagiarism, Pynchon wrote that, regardless of how much artistic license he might employ, "most of us who write historical fiction . . . feel some obligation to accuracy."[40] At the same time, though, David Cowart points out that Pynchon is an "unconventional historian" and that, for Pynchon, "narrow canons of accuracy may not be important to" a broader "historical vision."[41]

What we can say about David Mitchell's almost, but not quite, historically accurate language is that it is no further from the bounds of fabrication than other period details in contemporary writing. The fact that the diary has been altered, within the narrative framework of the text, yields a certain historiography to this linguistic mimesis, an admission of recovery and of incomplete historical knowledge. At the same time, however, Mitchell's language is almost entirely accurate—as accurate as one could feasibly hope for in a work of historical fiction. The question then becomes, What other markers might denote a historical effect to a contemporary readership in the early twenty-first century beyond etymological linguistic mimesis?

SIGNS OF THE TIMES

First and foremost, to achieve his historical stylistic imaginary, Mitchell deploys archaic language. Within the first few lines of the text we are given *Indian* to refer to any non-European, a *hamlet* to refer to a settlement, a spelling of *trousers* as "trowzers," a jacket of eighteenth-century origin (the "Pea-jacket"), an ampersand repeated for conjunction, and the term *eyrie* to refer to a homeland.[42] This "archaic overloading," as we might term it, is not strictly accurate. Looking at the first passage of *Moby-Dick* as a correlative text can provide an instructive example, since *Cloud Atlas* implicitly evokes this novel with its "'tis not down on any map" echoing Melville's famous "it is not down in any map; true places never are."[43] In the opening of *Moby-Dick*, however, ampersands do not appear instead of *and*, and several passages would be totally acceptable in contemporary spoken English (were they not so well known already): "Call me Ishmael" and "there is nothing surprising in this." That said, there are also a set of terms in the first paragraph of Melville's text that resonate with Mitchell's opening: Ishmael reports himself to be "grim about the mouth" and notes that "with a philosophical flourish Cato throws himself upon his sword; I quietly take to the ship."[44]

Second, I hypothesized that Mitchell might simply be using *uncommon* language to create the perception of a stylistic affinity with Victorian-era prose for the twenty-first-century reader. For, to achieve the effect of archaic language within an environment where readers do not know when words were actually first used, it might make sense to present a range of words that they are *less likely* to have encountered. This unfamiliarity might be construed as outside the bounds of conversational tone, which a reader could take to mean that the words are older than those used in day-to-day speech. Or more simply put, the less familiar the language, the more archaic it sounds.

To test this, I noted that the Merriam-Webster dictionary has a feature that ranks the "popularity" of words, and I decided to profile the first portion of the Ewing narrative using this tool. If, I thought, my hypothesis is correct, we could expect to see a distribution of words skewed dramatically toward the "unpopular" end of the spectrum. I also thought that it would be worthwhile and important here to profile a work by Melville of the time, to see whether these works, too, genuinely chose words "unpopular" in our present day (I chose "Benito Cereno"). The results of the experiment can be seen in figure 15. The graph of part 1 of "The Pacific Journal of Adam Ewing" is, indeed, interesting. It shows an approximately normal distribution (that is, a bell curve) of the vocabulary's range but with a strong positive skew applied by the fact that approximately 42 percent of the words used in the text fall within the *bottom 10 percent* popularity of the Merriam-Webster account. This seemed to confirm my thinking that unpopularity of terms was a better indicator of how to achieve a sense of the prose style of the 1850s than strict mimetic linguistic accuracy.

Perhaps more importantly, though, when we plot the same graph against Melville's "Benito Cereno," the patterns are *almost identical.* (Certainly, some of the reason for this curve can be seen in the dataset for "Benito Cereno" and for *Cloud Atlas*; I have removed neither names such as "Ghofan" nor hybrid words such as *fellowvoyager* or *userofthegoldenrod*—originally hyphenated—from the dataset, which, clearly, score in the lower popularity percentages. In the *Cloud Atlas* set, hyphenated terms such as *help-I* have become *helpi*. That is, for reasons that will shortly become apparent, I have not taken time to perform extensive data cleanup for this experiment.) The percentage of words that falls in the bottom 10 percent, according to Merriam-Webster, is just 0.5 percent different from that in *Cloud Atlas*. The remainder of the distribution is also

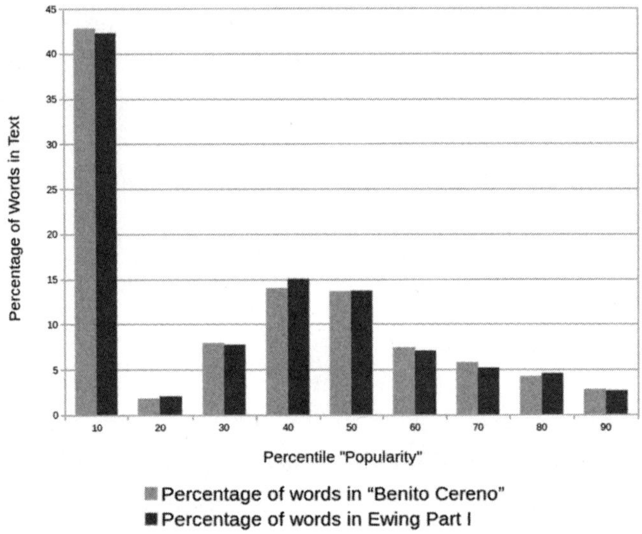

FIGURE 15. Word "popularities" in part 1 of "The Pacific Journal of Adam Ewing" in *Cloud Atlas E* and "Benito Cereno" according to Merriam-Webster (online).
Data Source: Digital Appendix 3: Figure 15.

nearly identical to that in Mitchell's subnovel. At this point in proceedings, I began to wonder whether there might be an underlying linguistic pattern at work here that pervades all language. Perhaps the long tail of these distributions is actually a feature that is intrinsic to language more generally? Or might it be, in fact, an underlying feature of how Merriam-Webster measures "popularity"?

Unfortunately, there is a problem with this methodology that I have not yet addressed. The underlying question that must first be answered is, What does the Merriam-Webster dictionary mean by *popular*? It turns out that the Merriam-Webster score for popularity is calculated by *the number of times that each word is looked up by users* online. In other words, *popularity*, as defined in the Merriam-Webster online dictionary, is not taken from any representative corpus of contemporary use but is determined by how frequently users visit the definition page in question. This, in turn, raises questions about what *popularity* might actually mean that hinges on the reasons for which people turn to online dictionaries. By Merriam-Webster's measure, "popularity" is actually constituted by a range of sociobehavioral and technological aspects.

To deal with the technological elements first, since they are the simpler to handle, it is unclear whether automated requests by search engines, repeated visits by the same users, fleeting "hits" on pages, and other nonhuman uses of the web page that contains the definition contribute to the "popularity" score. It could even be the case that by requesting how popular these terms are, my own data gathering actually ended up modifying the result. The length of time over which hits on pages are measured is also an unknown factor here. The patterns of linkage around the World Wide Web must also play a role in determining these values. Word definitions that are hyperlinked from prominent articles are likely to see more hits than those without such high-profile referrers.

Perhaps more interesting than these technical questions about how Merriam-Webster collects its popularity data, however, are the social reasons for which people might turn to online dictionary pages. For example, when a word scores in the "bottom 10%," does this mean that (1) the word is hardly ever searched for because it occurs so rarely in contemporary usage? (2) the word is hardly ever searched for because it is such a common word that everybody already knows how it is used? (3) the word is both uncommon in usage but also very well known? (4) the word is easy to spell? In contrast, when a word is scored as being very "popular," this could mean that (1) the word is extremely rare and not very well known; (2) the word is very common and is being searched for by nonnative speakers of the language; (3) the word has a subsidiary use that is less familiar; (4) the word has a specific grid pattern that fits with various word puzzles and is looked up disproportionately by players (*okapi*, for instance, is by far the most common crossword answer for any grid that reads: "o_a_i"); (5) the word has a difficult spelling and is frequently looked up not because it is uncommon in usage but for its composition; (6) the word has one or more homonyms, and users are seeking to disambiguate the term(s); (7) the word has an interesting and unapparent etymology; (8) the word has recently featured in a popular context, giving undue exposure to the term.

In actuality, how frequently a term is searched for in a dictionary will be made up of any number of the above factors in a randomly varying quantity per term. It is strangely the case that when I looked up the words *an* and *to*, the former was classified as among the most popular 10 percent of words while the latter scored in the bottom 10 percent. That said, the terms that I identified above (*pea-jacket* and *eyrie*) ranked in the bottom 10 percent and 30 percent of words, respectively. Likewise, words such as *convalescence*, *excoriating*, *pockmarked*, *bleating* and other less commonly used terms in *Cloud Atlas* do fall within the bottom 10 percent. Conversely, though, a word such as *ornery*, which could not be said to be frequently used in everyday contemporary speech and writing, features within the top 10 percent.

This is all to say that, in actuality, it is not really possible to use the Merriam-Webster "popularity" measure as an example of frequency of contemporary use, although it may appear as such at first glance. (This is also why I did not perform extensive cleanup on the dataset here. This is an excellent example of a humanities hypothesis for an experiment failing.) This is one of the methodological risks of close reading with computers: when we do not understand the composition and collection of the underlying data sources on which we draw for comparative evidence, we can be led astray. For, as Andrew Piper puts it, "unlike the imperious pronouncements of the literary critic who is only ever right, there is an element of uncertainty, error, and chance built into the task of computational criticism."[45] In this instance I am sure that Merriam-Webster has a definition of *popularity*. But the social and behavioral reasons that contribute to the final figure for "popularity" here are multivariate; many factors are condensed into a single measure, and it is almost impossible, from the outside of the black box, to determine whether the definition of *popular* matches the one for which I hope to search.

Instead, if we wished to get a true popularity measure of word-term usages in contemporary English, we would need a broad reference corpus against which to compare the language in our target texts. One such corpus is called the Oxford English Corpus (OEC), which is used by the makers of the *Oxford English Dictionary* to study evolving language use. It consists of approximately 2.5 billion words of twenty-first-century texts, which gives a far better sample basis for studying the most frequent words in contemporary usage. This is because the corpus is simply a range of texts on which one can measure frequency directly. This allows us to assume that the frequency of terms within the corpus will broadly correlate with the behavior that I am seeking to measure—that is, that Mitchell uses certain terms with far less frequency than in a broader corpus.

To study the relative frequency of terms within Mitchell's novel, I plotted the frequencies of the terms in Ewing part 1 as percentages of that text and then did the same for those terms within the OEC. The resultant overlaid graph can be seen in figure 16. This graph serves as a handy locating aide for those instances in which the usage differs between the texts. If we ignore all words that are below 1 percent of the total usage and only include those that have any degree of difference from the OEC, we find a number of interesting points. I refer to this as a "locating aide" rather than a definitive map of *Cloud Atlas*'s word frequencies, since there are all kinds of problems with the computational approach here, the most pressing of which is stemmatization. That is, usually, were we searching for uses of *abet*, we would need to make a conscious decision about whether to include *abetting*, *abets*, and a whole raft of other terms. As per the above exercise where I instead opted to narrow the problem ("find any but not all words after 1910"), the same might be said here: find instances of linguistic frequency discrepancy that we can use as a starting point for a more thorough, manual investigation.

First, the word *and* occurs only three times in Ewing part 1; a mere 0.04 percent of the text. In the OEC, the term occurs 57,716,722 times, a far higher 2.78 percent of the corpus. This astonishingly low usage of one of the most common terms in the English language can be attributed to Mitchell's frequent deployment of the ampersand in its stead—the same technique that Pynchon deploys in *Mason & Dixon* but also seen in China Miéville's *Railsea* (2012) to achieve a strange temporality for the "weird" environment of that novel.[46] Less common in contemporary usage, for sure, the ampersand was at one point in the nineteenth century taught to schoolchildren as the twenty-seventh letter of the English alphabet.[47] Although there are multiple convergent histories of the ampersand and its usage, there is no evidence that I have seen of such wholesale replacement of *and* with the ampersand in nineteenth-century printed prose, such as Melville. That said, the "Pacific Journal" is supposed to be a handwritten document, so, in the fictional landscape, the contraction of *and* to *&* would have saved writing effort.

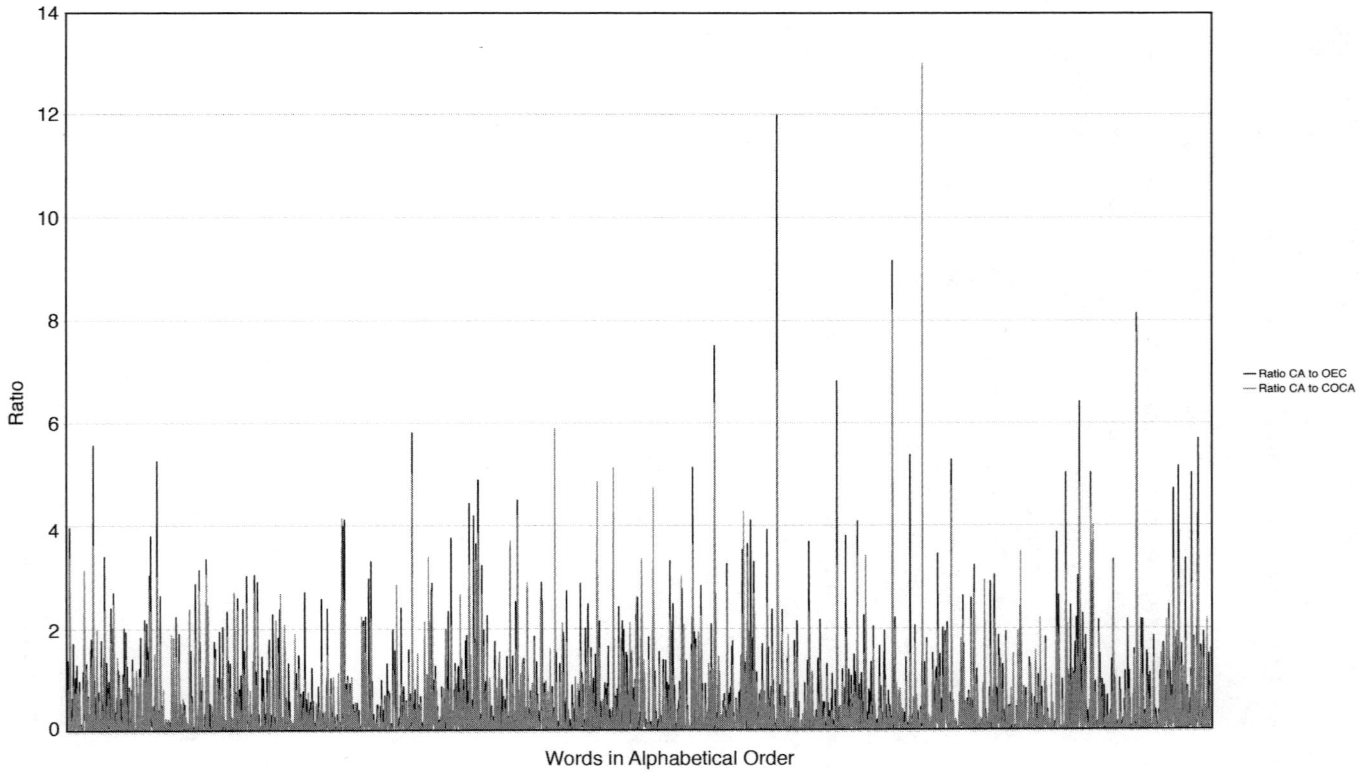

FIGURE 16. Relative percentage frequency of terms from part 1 of "The Pacific Journal of Adam Ewing" in *Cloud Atlas E* vs. the Oxford English Corpus and COCA. Where a lighter line appears higher, the usage in the OEC is higher than in COCA. Where a black line appears higher, the usage in the OEC is lower than in COCA. Higher bars represent significant and interesting outliers.

Data Source: Digital Appendix 3: Figure 16.

Again, owing to the first-person diaristic nature of this segment, we also see a far higher usage of the first-person pronoun *I* in *Cloud Atlas* than in the broader OEC (2.33 percent vs. 0.81 percent).[48] This is less a stylistic observation than simply a reflection on the specific object type that Mitchell uses. Likewise, there is a marked difference in usage of the term *is* between *Cloud Atlas*'s diary and the OEC (0.56 percent vs. 1.13 percent). This is curious. Certainly, the "Pacific Journal" moves between tenses; some portions of the diary-in-a-novel are written in the simple present and present continuous while others are written in various past tenses. One would assume that the same would be true, though, of the OEC.

Similarly, some of the other differences between Mitchell's frequencies and the OEC's are harder to understand. For instance, the term *in* has almost a half-percentage-point difference between *Cloud Atlas* and the OEC (2.03 percent vs. 1.55 percent). It is possible that the microtectonic shifts in word frequency that occur as a result of Mitchell's forced grammatical changes could have caused this difference. It is also possible that the difference has occurred purely by chance. The 0.4 percent difference between *of* also falls in this category, as do the differences for *the*, *that*, and *to*.

The challenge here, of course, is that the more frequent words (> 1 percent) tend, in both the OEC and the novel, to be function words. Yet those terms that are rarer in the OEC but that occur frequently in *Cloud Atlas*, such as *Moriori* (*Cloud Atlas*: 0.32 percent vs. OEC: 0.000004 percent), tend to be thematic words related to the novel's focus on the "Chatham" isles (Rēkohu). This coincides with a thematic focus on empire and tropical medicine alongside the use of racist language, prevalent in nineteenth-century English society (e.g., *blackamoor* at 0.01 percent in *Cloud Atlas*'s Ewing compared to 0.000003 percent in the OEC).[49]

Certainly, though, some terms are used that are just strange to our contemporary ear and that do not circulate in twenty-first-century parlance. *Hugger-mugger*, for instance, although occurring but once in *Cloud Atlas*, has a significant deviation from the OEC (0.007 percent vs. 0.0000005 percent). Similarly, the abbreviated *'kerchief* occurs at 0.015 percent in the novel but only at 0.00002 percent in the OEC. *Maladies* also has a 0.015 percent occurrence in *Cloud Atlas* but constitutes a mere 0.00005 percent of the OEC.

In fact, there is a relatively good (or, at least, better) way to identify terms that sound unusual to the contemporary ear: by comparison to the magazine portion of the Contemporary American Corpus of American English (COCA). This corpus consists of newspaper articles, fiction, academic writing, spoken word, and magazine articles from 1990 until 2015. As Ewing is supposed to be an American character, this US English corpus seemed appropriate as a comparison database. That said, COCA is itself a messy database. Examining the 2004 entry for fiction, I found

> ad Leila thought of him in those final seconds ? he knew the answerof course she had n't thought of him-but he could n't help entertaining the notion that the final image that came to her , the person she thought of , was him

and

> Or play it out . 113 OMITTED 113 114 OMITTED 114 <p> 115 NEWS FOOTAGE - AIRPORT ARRIVAL (VIDEO) 115 TV115 Raymond emerges from a private jet , waves to a crowd of TV115 supporters behind a chain link fence—116 EXT.

Clean, this dataset is not.

Nevertheless, I decided to take the 2004 magazine corpus from COCA and locate words that occur in *Cloud Atlas*'s Ewing part 1 that do not occur in the comparison dataset. This is an appropriate comparison since it comes from the same year as *Cloud Atlas*'s original publication and represents writing about the contemporary as opposed to the fiction corpus, which may contain historical fiction, for instance. The result is, indeed, a set of terms that are unusual to the modern ear, and these terms are shown in the following list (variants between versions are given here and numbers in parentheses represent *P* and *E* edition page references respectively):

abase (8, 8)
abet (34, 33)
aboriginal (28, 27)
aboriginals (16, 16)
abrogate (16, 16)
adzed (20, 20)
Aesculapian (18, 17)
affright (26, 25)
afore (31, 30)
ain't (35, 35)
alarum (28, 27)
alkali (37, 36)
Aotearoa (32, 31)
appurtenances (24, 23)
Arcadian (3, 3)
arrack (28, 27)
astraddle (494, 39)
Athenians (38, 37)
attainting (28, 27)
awa (13, 13)
aye (27, 26)
bamboozle (35, 34)
bank-notes/banknotes (37, 36)
banqueter (5, 5)
banqueting (3, 3)
banshee (4, 5)
barkings (20, 19)
basilisk (20, 20)
Bedlamite (4, 4)
bee-like/beelike (6, 6)
befell (18, 18)
besmirched (3, 4)
besought (8, 8)
bestial (29, 28)
bestir (35, 34)
bestirs (17, 17)
better'n (30, 29)
betwixt (11, 11)
bide (16, 16)
bilged (14, 14)
bizarreness (27, 26)
Blackamoor (7, 7)
blackballed (4, 4)
blackfella (6, 7)
Bonapartist (16, 16)
breakages (23, 23)
breakfasted (11, 11)
bridled (37, 36)
brokenly (30, 29)
bush-fires/bushfires (13, 13)
bystanding (39, 38)
cabal (7, 7)
cabin-mate, cabinmate (28, 27)
cannibals (18, 18)
canoed (30, 29)
captaincy (8, 8)
carrion (21, 20)
cartwheeling (19, 19)
castes (6, 6)
Castilians (23, 22)
Catholick (18, 18)
Cervello/cervello (36, 35)
Chathams (36, 35)
cindery (3, 3)
circumambulating (19, 19)
civilize (16, 16)
clap-trap/claptrap (17, 16)
clime (37, 36)
cocoa-nuts (3, 3)
combes (32, 31)
comeliest (7, 7)
commandeer (25, 24)
compleat (37, 36)
condign (32, 32)
confessor (18, 18)
conquistadores (14, 13)
cordially (9, 9)
curios (18, 18)
curtness (39, 38)
darkie (36, 35)
daunt (6, 6)
declaimed (12, 12)
delicto (7, 7)
Delphic (493, 39)
demarked (6, 6)
demotic (8, 8)
denture-sets/denture (3, 3)
desiderata (26, 25)
despoiling (13, 13)
Dimittis (8, 8)
disintegrated (19, 19)
disuse (11, 11)
dolorous (29, 28)
drachm (37, 36)
dropsy (22, 21)
duskier (6, 6)
dwarfish (19, 19)
dykey (10, 10)
emollient (5, 5)
Encantadas (31, 30)
enchanter (20, 20)
ere (7, 7)
evinced (32, 31)
excoriating (6, 6)
exterminating (16, 16)
extirpation (16, 16)
extricate (20, 19)
eyrie (3, 3)
farmhand (9, 9)
farmyard (23, 23)
fathered (32, 31)
fattens (38, 37)
fecundated (14, 14)
Feejee (5, 5)
feudin' (33, 32)
fie (37, 36)
filleted (15, 15)
filly (7, 7)
fish-hooks/fishhooks (36, 35)
fish-wives/fishwives (24, 23)
flagrante (7, 7)
fleetest (9, 9)
flogging (6, 6)
foremast (20, 20)
fore-noon/forenoon (494, 39)
forthwith (27, 26)
fripperies (24, 23)
frisk (11, 11)
gaoler (26, 26)
garbed (31, 30)
gnashers (4, 4)
God-speed/Godspeed (22, 22)
Gomorrah (9, 9)
grandee (6, 6)
grievously (19, 18)
grovelled/groveled (6, 6)
grubs (12, 11)
gun-dog/gundog (38, 37)
Gusano (36, 35)
Guttural (20, 19)
hailstones (18, 18)
hammerheads (38, 37)
harridan (3, 4)
hatefulness (25, 25)
hawser (24, 24)
heathen (21, 20)
henceforth (31, 31)
hidey-hole (30, 29)
hisses (38, 37)
hugger-mugger (11, 11)

husbandry (11, 11)
Icelander (28, 28)
idleness (18, 18)
importuned (14, 13)
importuning (11, 11)
imputations (3, 4)
Indiaman (35, 34)
instanter (33, 33)
intuited (26, 26)
Inverary (39, 38)
jackwood (23, 23)
Kossacks (16, 16)
lamentable (23, 23)
leakiest (23, 22)
learnt (10, 10)
leprosy (37, 36)
Lethean (37, 37)
lintel-pieces/lintel (6, 6)
litigants (20, 19)
madest (8, 8)
maggoty (36, 36)
mainmast (9, 9)
mannikin (19, 19)
manservants (23, 22)
Maoris (16, 16)
mast-head/masthead (25, 25)
masticates (4, 4)
maturer (18, 18)
medicament (37, 36)
Melanesia (36, 35)
mêlées/melees (28, 27)
merchantman (5, 5)
merchantmen (34, 33)
mercies (27, 26)
mixed-blood (16, 16)
mizzen-top (11, 11)
molars (3, 3)
Moriori (10, 10)
Morpheus (10, 10)
mulatto (16, 16)
Mutunga (15, 15)
narrating (36, 35)
neglectful (25, 25)
nephrite (6, 7)
Ngati (13, 13)
nib (36, 35)
nomenclatures (10, 10)
nonce (21, 21)
notarial (5, 5)
notary (10, 10)
Nunc (8, 8)
nut-brown (6, 6)
obdurate (8, 8)
oozes (38, 37)
orang-utan (18, 18)
ordure (14, 14)
orinoco (37, 36)
Owenga (13, 13)
Pakeha (10, 10)
parvenu (13, 13)
passeth (8, 8)
paua (12, 11)
pellucid (21, 20)
percipience (35, 34)
petrels (493, 39)
phantasms (12, 12)
pilfer (35, 34)
pilferers (29, 28)
pillory (26, 25)
pisco (5, 5)
piteous (6, 6)
play-act/playact (33, 32)
ploughman/plowman (17, 16)
vividly-plumaged / plumaged (30, 29)
Polack (16, 16)
Polynesia (36, 35)
ponga (6, 6)
Poorhouse (4, 4)
Popish (24, 23)
poultice (18, 18)
poxed (8, 8)
precluding (5, 5)
princelings (12, 12)
prize-fighter/prizefighter (6, 6)
prodigal's (31, 30)
Prophetess (4, 4)
proscribed (31, 31)
protuberance (21, 20)
provocations (14, 13)
pulsate (38, 37)
pulsed (21, 20)
pure-blooded/pureblooded (15, 15)
pusillanimity (14, 13)
pustular (6, 6)
pustule (25, 24)
putrescent (36, 36)
quadroon (9, 9)
quenched (8, 8)
rapine (15, 15)
reddened (493, 39)
refitting (13, 13)
remonstrated (7, 7)
renegado (9, 9)
rescuer (34, 33)
retched (21, 20)
retorted (7, 7)
rheums (22, 21)
rued (22, 21)
runes (6, 6)
sailcloth (22, 22)
Samaritans (14, 14)
satyr (39, 38)
scabby (25, 25)
scald (4, 4)
schema (25, 24)
scrofula (30, 30)
scuttlebutt (37, 36)
scuttling (28, 27)
sealers (13, 13)
seamen (24, 24)
semi-naked/seminaked (38, 37)
sentimentalist (21, 21)
serfs (32, 31)
shanties (28, 27)
shark-tooth (35, 34)
shipbuilder (4, 4)
Ship-mate/Shipmate (23, 23)
shirker (36, 35)
simulacrums (17, 17)
sinnet (39, 38)
sluicing (29, 29)
slumbers (28, 27)
smatterings (493, 39)
smoulder/smolder (13, 13)
smote (33, 32)
sneering (11, 11)
somnambulant (9, 9)
sonorous (8, 8)
spanker (35, 35)
spillage (15, 14)
spittoon (4, 4)
sprats (493, 39)
Stanislaus (25, 24)
stinking (21, 20)
stoppered (24, 23)
stratagem (9, 9)
subsisted (32, 32)
sufficiency (14, 14)
surprized (24, 24)
swilling (7, 7)
Tama (13, 13)
tameness (18, 18)

tapu (13, 13)
Taranaki (13, 13)
tarry (18, 18)
tatterdemalion (9, 9)
taverner (4, 4)
Teached (39, 38)
terraqueous (11, 11)
theorum (11, 11)
'tis (3, 3)
toilers (39, 38)
tolerably (10, 10)
tomahawks (14, 14)
topsails (39, 38)
transliterated (14, 14)
trebly (27, 27)
trespasser (21, 20)
trice (13, 13)
tricksy (7, 7)
trotters (11, 11)
tusked (19, 19)
'twas (21, 20)
twelvemonth (24, 24)
twittering (4, 4)
unguents (24, 23)
unheeded (33, 32)
unlettered (13, 13)
unpurged (37, 36)
unseaworthy (30, 29)
unsurveyed (18, 18)
untainted (10, 10)
unwonted (34, 33)
ursine (7, 7)
usurous (23, 23)
valetudinarian (37, 36)
viz (29, 28)
vouchsafe (5, 5)
Waitangi (13, 13)
Whanga (14, 14)
whorehouse (7, 7)
whosoever (12, 12)
windjammer (19, 19)
window-pane/windowpane (9, 9)
womenfolk (6, 6)
wretches (6, 6)
wuthering (8, 8)
yarned (5, 5)
yaws (22, 21)

Some of these terms are hybrid words that combine two others (albeit not quite portmanteau words) such as *sharktooth*, *twelvemonth*, *semi-naked*, and *mixedblood* (notably, *Cloud Atlas P* has a far greater propensity toward hyphenations, which were removed in the *E* edition's editing). Furthermore, according to the above hypothesis, several terms of outmoded address—*Blackamoor*, *blackfella*, *darkies*, *harridan*, *womenfolk*, *bedlamite*, *mulatto*, *quadroon*, and *mixedblood* again—fall within this category. Curiously, though, *nigger* appears several times in the 2004 magazine section of COCA but always in quotation marks or through a distancing inflection: "She remembered churchgoing folks in Kansas and Texas who also called people niggers."

Nonetheless, in some ways this list lends credence to my hypothesis: Mitchell does tend to use archaic/unusual terms with a greater frequency than we see in a general corpus of contemporary English. Specifically, colonial terms of racist abuse occur in the Ewing section of *Cloud Atlas* at a far higher frequency than in a broader contemporary corpus. There are, however, a number of additional limitations to this method that must be discussed. First, because the Ewing chapter is relatively small, a low number of usages is, as before, often enough to produce a distinctive skew against the OEC. For instance, the term *Blackamoor* is used only twice within the Ewing narrative, but this is enough to substantially weight its relative percentage against the OEC and COCA. This particular method, then, overweighs words with low frequencies in the smaller corpus. In a sense, though, this is helpful; the small number of usages here is a distinctive linguistico-thematic intersection to which we *should* pay attention.

Second, there is the question of the composition of the OEC. The blurb for the OEC indicates that it seeks to build a representative corpus of twenty-first-century English from across the spectrum of writing types:

> [The corpus] represents all types of English, from literary novels and specialist journals to everyday newspapers and magazines, and even the language of blogs, emails, and social media. And, as English is a global language, the Oxford English Corpus contains language from all parts of the world—not only from the UK and the United States but also from Ireland, Australia, New Zealand, the Caribbean, Canada, India, Singapore, and South Africa.
>
> The extensive use of web pages has allowed us to build a corpus of unprecedented scale and variety—the corpus contains nearly 2.5 billion words of real 21st-century English, with new text being continuously collected.[50]

Indeed, although the OEC is not composed entirely of fiction, the breadth it offers in terms of sourcing provides for a comparison environment that is more representative of global language usage in the early twenty-first century. Time and time again, Mitchell uses words that occur less frequently in the OEC. Certainly, this comparative frequency disjunct contributes to the stylistic historical imaginary of the nineteenth century in *Cloud Atlas*.

THEMES, LANGUAGE, AND STYLE

In the construction of literary style, where does the theme or topic end and language begin? Is it even possible to speak of literary style in terms of such subcomponents, crudely divorced from one another? Debates have raged for decades over the definition of style, and it is not likely that they will be resolved here.[51]

Mitchell himself has noted that the construction of a historical stylistic imaginary is not about total mimetic accuracy:

> Historical fiction isn't easy; it's not just another genre. How are they going to speak? If you get that too right, it sounds like a pastiche comedy—people are saying "thou" and "prithee" and "gadzooks," which they did say, but to an early 21st-century audience, it's laughable, even though it's accurate. So you have to design a kind of "bygone-ese"—it's modern enough for readers not to stumble over it, but it's not so modern that the reader kind of thinks this could be out of *House* or *Friends* or something made for TV—puff! Again, the illusion is gone. It's very easy to be wrong; it's very easy for the book to fail.[52]

In this reading, Mitchell believes that complete accuracy sounds alien and overperformed, though he does not go so far as to write about specific vocabularies and their (un)availability.

I want to turn, finally, to some thematic areas that Mitchell explores and that constitute this historical imaginary of the nineteenth century in *Cloud Atlas*, the ways in which thematic concerns interact with Mitchell's "bygone-ese." The main sources for the historical accuracy of this section of Mitchell's novel are well documented and implicitly include A. Shand's 1892 work in the *Journal of the Polynesian Society* on the Moriori genocide but also Jared Diamond's *Germs, Guns and Steel*, which Mitchell cites as the origin of *Cloud Atlas*, although Wendy Knepper also suggests a useful range of broader sources.[53]

The dominant driver of narrative action in this portion of the text is the slow poisoning of Ewing by the sinister Dr. Henry Goose. Indeed, it emerges—at first in the "Letters from Zedelghem"[54]—that Goose is a robber, intent on killing Ewing in order to retrieve the "entire estate" that he believes to be in Ewing's trunk.[55] Goose almost achieves this feat by convincing Ewing that an internal worm is causing his illness. The deceit works by Goose disguising his poison as medicine, substituting the toxin for the cure, while thereby also drawing a metaphorical parallel between the supposed parasite within Ewing's body and the parasite that is Goose within Ewing's confidence. Ewing so heartily swallows the lie—even if readers can perceive the threat and dramatic irony—that he proclaims that "Henry's powders are indeed a wondrous medicament."[56]

The technology of medicine from this historical period, then, is the most prevalent thematic strand that I identify in this first section of *Cloud Atlas*. This technology is situated within two epistemic contexts: empire and *pharmakon*. On the first of these aspects, as Pratik Chakrabarti has shown, "the history of modern medicine cannot be narrated without the history of imperialism."[57] While each of the very different world empires affected the development of medicine in different ways—be it through a "civilizing mission" or the "scramble for Africa"—the most important aspect for the Ewing chapter of *Cloud Atlas* is the intersection of tropical colonialism and parasitology.[58] For the discipline of "tropical medicine," although actually heterogeneous in its geographies and climates, which are collapsed into the single word *tropical*, has its roots in medicinal care for European colonial troops and expatriate civilians.[59] From this, as Michael Worboys points out, tropical medicine developed to become the "main scientific expression of Western medical and health policy for the Third World" throughout the twentieth century.[60] Specifically, the epistemology of "germ theory" was significantly revised as military doctors battled malaria. Charles Louis Alphonse Laveran's 1880 discovery of the protozoan cause of malaria, combined with Patrick Manson's work on filarial worms in 1877, created a hybrid discipline of parasitology and vector studies, merging into "tropical medicine," all within a colonial context.[61]

The colonial context that is needed for an exploration of tropical medicine is given within the first few pages of *Cloud Atlas*. The reader is shown an "Indian hamlet" in the novel's very first sentence, with an "Indian war-canoe" just a few pages later, alongside the colonial racism of a "sullen miss" who has a "tinge of black blood," coupled with the racist assumption that "her mother is not far removed from the jungle breed."[62] The text then quickly migrates to a "public flogging" of especial violence in which a "tattooed" crowd of "slaves" and the tribe's "chieftain" watch a "Goliath" of a "whip-master" work on a "beaten savage." The scene is ironically supposed to invoke the imperial logic of colonialism's "civilizing" morality as the "only two Whites present . . . swooned under each fall of the lash" even while raising the figure of colonial trade and human slavery when Ewing muses that the "pelt" of the whip-master would "fetch a fine price."[63] From the off, then, *Cloud Atlas* signals its colonial contexts, thereby reinforcing the earlier comparative frequency analysis.

It is against this racist epistemology that the central plot element of Ewing's story can be read best. Dr. Goose's claimed authority over parasitical worms—although in actuality slightly misaligned with the time line of the real-world development of parasitology—is crucial for the projected savage world of darkness, of "blood-frenzy" threat, and of scenes "at once indelible, fearsome & sublime" in which Ewing believes.[64] With Goose's encouragement Ewing constructs a worldview of the regions through which he is traveling as a "white man's grave," in which there is an innate danger from the climate (Goose tells Ewing that his fever is "caused by the clime") that poses a distinct threat to the "civilized" man, and the only option is to find a "specialist in tropical parasites."[65]

The flaws in this epistemology and its technological cure (Goose's medicine that is actually a poison) is shown through the stowaway episode of Ewing's narrative. Ewing discovers an "uninvited cabin-mate" in his quarters shortly into the voyage—the same man, Autua, who was whipped in the novel's opening.[66] The parallels with the "worm inside" are obvious here: the apparently "civilized" man has a parasite from the environment living off his body (the "worm") and now perceives that he also has an "Indian" parasitizing his living quarters. The "cure" to the stowaway situation (although not eventually carried out) yields the link to the second context for medicine in this part of *Cloud Atlas*: *pharmakon*. The captain wants to shoot Autua during his ascent of the mizzen.[67] The callousness of this proposed murder, as a supposed "remedy" or cure for the situation, underscores colonialism's toxicity by analogy. For the solutions derived from empire in this novel turn out to be as poisonous as Goose's attempted murder of Ewing. Colonial "medicines"—and their white "cures" of cultural domination—are genocidal, toxic technologies.

Such a reading sits well alongside Jacques Derrida's (in)famous work on the *pharmakon* in "Plato's Pharmacy." In this piece Derrida focuses on the fact that the Ancient Greek *pharmakon*—used by Plato in *Phaedrus*—is a "medicine . . . which acts as both remedy and poison."[68] Derrida writes that he aims "to display . . . the regular, ordered polysemy that has, through skewing, indetermination, or overdetermination, but without mistranslation, permitted the rendering of the same word by 'remedy,' 'recipe,' 'poison,' 'drug,' 'philter' etc."[69] Despite the fact that Mitchell pokes fun at the era of Derridean stylistics with his jibe of "MAs in Postmodernism and Chaos Theory," which I have already mentioned, the similarities between his novel and Derrida's *pharmakon* cannot be dismissed so easily.[70] Yet there is more to this than just medicine. For Derrida, the *pharmakon* can be seen in acts of translation and interpretation—violent destructions that must reduce the text "to one of its simple elements," thereby curing and killing—but also in "the *eidos*, truth, law, the *episteme*, dialectics, philosophy," all of which are "other names for the *pharmakon*."[71] In Derrida's reading, "what is at stake in this overturning [the *pharmakon*'s multiplicity of meaning that creates a constant 'non-identity-with-itself'] is no less than science and death."[72]

In *Cloud Atlas*'s first chapter, then, medicine acts at once as a cure and as a killing device, all within a colonial epistemology that produces an ironic imperial identity.[73] To understand the final claim here—that this technology creates an ironic imperial identity—requires a return to Mitchell's stylistics. For as with Derrida's characterization of the *pharmakon*, Mitchell's hyperbolic performance of colonial-style discourse contains its own nods at its opposite, even when "the charade was having its desired effect," as the text puts it.[74] There is, of course, a "worm inside" Mitchell's own text owing to the puncturing of linguistic mimesis by the etymological features I have traced above. This is furthered because this section of *Cloud Atlas*'s style is juxtaposed against six other linguistic registers that allow the reader to place each chapter in time.

Another form of historical mimesis in Ewing's narrative is the faux nineteenth-century redactions in the courtroom scene that act as markers of the period: "Unhand me you sons of w—s!"[75] This lineage of redaction is something to which I will return in my final chapter. From just this single instance, however, we can see the functioning of Mitchell's language registers and, again, they have a metaphorical parallel in the mediating technology in this chapter. For, in examples such as this redaction, the "sites of transaction between a knowing author and a knowing reader," as Lisa Gitelman puts it, are not merely concerned with decoding what lies beneath the blank but rather in correctly placing Mitchell's characters within a nineteenth-century imperial context.[76] Readers can see the irony of such overblown speech patterns—constructed by a contemporary novelist to critique empire—even while such speech serves the reader in determining the historical identity effect of Mitchell's characters. In this way the treacherous technology of medicine moves from a mimetic depiction conditioned by the spatial reach of empire to a metaphor that stands for Mitchell's stylistic play. This all stems from a linguistic cause amid an intradiegetic depiction of the *pharmakon* as a remedy and as a cure.

CLOSING WORDS

What I have shown in this chapter, through computational investigation, is that the construction of an imagined stylistic profile of a nineteenth-century text, as performed by David Mitchell in *Cloud Atlas*, has several unexpected characteristics. First, the construction of fictional historical language is not about etymological mimesis. Readers are poor at identifying the first-usage dates of words, and Mitchell's language—while extremely close to nineteenth-century reality—betrays itself in a small number of edge-cases. Even if, as Rose Harris-Birtill has suggested, Mitchell's texts are concerned with reincarnation and repetition, the reincarnation of the nineteenth-century prose style that *Cloud Atlas* presents is a *differentiated* repetition; it is the same but different, a reimagined representation of the target century from a twenty-first-century perspective, a historical imaginary of nineteenth-century stylistics, a "reincarnation time" for language.[77] It is as though there has been a transmigration of language, accurate for the most part but punctured by time.

Second, the comparison of the frequency of outlandish terms that Mitchell's Ewing uses against a contemporary English corpus seems to affirm my conclusion. Certainly, such a claim is on shakier ground, and there is a chance that some of the terms occur more frequently simply by chance. Future studies may test whether this hypothesis/tentative conclusion holds: that attempts to write in the style of the nineteenth century involve higher frequencies of archaic and racially abusive language than contemporary writing.

At the end of the day, though, it may be that the language in the Ewing section is not quite so outlandish compared to our own or compared to that in the "Sloosha's Crossin'" section of the novel. Thematic concerns (such as the text's focus on tropical medicine, even though mediated through a Derridean *pharmakon*, colonial violence, and seafaring narrative) inflect the word choices that Mitchell can make.[78] It is not as though the use of language is here selected in isolation from the thematic content. To set one's generic mode to the nineteenth century, in the early twenty-first century, requires not only a focus on *how* one writes but also *what one writes about*.

There is another side to the language usage in this section of Mitchell's novel to which I must finally turn. Thus far, aside from one mention, I have assumed that Mitchell aims to straightforwardly achieve a mimesis of a nineteenth-century prose style, and I have used various computational techniques to appraise this, even amid remarks on the self-aware historiography of the section. It could be, though, that the critique of colonialism in *Cloud Atlas* comes about through an element of parody or pastiche in Mitchell's writing that deserves closer attention (although, as above, Mitchell has claimed that this is not his intention). Theories of parody, such as Linda Hutcheon's famous formulation of ironic repetition and distancing, stress the need for both repetition and deviation.[79] A parody must resonate with but also clash against its target so that readers may at once identify the target work of parody but also feel a distance from it. This is, in a sense, akin to the broader claims about reading and interpretation with respect to information theory to which Letzler has recently turned.[80] That is, novelty and talent must be juxtaposed within a framework of pattern recognition and tradition. The fact that the language in Ewing part 1 "doesn't ring quite true," then, and that this is acknowledged in the text itself, should give us pause for thought. In the way in which the dissonance of etymological deviation can shine through—if one knows how and where to look—very little is lost in the "inaccuracy" of Mitchell's linguistic *parody*. It may in fact be this slightly off-kilter accuracy that transforms this section into a parody, thereby at least in part critiquing and neutralizing the offensive colonial discourses of its characters. There is, therefore, at least one way in which David Mitchell's language choices in "The Pacific Journal of Adam Ewing," whether conscious or not, must be read as political choices. For it is through the eyes of pastiche and parody that the discourses of this past space are made to seem ridiculous and outmoded.[81] At least part of this effect comes from a reimagined but punctured stylistics of the nineteenth century.

What I also hope to have shown in this chapter is that a close attention to quantitative aspects of *Cloud Atlas*, using computational methods, can bring us closer to understanding the text's features while unearthing fresh evidence that can then be reincorporated into our existing humanistic methods—a form of symbiosis between the so-called digital humanities and their longer-standing traditional disciplinary counterparts. Alone, the computational methods bring us data about the novel but little more. What we make of the statistics of word frequencies and dates, and how we understand their novelistic and political import, remains a matter of interpretation. Overall, we also need to remember, when reading "The Pacific Journal of Adam Ewing," that the language here is an excursion from our present, a mental voyage to an imagined stylistics of the nineteenth century, mediated through generic patterning. *Cloud Atlas* is a novel that asks us to focus on the interrelationship between our present period and Mitchell's imagined past; it is a novel that is about history *as* genre. It is also a text that reminds us that our trips to the past are but mental excursions—imaginary sabbaticals to constructed histories. And, as Frobisher puts it, no matter how much evidence we excavate to the contrary of the section's accuracy, our suspension of disbelief is likely to remain within Mitchell's authorial excursion from our present. For, even with its twenty-first-century intrusions, it seems likely that, for most readers, "time cannot permeate this sabbatical."[82]

Chapter 4

INTERPRETATION

> In some ways, titling this final chapter "Interpretation" rings false. I have already undertaken interpretation throughout this work; the data alone do not speak. In separating this chapter into its own domain, I run a structural risk of severing the digital work from its hermeneutic contexts. But a lone chapter that reintegrates the digital findings with the text, before finally turning its critical gaze back to the digital methods that have informed this book, seems an apt way to close a study endorsing "close reading with computers."

From the work in the preceding chapters I came to three high-level conclusions: (1) that *Cloud Atlas* is a novel about the manipulation of the archive; (2) that *Cloud Atlas* is a novel that draws attention to the specific against the general, or, at least, to the oscillation between these poles that is a part of historical knowledge-making; and (3) that *Cloud Atlas* deploys a slimmer range of mediated forms (both generic and linguistic) than we might believe, using a single narrow, yet also expansive, century to achieve its representation of a millennium-or-more's worth of imagined history and future. I dedicate this final chapter to the connections among these conclusions.

These aspects of the text have several important consequences, I will go on to argue, for the placement of the reader of *Cloud Atlas*. One traditional interpretation of the readerly position in the novel would see the furthest-flung reaches of history and argue that the reader must, somehow, be placed, in imaginative terms, *after* this period. Such a reading would consider all narrative within the text to be analeptic, relative to the reader's temporal placement. There is good logic behind such reasoning, for in *Cloud Atlas* all narratives are mediate. Encapsulation of narrative within object forms that are viewed by future historical periods is the name of the game, be it Frobisher reading Ewing's diary or Sonmi viewing Timothy Cavendish.

Another interpretation, though, would see the distant future of *Cloud Atlas* as an anticipation of retrospection, to appropriate Peter Brooks's phrase.[1] In such a model the reader can be placed anywhere on the time line of *Cloud Atlas*'s concertina-like progression. Sections that are ahead of the reader's temporal progression are to be viewed as SF worlds, as speculative imagined futures that reflect darkly back on the reader's present, amplifying the anxieties and concerns of the reader's moment in a quasi-satirical fashion.[2] This strikes me as a more plausible model for readerly placement. Clearly, on the one hand, the reader of *Cloud Atlas* is *not* actually placed beyond the far future of "Sloosha's Crossin'" at the proposed end of human history. The work is a 2004 novel, after all. On the other hand, the desire to imagine readers and writers into omniscient positions has a strong pedigree in the novel form, both realist and otherwise. Fundamentally, then, this chapter sets out to ask, Where is *Cloud Atlas*'s projected reader—as opposed to the actual reader of the early twenty-first century—to be situated?

ARCHIVES

A reasonable question, given my focus in Chapter 1 on the archive as a central precept of Mitchell's novel, would be, What textual evidence is there that the archive is really an important element of *Cloud Atlas* as a whole? After all, an imagined questioner might add, the analysis in Chapter 1 focused only on "An Orison of Sonmi~451," the sole chapter to mention the word *archive* in the text. Is it really fair to use the excuse of "close reading" to hone in on a single chapter of a work that spans a vast temporal range and then to claim that a logistical mistake in publishing practice could be the prompt for resituating a reading of the novel around the archive? Isn't this the very danger of "close reading," that it might conveniently cherry-pick some aspects of the text and ascribe them a central importance, while marginalizing other elements? Yet if we are to understand the imagined placement of the reader in this novel, it is crucial to grasp that reader's relationship to history, historiography, and critical reading of an archive.

I first aim to address these matters by showing how the archive sits implicitly beneath each of Mitchell's chapters and to show how this idea of an archive—documentations of a historical epoch encoded and made more or less legible to future readers—underpins Mitchell's novel. I argue, with extensive textual evidence, that moments of metatext in *Cloud Atlas* continually point to the presence of partial material encodings, inscriptions that gesture beyond their own bounds to broader historical contexts and other documents, even while signaling their own biases. I intend to pursue this in a chronological fashion of historical time through the text (that is, taking "Ewing" parts 1 and 2 as the first port of call, followed by "Letters from Zedelghem" 1 and 2, etc.), with the level of textual detail that one would expect from close reading—computational or otherwise.

In "The Pacific Journal of Adam Ewing" the most obvious signifier of the archive is the diary form itself and the various historical contexts that are recorded within it. Indeed, the entire novel opens with a historical date—"Thursday, 7th November [1850]"—although other parts of the chapter point back further than this to a prior entry for "15th October" of the same year.[3] As above, the precise year is not exactly specified in the text but can be located through calendar correlation of the named dates for the period. This initial focus on historic specificity in the text through dating, at one of the key points in the novel—the beginning, which usually receives more critical attention than other parts of the work—is significant.[4] For it not only dates the "object" that is being presented to the reader—thus providing the setup for the historico-mimetic language environment that I investigated in Chapter 3—but also *defines* the limitations of the item here shown. The Ewing diary is shown to be an imagined—and misdated, through anachronism—partial documentation of the personal historic record of the time. Indeed, this sly, one-off reference implies a broader documentary archive of the period, with additional details and material lost to time—as one would see in a true archive.

The Ewing diary is a fictional object that continually makes reference to its own privacy and the risk of its discovery by others—a not terribly subtle metafictional technique. To draw attention to its own form, Mitchell has Ewing write that he "remembered this journal," which is "visible to any drunken sailor who might break in," thereby situating the reader in both a voyeuristic and inebriated state.[5] It is an object of which the purported "author" believes that he "must be more vigilant than ever" to ensure that "this diary should not be read by unfriendly eyes."[6] At one point Ewing even arranges for the safe transfer of his diary to his family at the point in the text when he believes that his goose, so to speak, is cooked.[7] The text also continually calls attention to the act of writing, as seen in much postmodern metafiction.[8] For instance, the reader is told that an act is "easier written than done," reminded of a past time when the author "wrote this sunny sentence," shown how the writing has caused the author to have "worn away a nib" by his scribbling, persuaded that the writer is midact ("even as I write these words"), and prompted to note that the action is narrated from within an inscribed, mediated story that has its own internal chronology ("A continuance of yesterday's narrative," "Yesterday's entry," and the fascinatingly metatextual "The temptation to begin at the perfidious end is strong, but this diarist shall remain true to chronology").[9] These acts of writing draw attention to the object-document status of the Ewing diary as one of many, within a broader archive.

As with all diaries, Ewing's narrative, though, bursts the personal bounding of its pages and expands to encode historical events within its frame. For instance, we are given the extended subhistory of the Moriori genocide to which I have already devoted some attention.[10] This is explicitly framed as the recording of a "spoken history" that Ewing feels he must "record in these pages" for its significance.[11] Mitchell further supplements the explicit historical retelling through characters' personal lives and their intersections with the broader history. Thus, while the initial historical telling is simply a related history, Autua's personal life augments this background.[12] This historical expansion is not only a textual function that leads to the diary object appearing as though part of an archive; it is also one that Mitchell generically ascribes to other writers of the period for which he is aiming: "I recall the crimes Mr. Melville imputes to Pacific missionaries in his recent account of the *Typee*."[13]

Yet perhaps what is most significant about "The Pacific Journal of Adam Ewing," as forming part of the constituting archive that underpins *Cloud Atlas*, is its focus on historiographic bias within its record. Time and time again, Ewing reports his caution, or anxieties, about what is inscribed in the diary. At times the diary object is a space into which Ewing claims to pour his soul, a surface onto which anything and everything can (and must) be recorded in an act of *parrhesic* inscription: "I come to my journal as a Catholick to a confessor . . . steering as close to the facts as possible."[14] At other times, Ewing is a poor penitent, and he explicitly notes his difficulties in writing the truth, the whole truth, and nothing but the truth, confessing that his "initial resolve to report all I had seen . . . weakened as I approached" and that he is "still undecided what to report & to whom."[15]

This self-crafting of identity and admission of unreliable narration beckons toward the type of appraisal that one would expect a historian to make of an archival document; the diary object asks us to query its veracity (even as it appears within a work of fiction). Indeed, this is exactly the exercise that Frobisher undertakes in the "Letters from Zedelghem" when he discovers the diary. First, he remarks on the physical partiality of the text, which I noted above with reference to the diary's frame bursting: "It begins on the 99th page" / "It begins on the ninety-ninth page." It also, as above, is considered by Frobisher to be "too structured for a genuine diary."[16] These sentiments are repeated later in the second portion of the "Letters from Zedelghem," where Frobisher tells the reader that he has recovered all of the text from "the interrupted page until the end of the Ist volume." Interestingly, though, Frobisher's version remains partial. The journal is described as a "½ book" / "half-book"—another clear metatextual jab to which I will return shortly. Yet, even then, Frobisher historically contextualizes the Ewing diary, this time with ironic reference to World War I. For he describes Ewing as "happy, dying Ewing, who never saw the unspeakable forms waiting around history's corner."[17] This closing remark on the diary has two effects. First, it draws our attention once more to the partial perspective of the archive; it highlights what a historical speaker cannot know from his or her temporally bounded perspective and invites us, as critical historical readers, to appraise this. Ewing does not and cannot know of the war to end all wars, the unspeakable forms to which Frobisher must be pointing. On the second front, though, the line also carries a unique irony for Frobisher, who writes in 1931, just a short eight years before Europe will begin the war after the war to end all wars and witness the most abhorrent acts of genocide yet known to humanity.

The First World War looms large over the "Letters" chapter; Frobisher's brother, Adrian, was killed during those "days of bunting and cheering." This moment of historical exteriority is framed through an act of memorializing time dilation—we are, now, in the narrative "thirteen years since Armistice," but the years "seemed only as hours" to the writer—but also through historiography. The historiography of this moment that signals the wider archival context is, aptly for *Cloud Atlas*, twofold. In the first case, the text features historically situating remarks on the poor luck of the lost generation of World War I: "We cut a pack of cards called historical context—our generation, Sixsmith, cut tens, Jacks and Queens. Adrian's cut threes, fours and fives. That's all." The second context is more specific and centers, I would argue, on Paul Fussell's pioneering *The Great War and Modern Memory* (1975). As is well known, in this text Fussell was among the first to write of how, in the Uranian tradition, "given this association between war and sex, and given the deprivation and loneliness and alienation characteristic of the soldier's experience—given, that is, his need for affection in a largely womanless world—we will not be surprised to find both the actuality and the reality of front-line experience replete with what we can call the homoerotic."[18] For reasons of economy, I do not wish to delve extensively into Fussell's argument and the considerable volume of critical response that it generated. Instead, I wish to note that these intertwining thoughts around sexuality, war, and memory—of which Fussell is credited as among the loudest and earliest proponents—find a converging locus in *Cloud Atlas*. For it is immediately after searching for his sibling's grave that Frobisher wonders whether his "brother liked boys as well as girls too, or if that vice is [his] alone." We are told to "think of those troopers, lying together, cowering, alive; cold, dead," and to "wonder if he died celibate."[19] Certainly, a broader historical archive toward which the text gestures here helps us to contextualize such a conflation of history, sexuality, and modern memory.

The "Letters from Zedelghem" are also saturated with markers that point to their own mediation within a historical archive. The epistolary form with which the chapter opens—"Château Zedelghem, / Neerbeke, / West Vlaanderen, / 29th—vi—1931" (in block capitals in *Cloud Atlas E*)—is designed to provide an air of textual realism in both its detail and its own chronicle of postal materiality.[20] At the same time, there is a fictional displacement here. There is no village called "Neerbeke" in West Flanders, but there is a "Meerbeke" in East Flanders. There is also nowhere called "Zedelghem," as spelled here, but there is a "Zedelgem" in West Flanders, which plays host to Loppem Castle—possibly the model for Mitchell's château, containing, as it does, a lake within the grounds.[21]

Letters are not the only mediated and archivally traceable technology to appear in the "Letters from Zedelghem" chapter. For instance, early in the chapter, Frobisher bitterly reprimands Sixsmith for sending him a telegram: "A telegram, Sixsmith? You *ass*. . . . Telegrams attract attention!"[22] In this section of the novel communication technologies, in all their forms, serve as the way in which we can understand the situation within an archive of historical transmission. For instance, the very title of the chapter—invoking the history of the epistolary novel—refers to the inter-European postal service in the 1930s but, specifically, to the uniquely delayed temporality of this technology.[23] These communication technologies are also as prone to dangerous interception as was Ewing's journal. In addition to the attention attracted by the telegram, Frobisher notes that "it wouldn't do to leave *these* pages lying around for a certain seventeen-year-old snoop to come across."[24]

That said, consider, for instance, how the technology of the postal service is contrasted here with the aforementioned telegraph. At one point, Tadeusz Augustowski sends an "enigmatic telegram after the performance in Cracow," which reads: "FIRST TODTENVOGEL MYSTIFIED STOP SECOND PERFORMANCE FISTICUFFS STOP THIRD ADORED STOP FOURTH TALK OF TOWN STOP."[25] Here, the telegraph facilitates high-speed communication in hitherto impossible ways; the telegram arrives first, and the "newspaper clippings followed."[26] The era instigated by the telegraph is one in which the word *newspaper*—combining that which is new with the material technologies of print—becomes oxymoronic as paper becomes too slow to accommodate "the new." It is also hardly a stretch of the imagination to see, in the telegraph, the precursor of rapid communication over the internet.[27] The differences between the speed of electric transmission and hand-delivered mail are all the more prominent in *Cloud Atlas* when Frobisher complains of their conspicuous rapidity, blaming Sixsmith for drawing attention to him, even while later in the text he warns, "If you think I'll wait around for your letters to appear, I'm afraid you are much mistaken."[28] Yet Frobisher still falls back on technologies of manual inscription, "sitting at [his] escritoire" and seeking out "manuscript paper."[29]

The "Letters from Zedelghem" chapter also signposts beyond its own bounds to a set of other, missing letters that can be inferred to exist by the historiographically inclined reader. Frobisher's replies to Sixsmith make passing reference to Sixsmith's own letters that contain requests from Frobisher's parents in Cambridge for information on his whereabouts: "Shred my parents' request for information on my whereabouts and drop it into the Cam. . . . Mater is not 'frantic' " / "Fold my parents' mortifying letter into a paper boat and sail it down the Cam. . . . Mater is not 'frantic.' "[30] The reader is further given an instance in which Frobisher suggests that Sixsmith is fabricating letters from the former's parents: "Your tedious letter from my father's 'solicitor' was an Ace of Diamonds. Bravo. . . . Saffron Walden postmark also a masterly touch. Did you actually drag yourself away from your lab into the sunny Essex afternoon to post it yourself?" (Saffron Walden being quite some distance from Cambridge in the UK—indeed, in a different county).[31] We are told that Frobisher has also written several different versions of some letters: "If long letter is intercepted, another one is waiting in her dressing table."[32] The letters also contain signposts of their own future subjects in a way that feels, as Frobisher would put it, a little too well structured. For instance, the introduction to "Mrs. Dhondt" is closed with the assertion that "you'll meet her again in future letters, no doubt."[33]

Furthermore, this "Letters" chapter has its own peculiarities of typeface, as with Ewing's ampersands, at least in *Cloud Atlas P*. Significantly,

I would argue, the recurring contraction of fractional numbers into singular Unicode glyphs (or using Unicode fraction markers)—that is, not 1/2 or "half" but ½—is far from accidental in this version (indeed, popular word processing software such as Microsoft Word does not automatically convert "9/10ths" to "⁹⁄₁₀ths"). While this does not occur in *Cloud Atlas E* or in other translations, which tend to use terms such as *mezzo* or *half* written in full (of especial import in the Italian translation given the musical overtones of Frobisher's story), in *Cloud Atlas P* there is a near-constant typographic draw toward the fractional.[34] Instances include the following: "when we'd been alone ½ a minute," "my ½-packed valise," "my job is ⁹⁄₁₀ths anticipation," "the curtain ½ open," "½ past two," "another ½ year," "½ playful, ½ darkly," "½ expected," "½ as good a husband," "½ a ripped-in-two volume," "the ½-book," "½-way down," "½ hoped," "½ running ½ hobbling," and "½ forgot."[35] For a book composed of multiple half-books, *Cloud Atlas P* draws a great deal of typographical attention to its own splicing, all told within a narrative that is itself only a fraction of a life story. In fact, even were most of these instances written as the word *half*, as in *Cloud Atlas E* and its derivatives, they would still constitute a significant metatextual feature.

The historiography of the "Letters from Zedelghem" reflects back on the interpretation and reception of the Ewing chapter, as above, but also signposts forward with links for its own encapsulation. Perhaps the most trite of these motifs is the oft-remarked-on birthmarks that run through the novel and that are shared between characters across time periods: "She plays with that birthmark in the hollow of my shoulder, the one you said resembles a comet."[36] That said, regardless of how superficial the birthmark motif may seem, reincarnation and impossible foresight are clearly key themes for the work; the second Library of Congress classification for the novel in *Cloud Atlas E* is "Reincarnation," following "Fate and Fatalism." Ayrs apparently dreams of the future world of Sonmi~451 when he remarks that he "dreamt of a . . . nightmarish café, brilliantly lit, but underground, with no way out. . . . The waitresses all had the same face. The food was soap, the only drink was cups of lather."[37] And as with Ewing's chapter, "Letters from Zedelghem" gives instructions for the letters' own preservation—or, at least, the preservation of the *Cloud Atlas Sextet* that will later be discovered in the Luisa Rey Mystery chapter: "as we shook hands, he gave me his card, urged me to post a published copy of the score for his ensemble."[38]

Such a strange backward history, in which the textual future is reflected in the past, is also, as I have hinted, clear in "Half-Lives: The First Luisa Rey Mystery," set in 1975.[39] For it is here that we are told, by Luisa Rey, that she's "only a fucking *gossip columnist* in a magazine"; Mitchell says, as previously noted, that the source for the future Sonmi chapter is "gossip magazines."[40] The reader is also given a vision of the dark future of Nea So Copros within Luisa Rey's story:

> An underworld sweatshop clattering with five hundred sewing machines. . . . Limp Donald Ducks and crucified Scooby-Doos have their innards stitched. . . . Each woman—Hispanic or Chinese only—keeps her eyes fixed on the needle-plates. (*Cloud Atlas P* 443)

> An underworld sweatshop clattering with five hundred sewing machines. . . . Limp Donald Ducks and crucified Scooby-Doos have their innards stitched. . . . Each woman keeps her eyes fixed on the needle plates. (*Cloud Atlas E* 425–26)

The Fordist production-line workplace here, coupled with both the Disneyfication of culture and (although notably only in *Cloud Atlas P*) the racial imbalance of those who conduct such physical labor, all combined within a frame of gossip columns, implies that just as the future will read the Luisa Rey mystery, it may be that the past Luisa Rey is equally well writing the future as an obverse futurography.

Furthermore, the Luisa Rey chapter contains within it the most explicit metatextual remarks on historiography within the entire novel. In a passage that is worth citing at length, Isaac Sachs writes in his notebook:

> • *Exposition: the workings of the actual past + the* virtual *past may be illustrated by an event well known to collective history such as the sinking of the* Titanic. *The disaster as it* actually *occurred descends into obscurity as its eyewitnesses die off,*

documents perish + the wreck of the ship dissolves in its Atlantic grave. Yet a virtual *sinking of the* Titanic, *created from reworked memories, papers, hearsay, fiction—in short, belief—grows ever "truer." The actual past is brittle, ever-dimming + ever more problematic to access + reconstruct: in contrast, the virtual past is malleable, ever-brightening + ever more difficult to circumvent/expose as fraudulent.*

- *The present presses the virtual past into its own service, to lend credence to its mythologies + legitimacy to the imposition of will. Power seeks +* is *the right to "landscape" the virtual past. (He who pays the historian calls the tune.)*
- *Symmetry demands an actual + virtual* future, *too. We imagine how next week, next year, or 2225 will shape up—a virtual future constructed by wishes, prophecies + daydreams. This virtual future may influence the actual future, as in a self-fulfilling prophecy, but the actual future will eclipse our virtual one as surely as tomorrow eclipses today. Like Utopia, the actual future + the actual past exist only in the hazy distance, where they are no good to anyone.*
- *Q: Is there a meaningful distinction between one simulacrum of smoke, mirrors + shadows—the actual past—from another such simulacrum—the actual future?*
- *One model of time: an infinite matrioshka [matryoshka* in *Cloud Atlas E] doll of painted moments, each "shell" (the present) encased inside a nest of "shells" (previous presents) I call the actual past but which we* perceive *as the virtual past. The doll of "now" likewise encases a nest of presents yet to be, which I call the actual future but which we* perceive *as the virtual future.*[41]

The reversibility of the construction of history presented herein delimits Mitchell's writing from other British historiographic metafiction. While, at first, the passage reads as though it were simply another metatextual mediation on the twinned nature of encoded history and fiction—emplotment, as in the Sonmi narrative—the focus on the virtual and actual futures here changes the stance.

In the model of time that Mitchell's Sachs proposes here, there is a hierarchy of historical power. The absolute ("brittle") past is eclipsed, over time, by the ("malleable") virtual past. The present creates this virtual past in service of political acts ("the present presses the virtual past into its own service"). Symmetrically, and stretching into the future, the present creates a virtual future of "wishes, prophecies + daydreams." Such a virtual future influences and partially constructs the actual future "as in a self-fulfilling prophecy." The actual future, though, it is claimed, "will eclipse our virtual one" as it becomes materially concrete. This actual future will be a present, of course, that will construct the virtual past that will, in turn, eclipse the absolute past and the virtual future that will both condition and be eclipsed by its actual future-present.

In the "Luisa Rey Mystery" chapter—itself notably only the "First Luisa Rey Mystery," pointing to a series of crime novels that, again, exist beyond the pages of the novel *Cloud Atlas* in the reader's hands—the detective character is used as the by-now traditional substitute figure for the historically inclined reader.[42] Again, it is the mass of material traces, the "documents" that will "perish," that are the key to the constitution of the virtual past that the detective-reader now understands him- or herself to be involved in reconstructing. As one might expect, the "Luisa Rey Mystery" is full of such documents, but it focuses particularly on the Sixsmith dossier. This item, a "vanilla binder," "a secreted-away copy," is supplemented by other archival units: "a folder labeled #LR2," a "padded khaki envelope," and "academic papers, data, notes, early drafts," among other instances of physical documents.[43] The chapter also contains three typeset newspaper pages (more convincingly produced in a double-column layout in *Cloud Atlas P*), the falsified virtual construction of a mediated recent past: quasi-independent documents that the text implies will exist beyond its pages in their faux-documentary nature.[44] Such reference to outside artifacts through alterations in typeface and layout are supplemented by discussions between Luisa's newspaper-room colleagues about articles that will go to print—and thus into the historical archive—but that are never seen or mentioned again.[45]

That said, the Luisa Rey chapter is, at the time the reader first encounters it, *less* explicitly metatextual in its approach to writing than either the Frobisher or Ewing sections. Aside from the titular metadata setting up the chapter as a detective story, the "Luisa Rey Mystery" is neither a letter nor a diary; its object status only becomes totally clear in the subsequent section. That said, the chapter remains saturated with writing and its genealogies. For instance, Luisa Rey exhorts herself to "*go home and just dream up your crappy words for once*."[46] We are also given an extensive history of Luisa Rey's father's journalistic career and the acts of heroic documentation that he undertook in Vietnam.[47] This back-history inscribes a set of humanitarian writing principles almost in DNA through inheritance, albeit one that feels difficult to live up to: "Luisa Rey is no Lester Rey," she remarks.[48]

Conversely, the Luisa Rey section contains the clearest examples of the object mediation of the chapters that the reader has encountered thus far. The chapter opens, for instance, with a strong focus on the now-recorded nature of music when Rufus Sixsmith hears booming "disco music" from the "next apartment."[49] This then progresses to Luisa Rey tracking down a rare vinyl recording of Frobisher's *Cloud Atlas Sextet* from the Lost Chord Record Store—another instance of object hunting as emblematic of archival practices, in this case the librarian or archivist being substituted for a record-shop clerk.[50] The reader is also given a precise account of how Frobisher's letters come to be in Luisa Rey's possession. Sixsmith places the "nine read letters"—corresponding to the nine that the reader has thus far read—inside the "Gideon's Bible" in his "bedside cabinet."[51] These letters are then found by "the maid," who gives them to Luisa Rey, herself masquerading as Sixsmith's niece Megan at this point.[52]

The encapsulation of these letter objects is more bounded than, say, the Ewing diary, at least in one version of the text. When, in *Cloud Atlas P* only, Luisa Rey reads the "first long letter found in Sixsmith's possession," this correlates to the correspondence of June 29, 1931, which is indeed a long letter.[53] While the letters certainly gesture beyond their own bounds by the very fact that they are disaggregated objects, within the "Luisa Rey Mystery," the reader is not given an instance of a Frobisher letter that eludes sight. The final letter also feels distinctly bounded since Frobisher kills himself immediately after writing it. In this instance the archive does appear to be more definitively circumscribed than in other cases, aside from Sixsmith's replies. That said, the uncanny connections that Mitchell forces on the reader—such as the appearance of the schooner on which Ewing sailed, the *Prophetess*—is designed both to unsettle expectations of a closed world and to disturb the idea that the temporality of writing's power extends backward only into the virtual past.[54]

Moving into "The Ghastly Ordeal of Timothy Cavendish," the virtualization of this past is intensified when it is revealed that the Luisa

Rey chapter is, itself, supposed to be a work of fiction, written by a "lady author," the "dubiously named Hilary V. Hush."[55] The comedy touch is here provided by this pseudonymous author claiming that, at age nine, she saw a vision of Alain-Fournier at Lourdes and that this inspired her formulaic crime fiction. It also provides a link to Mitchell's semiautobiographical bildungsroman *Black Swan Green* (2006) and his earlier novel *Number9Dream* (2001), both of which contain characters who read *Le Grand Meaulnes* (1913).

Concerned as it is with the trade publishing industry, "The Ghastly Ordeal" is a chapter replete with material objects that compose an archival constellation. Aside from the book manuscript of the Luisa Rey chapter, the reader is presented with an array of artifacts, both genuine and fabricated. In the latter category Cavendish's attempt to sell "Charles Dickens's own, original, authentic, writing-desk" goes nowhere since it is clear that he possesses no such item, another instance of the potential forgery of archival artifacts.[56] Elsewhere in the chapter we are told of an "autobiography" that has been "edit[ed] and print[ed]," and of memoirs that have been written "in longhand" so that the author cannot "go changing" what has already been "set down."[57] Cavendish is, here, a highly unreliable narrator who seeks credibility through defense by media. A liar by nature—in his attempt to sell the writing desk, for example, and to avoid his debts to the gangland brothers of his vanity press client—Cavendish also purports to be writing this chapter by hand, thereby justifying the convoluted narrative path but also the indisputability of what he has already written. Hence, his digressions and remarks on how it is "odd how the wrong stories pop into one's head" are comments on both the inscription status of this chapter and the act of archival filtering. Just as the novel's metastructure is one where stories interrupt and disrupt others—popping into one's head at the wrong moment—the disentanglement and sorting of documents into individuated components is core to the archival research that sits at the novel's center.

The curious aspect of the mediation of "The Ghastly Ordeal," though, is that although it purports to be a *written* memoir—and, in the sense of the novel *Cloud Atlas*, it *is* a written chapter—and although its many literary references are mostly to written texts (*Le Grand Meaulnes*, *A Christmas*

Carol, *Gulliver's Travels* [1726], *Moby Dick*, *The Gulag Archipelago* [1973], *An Evil Cradling* [1991], Tolstoy, *All Quiet on the Western Front* [1929], *The Drowned and the Saved* [1986], Chekhov, *The Lion, the Witch and the Wardrobe* [1950], *Titus Andronicus* [c. 1588]), there are foreshadows of the *filmic* nature of the chapter.[58] For, as Sonmi remarks, this chapter is, in her mediated world, a "film" / "disney" that she previously "began watching" / "once began."[59] In particular, several reference points in the Cavendish chapter highlight the visual media of film and television that dominated its twentieth-century setting: *Mary Poppins* (1964), *Soylent Green* (1973), *Crimewatch UK* (1984), *One Flew Over the Cuckoo's Nest* (1975), *The Great Escape* (1963), John Wayne, the *Six O'clock News*, a "history programme on BBC2," *Close Encounters of the Third Kind* (1977).[60] Without wishing to elide the differences between television and film, this televisual mode is explicitly highlighted as somehow less mediated than text, when the novel claims that it is "so much more *Real* for ordinary people" than books.[61] Aurora House literally becomes, for Cavendish, a "B-movie asylum."[62] The character also speculates on the day when "*The Ghastly Ordeal of Timothy Cavendish* [will be] turned into a film" and gives instructions to an imaginary moviemaker: "Lars: zoom the camera in from the outside car park."[63]

I explored the archival implications of the Sonmi chapter in Chapter 1, where I noted that the transtextual variance of the novel leads to a destabilized archive that is unable to accurately preserve its own material. What was perhaps less clear there was how the authority of such an imbalanced archive is transmitted to the future world of "Sloosha's Crossin'." In this regressed future world the denizens "pray to Sonmi," indicating that the speculative future of Nea So Copros has been enshrined in oral mythology.[64] Sonmi, here, has become "the map an' the edges o' the map an b'yonder the edges."[65] Furthermore, the Swannekke Island of the Luisa Rey narrative has become a designation for a tribe: the "Swannekke people."[66] In a reverse of the well-known patterns of orality and literacy charted by Walter Ong, Mitchell's far future is a culture that has inverted the trend: a world in which a culture has moved from the written to the spoken word.[67]

Of course, Mitchell's novel, itself a written text, must convey a sense of orality through writing. The very inscribed phonetics that Mitchell presents in the final future chapter are a self-undoing of a future culture that is primarily oral. They are also themselves the archival inscription of an authority that has been gradually diluted throughout the novel, moving from a self-redacted (and potentially published) diary, through a set of intercepted letters, into the pages of a manuscript-within-a-novel, through a farcical film, into an encoded and duplicated testimony, up to the proliferation of theological myth. Transmission and mistransmission, predicated on archival authority, are key. For, indeed, the entire "Sloosha's Crossin'" chapter is revealed, in the final instance, to be a story related by Zachry's son, who is in possession of Sonmi's orison, a matter to which I will return shortly.[68]

When taken in aggregate, the above evidence—coupled with the earlier chapter's work on version variance—lends itself to a clear conclusion: *Cloud Atlas* is a novel about the archive and its reception, a text about mediated object transmission. In many ways *Cloud Atlas* is a novel about textual scholarship and historiographic interpretation, parodying the ways in which texts are received, corrupted, remediated, and circulated over time on the historical scale. The text provides documents for a reader to scrutinize amid its consistent archival framing. The reader is, therefore, a future historian and textual critic of the many archival documents and objects in *Cloud Atlas*, which have, nonetheless, all been forged.

THE SPECIFIC AND THE GENERAL

My second contention, from Chapter 2, is that *Cloud Atlas* is a text that draws attention to the relationship between the specific and the general, between parts and the whole. This is important for considering readerly placement since it pertains to the reading style that the text encourages—namely, the critical unveiling to which I referred in my introduction. For one of the further, noncomputational ways in which we might consider *Cloud Atlas* to be a novel that focuses on the specific against the general is through an analysis of redaction in "The Pacific Journal of Adam Ewing." Redaction in the novel is related to the historical imaginary to which I earlier drew attention. It is not, however, a feature of the text that requires computational methods to examine. Indeed, the diary is littered with "b—s" and other redacted terms of profanity, as noted in Chapter 3. This redaction, though, is a perfect questioning of the type of interrelation of the general and specific to which I made reference. Such redaction is, in one sense, an ultrageneralization: an abstraction to the broadest level of category; the generic blank or floating signifier. Even so, it is clear to the twenty-first-century reader precisely what sits behind such redaction: the specific. The literary effect, of course, is to paint the claimed 1850s prose as from an era of delicate sensibilities. What we make of such redaction, though, is far more complex.

There is a long literary history behind this tradition of redaction, particularly when it comes to names and expletives. As a mode that self-consciously and ostentatiously withholds information from the reader through either the use of consecutive dashes or through a deliberate placement of a black "block" over text, it is difficult not to read redactions instituted by the author as unplumbed textual depths that should be excavated by the canny reader—a second text beneath the text, in the symptomatic vein. This contrivance appears prominently with respect to names and addresses in the nineteenth-century novel; *Jane Eyre*'s references to ". . . shire" are among the first to spring to mind. Heinrich von Kleist's 1808 novella *The Marquise of O. . .* even features a redaction in its title. Such redaction, however, is different from the Heideggerian or Derridean phenomenon of writing *sous rature*. Instead, as John Barth notes in his playful creative/critical postmodern work *Lost in the Funhouse* (1968), these redactions or blanks often serve as an artificial realist device that attempts to blur the distinction between the fiction and some underlying facticity: "Initials, blanks, or both were often substituted for proper names in nineteenth-century fiction to enhance the illusion of reality. It is as if the author felt it necessary to delete the names for reasons of tact or legal liability. Interestingly, as with other aspects of realism, it is an *illusion* that is being enhanced, by purely artificial means."[69]

That said, it is surprising that there is so little scholarship that deals with redaction in the novel. Certainly, there are the readings by Jacques Lacan, Jacques Derrida, and Barbara Johnson in the late 1970s of Edgar Allan Poe's *The Purloined Letter* (1844), disagreeing variously on the meaning of the absent content of the letter in the midst of the structuring narrative.[70] There are also the early prehistories of the novel that note the complex interrelations among sociolegal responsibility, historiography, and the world represented within the text, particularly in the *roman à clef*.[71] But the most extensive treatment of redaction (or, at least, blanks) is given by Lisa Gitelman, although this treatment still only comprises two pages of her excellent *Paper Knowledge* (2014), and she confesses up front that "it would probably be fruitless to search for the precise origins of this kind of blank."[72]

Gitelman rightly traces at least a portion of the redaction in the eighteenth century to the potential for libel, as does Lennard J. Davis.[73] Quoting Jonathan Swift's pronouncement that "we are careful never to print a man's name out at length," Gitelman highlights the fact that "everybody alive" will have known to whom Swift was referring at the time of his writing. Although the fame of these characters is now faded in the twenty-first century, for contemporaries of Swift, as Gitelman notes, these blanks are only nominal; "they are not really blank but only virtually so," and they are "sites of transaction between a knowing author and a knowing reader."[74] In such cases the reader is supposed to be able to infer what lies beneath. Yet in other instances it is clear that the blanks are not meant to be uncovered, perhaps merely implying a protofacticity, as Barth noted, or a specific perceived (imagined) sensibility of an era, as I pointed out above.

The degree of inference that is logically possible for a reader encountering a literary redaction depends not only on historico-contextual elements but on more proximate textual-structural aspects. Indeed, *close reading* of blanks is conditioned by surrounding and broader structural contexts. These contextual elements are a type of "metadata" that allow us to read specifics into otherwise *unformed* aspects of a text. They apply to written words as much as they do to blank spaces. That is to say: close reading does not function independently of a more distant surrounding context.

Literature is surrounded by and represents metadata in ways with which all readers are familiar. Consider, for example, figure 17. Most readers will instantly recognize this document, although it has no visible text. It is the copyright frontispiece to a contemporary book with the textual elements redacted. Yet, despite this redaction, most viewers will have accurately recognized that the blocks separated by commas and obliterated by larger chunks are text. Without seeing any of the content, the mere shape, document flow, and spacing here gesture toward words, even without access to the underlying language. The direction of the commas that I have left visible, along with the placement of the © sign, may also allow a reader to infer that this is a European alphabet with a left-to-right reading pattern.

Some of the characters, though, can be deduced to be numbers, rather than text. This is because we recognize certain structural and contextual features of this metadata and can make assumptions about the validity of specific character sets and data types beneath the blanks. Conspicuous silence sometimes speaks loudly of itself to readers. For instance, look at the lines that contain the copyright symbol. We know that the syntax for a standard copyright declaration in English is "© *FirstName LastName Date*." Given that there are two consecutive lines ending in a roughly uniform block size that could accommodate a Gregorian-calendar-style date signifier, it makes sense to assume that this redaction is likely to be a date and that the character set is numerical. With a little background knowledge we can also pinpoint the ISBN lines of this page and work out some of the specific characters (they are the lines situated approximately three-quarters of the way down the page). One might know that this is an ISBN because most book publications are likely to have an ISBN and, in this case, the blanks appear to signify ISBN-13-style formatting (e.g., 978-1-107-09789-6) in their spacing. These lines are also preceded by a four-character block that could read "ISBN" and followed by a redacted block that could denote a publication type (perhaps "Hardback" or "Paperback"). We can also, with some sleuthing, guess at some of the digits in the ISBN. It is highly probable that the ISBN begins with the numbers 978, since this EAN-13 identifier occurs in the majority of assigned ISBN-13 numbers. Although the 979 prefix is also becoming more common, 978 is the most likely set of digits here. The next digit seems to be a lone number, probably either a 1 or 0, which would indicate that the book in question comes from a majority English-speaking country.

It also seems clear that the first redacted block of text at the head of the page is some form of press logo. The second, comma-separated line could potentially be an address. The following line would likely be some type of mission statement. The large blocks of text that are totally redacted are probably tedious legal disclaimers that are seldom read until people find themselves taken to court. In fact, given that such legal disclaimers are usually ignored, the way in which most readers "read" these blank blocks is identical to the

FIGURE 17. Redacting copyright.

way in which they read them when the text is available. Sometimes, redactions are as much use to readers as though the full text were legible. There are also a number of lines that look likely to be website URLs.

The purpose of this exercise, which I owe to Geoffrey Bilder, is to demonstrate a simple fact pertinent to the reading of literary redaction. Known generic forms and structuration principles—that function similarly to the structural metadata in the example above—texture and color the valid interpretative pathways for redacted text. Brontë's ". . .shire" denotes an English county by the common suffix; Kleist's "Marquise of O. . ." yields a place and a name.

The structuring elements that surround the blank redactions in *Cloud Atlas* are designed to bring to the fore the claimed historical specificity of the Ewing chapter. The clearest instance of this is when Goose—mirrored in the text's later ornithologically named MD, "Dr. Egret"[75]—claims that Ewing has begged him to "keep that d—d nigger away from me."[76] The alienating shock effect here is the same as that exemplified in my earlier corpus percentage analysis: that the word *damned* might require censoring while the truly more offensive racial slur remains in plain sight disconcerts the reader. This is a type of uncanny effect in which we realize that we are not at home in our own time period—which is itself nonetheless replete with structural (and still, often, overt linguistic) racism—but instead in a world of hegemonically accepted, explicit, linguistic racial abuse. In this case the reader is asked to question what is here generic and what is specific. At this point terms of abuse (*damn* or the earlier *bitch/bastard*[77]—although *bitch* occurs in plaintext, too)[78] are redacted; they are made into generic forms that are cross-substitutable with others. At the same time, the knowing reader is expected to interpolate a specific term within the blank mark on the page. The juxtaposition of the more offensive term also complicates our ability to read generically. For if we assume that we know the set of terms that might fit beneath generic redaction—those that are offensive—then the twenty-first-century reader should be disconcerted at the proximate inconsistency of encountering the unredacted, specific term, *nigger*.

In some ways, though, this is also what *Cloud Atlas* does at its broadest textual level. In billing itself as a novel, the work engenders a pretense toward a coherent specificity of genre, only to undermine this. The novel gives a diffuse set of generically specific practices, in contrast to the expected form of "a novel." In each shifting genre sense, *Cloud Atlas* undermines our expectations of the genre of a novel, even while using generic practices from the novel's history to achieve that. The reader is at once supposed to recognize the specifics of the generic segment and its antecedents even while feeling that the master structure of the book has been undermined. In other words: the focus on the generic and the specific that I highlighted in Chapter 2 runs at the metalevel throughout *Cloud Atlas*'s form and casts the reader as a critical reader, one who should question the surfaces and depths of the words on the page and the "documents" within the fictional archive.

READERLY PLACEMENT AFTER THE END OF HISTORY

Fundamentally, *Cloud Atlas* makes a joke about and mounts a critique of the "end of history." As above, the temptation with the book is to place the text's imagined/interpellated reader *after* "Sloosha's Crossin,' " since this would be, in theory, the only place at which such a constructed reader could possibly view the entire historical narrative offered by the text.[79] Such a narrative perspective on history always assumes a looking back. Yet *Cloud Atlas* is a novel that deals with strange warpings and loops of time, and it does so, primarily, by using genre forms and a nonlinear narrative flow. Through its structure and narrative contents, it "problematizes the arrow"—that symbol of linear time—"in terms of narrative teleology," as Diletta De Cristofaro puts it.[80]

In Mitchell's grand universe of his multiple novels, time assumes many forms. It is telescopic, fractal, and it runs at different speeds, as just three examples.[81] The single novel on which I am here focused is also a *compressor* of time. The text itself functions as a means of compacting thousands of years of history and future speculation into the space of a few days' worth of reading, making it an apt novelistic space for a distant close reading, as I noted in my introduction. Of course, many novels achieve such a feat; few, however, cover so vast a terrain as *Cloud Atlas*.

Most importantly, the specific compression that the novel achieves (at least when using the specific measures that I have covered in this book) is to pack its narrative to between approximately 1950 and 1980, through both its generic and linguistic mediation. On the one hand, I have shown how the text attempts in terms of language to place its lower boundary at 1850 but actually ends up closer to the mid-twentieth century in terms of etymology. On the other hand, the mediation of the last, far-future section of the novel is achieved through direct imitation of Russell Hoban's seminal language-bending 1980 novel, *Riddley Walker*. A combination of linguistic and generic readings substantially narrows the novel's referential time frame.

That Mitchell's novel uses the regressed language of Hoban's dystopia, written almost forty years ago as of this writing, for its most far-flung section narrows one reading of the time frame within the novel substantially. As a result, the text is dated to the precise period detailed in Francis Fukuyama's well-known (although now, also, fairly old) anti-Marxist (although still dialectical) take on "the end of history," in which, he contends that liberal democracy and capitalism become an endpoint from which no further change is possible or desirable: at the birth of high neoliberalism in the 1980s.[82] This is the period in which the logic of capital becomes one of no alternative with an impossibility of failure. Every time capital fails, it is simply asserted that this is merely because of problems of implementation: capitalism "has never been seriously tried."[83] Indeed, for Peter Fenves, the "fact that Fukuyama's announcement of the end of history enacts nothing, makes no demands, and discovers no new desires converges with the ineluctable fact from which the case for this announcement seeks confirmation: the fact that there is a lack of alternatives to speaking the language of liberal democracy."[84]

As I noted in Chapter 1, there are several ways in which Mitchell's text gestures specifically toward Fukuyama's thesis. In *Cloud Atlas E* the archivist holds a (potentially false) belief that "future ages will still be corpocratic ones."[85] Such a belief chimes with Fukuyama's contended thesis that liberal capitalism will triumph as the final economic form of history since "the dynamism of capitalist economies tends to break down many conventional and cultural barriers to equality through its continually changing demand for labor."[86] The inequality of economic slavery that Mitchell depicts in Papa Song's diner is a direct challenge to this claim.

The novel itself is also concerned with motifs of repetition; its object-mediated connections between characters over vast time periods and the physical inscription of legible (l)inks through birthmarks is intended to represent exhausted possibilities, albeit in permutation. The fact that neither any generic precursor for Mitchell's text, nor any new linguistic coinage within the novel (beside Mitchell's own neologisms), is to be found from after 1980 also limits the futurity of the novel, even when the text's setting is the far-flung future.

Such a thesis is problematic, however. For Mitchell's novel joins the ranks of those who are critical of Fukuyama's argument.[87] The locutor—the archivist—is, to reiterate, an agent of a secretive future state, which is attempting to instill fear into its population by fabricating a rebellion that would not have otherwise existed. In doing so, the system uncovers the real dissent of Sonmi~451, even though she is unable to avert her own death. This is hardly the liberal state of Fukuyama's text. Indeed, in this way *Cloud Atlas* becomes a focalized critique of the end-of-history thesis, for the future world of Sonmi~451 is accurately described by Jacques Derrida in his 1994 *Specters of Marx*: "never have violence, inequality, exclusion, famine, and thus economic oppression affected as many human beings in the history of the earth and of humanity."[88]

Further along on this same thread, a central plank of Fukuyama's argument is that human beings crave a type of recognition for their basic dignity and humanity: *thymos*. Certainly, many have criticized the insufficiency of this portion of Fukuyama's argument.[89] Yet, for Fukuyama, only liberal-democratic capital is capable of fulfilling this desire. *Cloud Atlas* claims otherwise, particularly in *Cloud Atlas P*. In the *P* text, as in the above chapter on textual variances, there is a more strident emphasis on the degraded conditions of slavery or bonded labor (tied to race) that are engendered under a future corpocratic (capitalistic) state. It is an important feature of the market circulation of Mitchell's novel that in the US—the shining emblem of Fukuyama's thesis—the extremities of such criticisms were excised from the novel. In the land of free speech it seems that some criticisms, especially those addressing the fracturing and sensitive histories of race and slavery that have shaped the modern republic, are more welcome than others. Indeed, a strong criticism of Fukuyama's end of history is that while he scoffs at the idea that "slavery may recur," a 2017 report indicated that more than forty million people around the world *are* still living under conditions of slavery, with two million of those based within the Americas.[90] *Cloud Atlas* makes this argument about the working conditions of capital, even while purporting a different type of recognition for its people: pattern recognition. Through its cycling histories, *Cloud Atlas* shows commonalities of personhood and dignity based on commonalities across time rather than on any characteristic of the political system under which its characters exist. Even if, as Joanna Bourke has convincingly argued, "the concept of 'the human' is very volatile" and that distinctions between humans and animals are "both contested and policed," *Cloud Atlas* seeks a historical continuity of recognition of a loosely defined personhood, over its differing historical contexts.[91]

The cyclical structure of history in *Cloud Atlas*, in which a grand eternal recurrence is framed, also sits badly alongside Fukuyama's text. For Fukuyama claims that "mankind does not return periodically to the same state of ignorance" and that "a truly cyclical history is conceivable only if we posit the possibility that a given civilization can vanish entirely without leaving any imprint on those that follow," both statements being premised on the idea of a positivist direction of technological development.[92] Fukuyama does note that science fiction novels since the Second World War have frequently represented the "possibility of the cataclysmic destruction of our modern, technological civilization," but this possibility is brushed aside as unrealistic fiction, since Fukuyama claims that the knowledge of modern science cannot be unlearned.[93] One might retort: if stranded on a desert island, how many laypeople would be able to build that most basic of contemporary technologies, a working refrigerator?

By reading its literalization of Fukuyama's title, we can also see in *Cloud Atlas* a swipe at the idea of the "last man" at the end of history. Within the narrative chronology, the final protagonist offered by Mitchell's text is Zachry. He is, the reader is led to believe for most of this chapter, literally the "last man" of Mitchell's novel—the final central character to whom we will be introduced. Yet, in just a few lines at the end of "Sloosha's Crossin'," Mitchell undoes this thesis. The reader is, out of the blue, given a line from Zachry's son: "Zachry my old pa was a wyrd buggah, I won't naysay it now he's died."[94]

Furthermore, depending on whether one takes historical or narrative time, technically the "last man" of the novel is also the first: Ewing. The last man turns out to be anything but, and the apocalypse at Mitchell's end of history becomes just another transient episode amid constant repetition with difference; every story is narrated from a future, historically mutated vantage point, and the final, yet also middle, tale of *Cloud Atlas* is no different.

Cloud Atlas, in many ways, then, is more cynical yet also more optimistic than Fukuyama's conservative, anti-Marxist theory. It is a skeptical and cynical novel because it envisages a future historical regression, one in which the human desire for recognition—*thymos*, in Fukuyama's terms—is achieved through historical pattern recognition. This is the pessimism to which Fukuyama constantly refers. Indeed, *Cloud Atlas* is therefore, as Fukuyama once put it, a deeply "postmodern" novel that posits, from a comfortable position, that there is no rational pattern to history that can be discerned: no universal logical key.[95] Yet it is a more hopeful—or, at least, imaginative—novel of history than Fukuyama's thesis: the endpoint of liberal capital is revealed as a mere comforting illusion based on radical economic inequality, and pattern recognition can bind us throughout history.

Cloud Atlas is not, at the end, though, a pessimistic text: how could it be, when its final line reminds us, in the face of an ocean of indifference, of what an ocean is composed: drops? A textual believer in the power, but also potential misprision, of narrative and object-mediation, *Cloud Atlas*'s focus on drops, on oceans, on the specific, and the unique, ultimately also applies to the text's own ideas of time and change. Despite the coming so-called postcritical age, *Cloud Atlas* is a novel that asks us to read the long 1980s in a critical light, against a world of indentured servitude, of potential cures that merely serve to poison us further, and against the seeming momentum of perpetual imperial rise and fall. It is a text that shows us the end of history, in more senses than one, before turning its back on them all, in favor of a critical present.

CONCLUSION

> Every six months or so, the higher-education press appears to run out of stories. Bereft of material, journalists turn to the loosely grouped digital humanities as their punching bag of choice. There is no shortage of conventional literary critics and historians who are all too willing to take up the fight against this straw figure. It is claimed that because digital humanities receives funding and sometimes builds technologies, it must be neoliberal.[1] It is claimed that quantification will destroy the human element of the humanities.

It is time that we abandoned these comforting arguments. Conventional literary studies has nothing to fear from digital technologies. At some point, all scientism about literature must encounter a fundamental truth: it is attempting to describe something—an artwork—that defies empirical logic and replaces intersubjective with individual and subjective truth. This is not to say that we cannot find worth from close reading with computers. As with all good criticism, elucidatory approaches that bring fresh evidence to light can increase our engagement with, understanding of, and pleasure within a work of fiction. Computational methods can help us with the *empiricism* that is crucial to accurate close reading.

The other core aspect that I have explored throughout this book is that general assumptions about computational methods and labor reduction, especially in relation to the scale of depth, do not necessarily hold true. The digital humanities are often branded as solely concerned with functioning at scale, at a size greater than human labor power will permit. Clearly, the activities for which I have used computational methods in this book would still have been possible without the use of computers; they would just have been immensely tedious. For the legal reasons that I outlined in my introduction, though, the labor in preparing the corpus for these techniques was huge and probably beyond any reasonable level of work that could be conducted at scale. The type of medium-distance approach that I have used in this book, then, warps our conventional definitions of close and distant reading. For one thing, it is a form of close reading that uses distant reading's data- and text-mining approaches. For another, it uses techniques that save us from quantities of tedious labor, even while itself demanding much preparatory (and tedious) labor. Finally, it is a technique that knows a truth that close reading has concealed for many decades: that single texts contain unfathomable depths and large-scale distances, Mariana Trenches of size concealed beneath the surface waves.

I have also attempted throughout this book to weave my data-driven approaches back into a more traditional set of literary hermeneutics—that is, to use the computational methods as data gathering for literary interpretation. If, in one sense, this is what close reading has always done—looked closely for features that could serve to promote or discredit an interpretative standpoint—then it is actually somewhat the case that there is little difference between close and computational distant reading. For, where close reading might seek textual features (albeit valuing them for their intrarelations within single or a small set of texts), distant reading might look for such features at scale across a large number of novels. Once distant reading has amassed its evidence, it must then look for explanations, narratives, and historical stories within which to weave its findings, just as close reading must, on the micro scale.

The title of this book uses the phrase "computational formalism," a matter that I have not yet addressed. This term is derived, obviously, from the longer histories of formalist literary study but also from the Stanford Literary Lab's first pamphlet, "Quantitative Formalism." The reason for the change of the first term is clear enough. I wanted a phrase that indicated, specifically, the repetitious task-based nature of the work here conducted using computers, as opposed to the purely numerical approach signaled in the Stanford Lab's publication. But I have stuck with the term *formalism*, which perhaps requires a little more justification. *Form*, as Caroline Levine has reminded us, is a broad term.[2] It is also the case that form cannot be confined to internal textual observations within the aesthetic realm; all readings are embroiled within networks of social understanding, and literary linguistics collide with readerly contexts. Formal adherence to generic conventions, for instance, requires correlation with other texts and extratextual social realities.

Yet, for the most part, this book has looked at the structures of language, of internal structural ordering, and of aesthetic matters of the text (even as the final close reading examined the political import of these aspects). These are, after all, both the subject matters of close reading and the easiest elements of a text to quantify for processing purposes. This is not to say that a computational approach that looked at more social aspects of literary works is impossible. It is also the case that in the comparative study of literary etymology and word frequencies, the study of the novel's language choices only made sense when compared to the choices made in other texts. It is the differentiation of literary choices, made by an author, from the choices made across the writings of the broader social body that matters.

Finally, there is a looming challenge for literary studies as such computational methods become more prevalent, toward which I have already gestured on a few occasions. In this book I have stuck with tried-and-tested (and, in technological terms, relatively dated) digital approaches. On the one hand, this has the advantage of making it easier to draw firmer conclusions, albeit then not having had cutting-edge technology at my disposal. On the other hand, at present the trend in the field is toward statistical-literary modeling. Such techniques use advanced machine-learning approaches to create a model, based on known inputs, that can then make predictions about broader sets of data. The problem is that with the growth of such sophisticated techniques comes a commensurate difficulty in understanding and using them in a responsible fashion. That is, even while think pieces seem, on a daily basis, to ask for new forms of information literacy in the humanities ("learn to code," etc.), these very forms are rapidly becoming necessary but insufficient for an understanding of the latest statistical machine learning models.

The obverse of this problem/challenge, though, is that while an obvious answer would seem to be to create interdisciplinary teams, partly from information studies and partly from literary studies, such teams quickly become lopsided. As Alexander R. Galloway put it: "Ultimately it comes down to this: if you count words in *Moby-Dick*, are you going to learn more about the white whale? I think you probably *can*—and we have to acknowledge that. But you won't learn anything new about *counting*."[3] It is this asymmetry of interdisciplinary approaches—in which a home discipline uses techniques from another, but only the home discipline truly benefits—that creates at least part of the problem once noted by Stanley Fish (no particular friend himself of the digital humanities), namely that interdisciplinarity is so very hard to do.[4]

In turn, this leads to a challenge for close reading itself. What would it mean to conceive of an interdisciplinary team effort for close reading? For many this might seem a strange concept; close reading has, I would suggest, become understood as an activity undertaken in solitude both by and for oneself. Even when taught in communal spaces, the aim appears to be to empower the reader to leave the group environment and to perform his or her own close readings. Yet in many ways such a view ignores the history of close reading pioneered by Richards and the pedagogical form through which close reading is taught today. After all, these two bases for close reading rely on the seminar, a communal space wherein many pairs of eyes and many different types of expertise come together to collaboratively discuss and work with texts. Regardless of the romantic individualist lens through which close reading is often viewed at this moment, its historical genesis and its continued teaching are linked to interpersonal spaces.

Perhaps, then, the fear is not really of interdisciplinary groups per se but rather a reservation about the cultural status and prestige of literary studies within such groups. As a disparate field with not even a concretely defined object of study, the constant professionalizing desire of the discipline of literary studies balks at the idea of other spaces encroaching on close reading. Indeed, the nightmare of English literature (but also of other national literatures), to twist a Joycean phrase, could be articulated thus: if close reading becomes an activity that works across disciplinary boundaries, what domain of expertise will remain within literary studies? What is it that literary studies, in particular and distinctly from other disciplines, can discern for the empirical and hermeneutic practices of close reading? What might it mean that statistical literacy could be as important to understanding close readings of the future as verbal literacy? The growing fear here points to literary studies' own anxiety of obsolescence.

I do not have answers to these challenges of knowledge and collaboration for the future direction of English studies. It is not clear to me, at the time of this writing, whether quantitative methods will come to dominate the field of literary research. For instance, the teaching pipeline of higher education does not, at present, do a good job of training students in the use of quantitative methods. That said, there is certainly ever more pressure to adopt scientistic methods, both as a funding imperative and as a practical necessity for dealing with the volume of literary material that is published. Yet the *experience* of reading statistically and reading as a human remain very different from one another. Students do not come to interview at undergraduate level and profess their love of statistically modeling texts; they say that they love reading. This signals the persistence of conventional close readings for the immediate future. The same differentiation, though, could be posited between the experiences of reading "academically" and of reading for pleasure. Many students also claim, at the close of their literary degrees, that the fun has been sucked out of reading. Regardless, though, I hope that I have shown at least some of the merits that a digital approach could bring to our close readings. Where next such computational formalism may take us remains an unknown on which I am unwilling to hazard a guess.

APPENDIXES

Appendix A
TEXTUAL VARIANTS OF CLOUD ATLAS

For reference purposes I present here a concordance of excerpts from P and E editions with the numbering referring to the question count (Q1, Q2, etc.) from the start of the Sonmi narrative. To comply with copyright, these are redacted in most cases, except where I have analyzed the works above, but enough information is included to allow the identification and verification of the textual editions detailed herein.

TABLE 3. Textual Variants of *Cloud Atlas*

Variant	*P* page	*Cloud Atlas P* text (UK)	*E* page	*Cloud Atlas E* text (US)
Q1	187	"Historians still unborn will appreciate your cooperation in the future, Sonmi~451. We archivists thank you in the present. . . .Once we're finished, the orison will be archived at the Ministry of Testaments. . . .Your version of the truth is what matters."	185	"On behalf of my ministry, thank you for agreeing to this final interview. Please remember, this isn't an interrogation, or a trial. Your version of the truth is the only one that matters."
R1	187	"No other version of the truth has ever mattered to me."	185	"TRUTH IS SINGULAR. ITS 'VERSIONS' ARE MISTRUTHS."
Q2	187	"Let's begin. Usually, I start by asking interviewees to recall their very earliest memories. You look uncertain."	185	"Good. Ordinarily, I begin by asking prisoners to recall their earliest memories to provide a context for corpocratic historians of the future."
R2	187	"I have no earliest memories, Archivist. Every day of my life in Papa Song's was as uniform as the fries we vended."	185	"Fabricants have no earliest memories, Archivist. One twenty-four-hour *cycle* in Papa Song's is indistinguishable from any other."

Variant	*P* page	*Cloud Atlas P* text (UK)	*E* page	*Cloud Atlas E* text (US)
Q3	187	"Then would you please describe that world"	185	"Then why not describe this 'cycle'?"
R3	187	"It was a sealed dome about eighty metres across, a dinery owned by Papa Song Corp. Servers spend twelve working years without venturing outside this space, ever. . . . North was the Seer's office; west, his Aides' room; south, the servers' dormroom. Consumers' hygieners were ingressed at north-east, south-east, south-west and north-west. The Hub sat in the centre."	185	"If you wish. A server is woken at hour four-thirty by stimulin in the airflow, then yellow-up in our dormroom . . . .At hour five we man our tellers around the Hub, ready for the elevator to bring the new day's first consumers. For the following nineteen hours we greet diners, input orders, tray food, vend drinks, upstock condiments, wipe tables, and bin garbage. Vespers follows cleaning, then we imbibe one Soapsac in the dormroom."
Q4	188	"Antics?"	186	"You have no rests?"
R4	188	"Various 3D conjuring tricks; . . ."	186	"Only purebloods are entitled to 'rests,' Archivist. For fabricants, 'rests' would be an act of time theft. Until curfew at hour zero, every minute must be devoted to the service and enrichment of Papa Song."
Q5	188	"How many staff worked in the dinery?"	186	"Do servers—unascended servers, I mean—never wonder about life outside your dome, or did you believe your dinery was the whole cosmos?"
R5	188	"Fourteen, approx. . . . Four hundred consumers could be seated."	186	"Oh, our intelligence is not so crude that we cannot *conceive* of an outside. Remember, at Matins, Papa Song shows us pictures of Xultation and Hawaii, and AdV instreams images of a cosmology beyond our servery."

Variant	*P* page	*Cloud Atlas P* text (UK)	*E* page	*Cloud Atlas E* text (US)
Q6	188	"Can you describe a server's schedule?"	186	"What about your sense of time? Of the future?"
R6	188	"Hour four thirty is yellow-up. . ."	186	"Papa Song announces the passing hours to the diners, so I noticed the time of day, dimly, yes. . . . We had only one long-term future: Xultation."
Q7	188	"You have no rests?"	186	"Could you describe this annual 'Star Sermon' ceremony?"
R7	188–89	" 'Rests' constitute time-theft, Archivist!"	186	"After Matins on First Day, Seer Rhee would pin a star on every server's collar. The elevator then took those lucky Twelvestarred sisters for conveyance to Papa Song's Ark."
Q8	189	"Is it true, Fabricants really dream, just like us?"	187	"I'd like to ask about the infamous Yoona~939."
R8	189	"Yes, Archivist."	187	"I knew Yoona~939 better than any fabricant. . . .Her sullenness hid a subtle dignity."
Q9	189	"What have your dreams been about here in prison?"	187	"This 'subtle dignity' you mention—was it a result of her ascension?"
R9	189	"Dreams are all I have ever truly owned."	187	"Postgrad Boom-Sook's research notes were so sparse I cannot be certain when Yoona~939's ascension was triggered."
Q10	189	"Do servers never wonder about the bigger world. . .?"	187	"Popular wisdom has it that fabricants don't have personalities."
R10	189	"Our cosmology is not so crude, or our intelligence so limited."	187	"This fallacy is propagated for the comfort of purebloods."

Variant	*P* page	*Cloud Atlas P* text (UK)	*E* page	*Cloud Atlas E* text (US)
Q11	189	"It's difficult to imagine, living with so many. . . imponderables."	187	" 'Comfort'? How do you mean?"
R11	189	"When you were three or four, Archivist, your father vanished to a realm called 'Work', did he not?"	187	"To enslave an individual troubles your consciences, Archivist, but to enslave a clone is no more troubling than owning the latest six-wheeler ford, ethically."
Q12	189	"So you never wanted to step in the elevator and just. . . y'know, go see?"	187	"When did Yoona~939's deviances—perhaps I should say singularities—first become apparent to you?"
R12	189	"No elevator functions without a Soul aboard."	187–88	"Ah, questions of when are difficult to answer in a world without calendars. . . . I became aware of Yoona~939's irregular speech."
Q13	190	"Did you have a sense of time?"	188	"Irregular?"
R13	190	"Yes: as governed by Catechism Six."	188	"Firstly, she spoke more. . ."
Q14	190	"Which states?"	188	"How could Yoona~939 . . .acquire verbal dexterity. . .?"
R14	190	"*One Year, One Star, Twelve Stars to Xultation!*. . .They xhorted us to. . .join them on Xultation as soon as possible."	188	"An ascending fabricant absorbs language."
Q15	190	"I thought your working life was set at twelve years?"	188	"were you happy, back in those days?"
R15	190	"If a server reports. . ."	188	"of all Nea So Copros's slaves we surely are the most miserable"
Q16	190	"Ah yes, the notorious Yoona ~939. Can you remember meeting her?"	189	"Slaves, you say?"

Variant	*P* page	*Cloud Atlas P* text (UK)	*E* page	*Cloud Atlas E* text (US)
R16	190	"I can."	189	"Corpocracy is built on slavery. . . . Why has my case been assigned to an apparently inxperienced corpocrat?"
Q17	191	"were they a result of her ascension?"	189	"The xecs at the Ministry of Unanimity insisted that you, as a heretic, had nothing to offer corpocracy's archives but sedition and blasphemy. Genomicists, for whom you are a holy grail, as you know, pulled levers on the Juche to have Rule 54.iii—the right to archivism. . ."
R17	191	"Student Boom-Sook's research notes were so chaotic. . ."	189	"So you are gambling your career on this interview?"
Q18	191	"Why do you say that?"	189	"That is the truth of the matter, yes."
R18	191	"To enslave an individual distresses the conscience."	189	"Your frankness is refreshing after so much duplicity."
Q19	191	"When did Yoona~939's deviances become apparent to you?"	189	"A duplicitous archivist wouldn't be much use to future historians, in my view."
R19	191	"Questions of 'when' are difficult to answer in a world with no calendar."	189	"Poor Seer Rhee was corp man."
Q20	191	"What over deviances showed themselves?"	189	"*His* cuckolds?"
R20	191–92	"Yoona~939 mimicked the consumers."	189–90	"Yes. Seer Rhee should be understood in the context of his wife."
Q21	192	"And when did Yoona~939 actually violate a Catechism in public?"	190	"Yoona~939's notoriety must have threatened the seer's 'blemishless record' severely, wouldn't you agree?"
R21	192	"During Month Eight. . ."	190	"Certainly. . ."

Variant	*P* page	*Cloud Atlas P* text (UK)	*E* page	*Cloud Atlas E* text (US)
Q22	192	"She said *that*. . ."	190	"When did Yoona~939 first attempt to make you complicit in her crimes?"
R22	192	"Her amazement equalled your own."	190–91	"I suppose the first time was when she xplained a newfound word, *secret*, one slow hour at the teller. . . . This confession shocked me most of all, in a way."
Q23	193	"Why didn't the mother. . .?"	191	"How so?"
R23	193	"Maybe the woman was numb."	191–92	"Catechism Three teaches. . . . Greatest of all, however, was a book, a picture book."
Q24	193	"There were no other witnesses. . .?"	192	"Not many of those around these days."
R24	193	"she let Yoona's outburst go unreported"	192	"Indeed not."
Q25	193	"How did Yoona develop her verbal skills. . .?"	192	"How many 'next times' were there?"
R25	193	"Ascension absorbs language."	192	"Ten, or fifteen, approx. . . ."
Q26	193	"Were you happy in those days?"	192	"What shapes did these doubts take?"
R26	193	"of all Nea So Copros' slaves we surely are the most miserable."	192	"Questions: . . ."
Q27	193	"There are no slaves. . . !"	192	"How did you respond to such blasphemous hubris?"
R27	193	"Is your youth genuine or dewdrugged?"	192–93	"I begged Yoona to stop."
Q28	193–94	"Unanimity insisted that a heretic had nothing to offer the state archives but sedition."	193	"Two un-Souled fabricants, fleeing their corp, unaided?"
R28	194	"So you are gambling."	193	"But how could Yoona know that?"

Variant	*P* page	*Cloud Atlas P* text (UK)	*E* page	*Cloud Atlas E* text (US)
Q29	194	"That is more or less the truth of the matter, yes."	193	"Are you saying mental illness triggered the Yoona~939 Atrocity?"
R29	194	"I learned to expect only duplicity."	193	"I am, emphatically."
Q30	194	"A duplicitous archivist wouldn't be much use to anyone!"	193	"Would you describe the events of that New Year's Eve from your vantage point?"
R30	194	"Seer Rhee was corp man."	193–94	"I was wiping tables."
Q31	194	"Did you say 'his many *cuckolds*'?"	194	"She hadn't told you of her escape plan?"
R31	194	"Seer Rhee must be understood in the context of his wife."	194	"As I said, she had ceased to acknowledge my xistence."
Q32	194	"How come she never used this influence on her own husband's behalf?"	194	"Media reported that Yoona~939 stole the child to employ as a pureblood shield on the surface."
R32	194–95	"I don't know the inner mechanics of their marriage."	194	"Media reported the 'atrocity' xactly as Unanimity directed."
Q33	195	"Why did Seer Rhee tolerate . . .?"	194	"You sound very sure of your thesis."
R33	195	"First: . . ."	194	"If my xperiences do not give me the right to be sure, whose do?"
Q34	195	"Did Yoona~939 threaten Seer Rhee's blemishless record, do you think?"	194	"Nonetheless, please describe the Yoona~939 Atrocity, as you saw it."
R34	195	"I am certain she did."	194–95	"Very well."
Q35	195	"At what point did Yoona ~939 make you complicit. . .?"	195	"When Unanimity confirmed the fabricant was a genuine Yoona. . . we. . . I. . . "
R35	195–96	"Yoona attempted to xplain the meaning of a newfound word, *secret*."	195	"You felt the corpocratic world order had changed, irrevocably."

Variant	*P* page	*Cloud Atlas P* text (UK)	*E* page	*Cloud Atlas E* text (US)
Q36	196	"Why so?"	196	"What happened down in your dinery, meanwhile?"
R36	196–97	"Catechism Three teaches . . . Then she showed me the finest treasure of all. 'This book,' she said. . ."	196	"Unanimity arrived in force."
Q37	197	"Could Yoona read like a pureblood as well as talk like one?"	196	"I still find it incredible."
R37	197	". . .we read the pictures. . ."	196	"Such was the shock, the panic."
Q38	197	"There was a next time?"	196	"Would you recount what you remember for my orison?"
R38	197	"Ten Tenth Nites, or fifteen. . ."	196–97	"Our Logoman's head filled half the dome."
Q39	198	"What shapes did these doubt takes?"	197	"You said in your trial that Yoona~939 couldn't have been a Union member. Do you still maintain that position?"
R39	198	"Doubts about the sureties of the fabricant world. . ."	197	"Yes."
Q40	198	"How did you respond?"	197	"I'm puzzled."
R40	198	"I begged Yoona to stop voicing crimes of blasphemy."	197	"Because my own ascension had already begun."
Q41	198	"But two Inside servers, fleeing their corp, unaided. . ."	197	"So. . . after the Sermon, New Year's Day was business as usual?"
R41	198–99	"How could Yoona~939 know that?"	197–98	"Business, yes; usual, no."
Q42	199	"Did anything trigger the Yoona~939 deviancy. . .?"	198	"Your birthmark? I didn't know fabricants have birthmarks."
R42	199	"The deviancy was an inevitability awaiting a trigger."	198	"We do not."
Q43	199	"Did you tell Yoona~939 your fears?"	198	"Would you show it to my orison. . .?"

Variant	*P* page	*Cloud Atlas P* text (UK)	*E* page	*Cloud Atlas E* text (US)
R43	199–200	"My sister had ascended."	198	"If you wish."
Q44	200	"Can seers inflict. . .?"	198	"Xtraordinary. It looks like a comet."
R44	200	"Seers manage."	198	"Hae-Joo Im made xactly. . ."
Q45	200	"But the Yoona~939. . ."	198	"Did Seer Rhee retain his position?"
R45	200–201	"I was wiping tables."	198	"Yes, but it brought the unlucky man little solace."
Q46	201	"Media reported. . ."	198	"And it was around this time that you grew aware of your own ascension?"
R46	201	"Media reported what Unanimity told them to report."	198–99	"Correct."
Q47	201	"She didn't discuss her escape attempt with you?"	199	"How long did you have to endure that state?"
R47	201–2	"Yoona had stopped discussing anything with me."	199	"Some months."
Q48	202	"I saw that image too."	199	"Rhee was dead?"
R48	202	"You felt the world would never be the same."	199	"Whatever the official verdict, the office stunk of Soap soporifix."
Q49	202	"What happened down in your dome?"	199	"You said you envied your unthinking, untroubled sisters."
R49	202	"The two other Yoonas. . ."	199	"That is not quite the same as wishing to be one."
Q50	202	"I was amazed."	200	"That decision didn't cause you any guilt, later?"
R50	202–3	"Such was the level of panic."	200	"Not much: . . ."
Q51	203	"Can you recount. . ."	200	"He sounds like an enforcer."
R51	203–4	"He said that. . ."	200	"The man introduced himself as Chang."

Variant	*P* page	*Cloud Atlas P* text (UK)	*E* page	*Cloud Atlas E* text (US)
Q52	204	"Wasn't Yoona~939 a Union member. . .?"	200	"Not much of a choice."
R52	204	"How and when could Union recruit her?"	200	"No."
Q53	204	"So after the Sermon. . ."	201	"Please, describe xactly what you saw."
R53	204	"Business: not quite as usual."	201	"Chongmyo Plaza, predawn . . . ."
Q54	204	"I didn't know fabricants had birthmarks."	201	"It must have been overwhelming."
R54	204	"We don't: they are genomed out."	201	"Even the smells were new."
Q55	205	"Please show it to the orison [. . .] It resembles a comet."	201	"Didn't you ask where you were being taken?"
R55	205	"Hae-Joo Im made the same observation."	201–2	"Why ask a question. . .?"
Q56	205	"So, I assume you passed the Medic's xamination?"	202	"What else caught your eye?"
R56	205	"Yes."	202	"Oh, the greenness of green."
Q57	205	"Did Seer Rhee. . .?"	202	"So you were taken to the University straight from Papa Song's?"
R57	205	"Yes."	202–3	"To reduce xperimental contamination, yes."
Q58	205	"Servers' memories are genomed weak."	203	"What did you think of your new quarters?"
R58	205	"A simple question. . ."	203–4	"Dirty."
Q59	205	"Go on."	204	"Had you never seen insects before?"
R59	205–6	"First, a voice. . ."	204	"Only rogue-gened roaches and dead ones. . ."
Q60	206	"What did you intend to do?"	205	"What. . . were you supposed to do for the next three days?"

Variant	*P* page	*Cloud Atlas P* text (UK)	*E* page	*Cloud Atlas E* text (US)
R60	206	"What could I do. . .?"	205	"Xcept watch the rolex hand erode the hours. . ."
Q61	206	"And how long did you have to endure. . .?"	205	"Did your second day outside provide any answers?"
R61	206–7	"On Fourth Month. . ."	205–6	"Some: but yet more surprises."
Q62	207	"Rhee was dead?"	206	"What sort of fabricant was Wing~027?"
R62	207	"I smelt lethe. . ."	206–7	"No, a disasterman."
Q63	207	"Did that decision cause you any guilt?"	207	"So Wing~027, not Hae-Joo Im or Boardman Mephi, mentored you first?"
R63	207	"No."	207–8	"That is not true, strictly."
Q64	208	"An enforcer?"	208	"What about his Ph.D. xperiments on you?"
R64	208	"He was a chauffeur."	208	"Boom-Sook Kim's concerns were not his Ph.D."
Q65	208	"Not much of a choice."	208	"But how was Boom-Sook planning to graduate?"
R65	208	"It was the first choice of my life."	208	"By paying an academic agent."
Q66	208	"I almost envy you."	208	"Wasn't Boom-Sook Kim's tutor aware of this outrageous plagiarism?"
R66	208–9	"Chongmyo Plaza. . ."	208	"Professors who value tenure do not muckrake the sons of future Juche Boardmen."
Q67	209	"It must have been overwhelming."	208	"Did Boom-Sook never even talk to you . . . interact with you, in any way?"
R67	209–10	"Overwhelming: the apposite word."	208–9	"He addressed me like purebloods speak to a cat."
Q68	210	"Didn't you ask. . .?"	209	"So for nine months nobody observed your skyrocketing sentience?"

Variant	*P* page	*Cloud Atlas P* text (UK)	*E* page	*Cloud Atlas E* text (US)
R68	210	"Why ask a question. . ."	209	"So I believed."
Q69	210	What else caught your eye?"	209	"What is 'poker'?"
R69	210–11	"Back below the canopy . . ."	209	"A card game . . ."
Q70	211	"So you were taken. . .?"	209	"Why was it that you never met Wing~027 again?"
R70	211–12	"To reduce xperimental contamination, yes."	209–10	"One humid afternoon [. . .]"
Q71	212	"What did you make of your new home?"	210	"Why is that unusual?"
R71	212	"I was struck by its dirt. . ."	210	"Purebloods see us often but look at us rarely."
Q72	212	"Had you never seen insects before?"	210	"Did you feel . . . well, what did you feel?"
R72	212–13	"Only rogue-gened. . ."	210	"Fury."
Q73	213	"What. . . were you supposed to do for the next three days?"	210	"What happened to you over summer recess?"
R73	213–14	"I had no idea."	210–11	"Boom-Sook should have deposited me. . ."
Q74	214	"When you woke. . .?"	211	"So you never set foot outside Boom-Sook's lab in five weeks?"
R74	214–15	"The Soap had less. . ."	211	"Not once."
Q75	215	"What sort of fabricant was Wing~027?"	211	"But that's fifty days of unbroken solitary confinement!"
R75	215–16	"A disasterman, he boasted. . ."	211	"Fifty glorious days."
Q76	216	"So Wing~027, not Hae-Joo Im or Boardman Mephi, mentored you first?"	211	"And you were still Boom-Sook's thesis specimen. . .?"
R76	216–17	"Wing~027 could have mentored me further."	211–12	"Yes."
Q77	217	"What about his Ph.D. xperiments on you?"	212	"Did it snow?"

Variant	*P* page	*Cloud Atlas P* text (UK)	*E* page	*Cloud Atlas E* text (US)
R77	217	"Boom-Sook Kim cared not for xperiments."	212	"Ah, yes, snow."
Q78	217	"Then how was Boom-Sook planning to obtain his Ph.D.?"	212	"You speak like an aesthete sometimes, Sonmi."
R78	217	"By paying an academic agent. . ."	212	"Perhaps those deprived of beauty perceive it most instinctively."
Q79	217	"Was Boom-Sook Kim's mentor aware of this plagiarism?"	212	"So it must be around now that Dr. Mephi enters the story?"
R79	217	"Professors value tenure too much to muckrake the sons of future Boardmen."	212–13	"Yes, Sextet Eve."
Q80	217	"Did Boom-Sook never talk to you. . .?"	213	"Fang seems to have been the ringleader."
R80	217–18	"He addressed me like purebloods speak to a cat."	213–15	"He was, yes. . . ."
Q81	218	"So for nine months nobody observed your skyrocketing sentience?"	215	"Boardman Mephi?"
R81	218	"Boom-Sook Kim's only regular visitors. . ."	215–16	"Yes, but let us be thoro. . ."
Q82	218	"What is 'poker'?"	216	"Yes, I'm curious to hear that, too."
R82	218	"A card game. . ."	216	"Boom-Sook tried everything."
Q83	218	"Why was it that you never met Wing~027 again?"	216	"That must have been very welcome news."
R83	218–19	"One humid afternoon. . ."	216–17	"Yes, xcept for the loss of my sony."
Q84	219	"Why is that unusual?"	217	"What reason did the Boardman give for your timely rescue?"
R84	219	"Purebloods always see us but rarely look at us."	217–18	"None, as yet."

Variant	*P* page	*Cloud Atlas P* text (UK)	*E* page	*Cloud Atlas E* text (US)
Q85	219	"Did you feel. . . well, what did you feel?"	218	"A bewildering evening—crossbolts one moment, art history the next. . . "
R85	219	"Fury."	218–19	"Certainly."
Q86	219	"What happened to you over summer recess?"	219	"Denial was plainly pointless."
R86	219–20	"According to regulations, Boom-Sook should have deposited me. . ."	219	"Indeed: . . ."
Q87	220	"So you never set foot outside Boom-Sook's lab in five weeks?"	219	"Obviously, none of them got their way."
R87	220	"Not once: . . ."	219	"No."
Q88	220	"But that's fifty days of unbroken solitude."	219	"And what did Boardman Mephi intend to do with you now?"
R88	220	"My mind traveled. . ."	219–20	"Frame a new compromise. . ."
Q89	220	"Were you still Boom-Sook's thesis specimen. . .?"	220	"Did Sonmi~451's interests enter this simultaneous equation?"
R89	220–21	"I was."	220	"To a degree, yes."
Q90	221	"What was your reaction to snow?"	220	"If Boom-Sook Kim was such a buffoon, how had he attained this holy grail of psychogenomics—stable ascension?"
R90	221	"It is beautiful."	220	"Later, I asked Hae-Joo Im the same question."
Q91	221	"And it must have been around then that Dr Mephi enters the story?"	221	"And all the while Boom-Sook Kim was blissfully unaware of the furor his plagiarized Ph.D. was causing?"
R91	221–22	"Yes, on Sextet Eve."	221	"Only an obdurate fool. . ."

Variant	*P* page	*Cloud Atlas P* text (UK)	*E* page	*Cloud Atlas E* text (US)
Q92	222	"Fang seems to be the ringleader."	221	"How did you find your new regime in the Unanimity Faculty. . .?"
R92	222–24	"He was: . . ."	221	"As I was moved on Sextet Eve. . ."
Q93	224	"Boardman Mephi?"	221	"What was your first lecture?"
R93	224–25	"Unanimity Professor. . ."	221–22	"Swanti's *Biomathematics*. . ."
Q94	225	"I'm curious to hear that, too."	222	"Did Professor Mephi know about the students' unfriendliness?"
R94	225	"Boom-Sook tried everything."	222	"I think so."
Q95	225	"That must have come as very good news."	222	"It must have taken courage to return."
R95	225	"Yes, xcept for my sony"	222	"Not really: an enforcer escorted me."
Q96	225	"What reason did the Boardman give for your timely rescue?"	223	"Did you brave any more lectures?"
R96	225–27	"I didn't ask."	223	"One, on Lööw's *Fundaments*."
Q97	227	"A bewildering evening—crossbolts one moment, art history the next. . . "	223	"Media? On a corpocratic campus?"
R97	227–28	"Certainly. . ."	223	"No. . ."
Q98	228	"Denial was plainly pointless."	223	"What about the xperiments you were obliged to undergo?"
R98	228	"Indeed."	223–24	"Ah, yes, a daily reminder of my true status."
Q99	228	"Obviously none of them got their way."	224	"Out where?"
R99	228	"No."	224–25	"Next ninthnite."
Q100	228	"So. . . what did Boardman Mephi intend to do with you now?"	225	"Didn't he irritate you a little?"

Variant	*P* page	*Cloud Atlas P* text (UK)	*E* page	*Cloud Atlas E* text (US)
R100	228–29	"Frame a new compromise."	225–26	"Initially, he irritated me a lot."
Q101	229	"Did Sonmi~451's interests enter this simultaneous equation?"	226	"Were you nervous about leaving Taemosan?"
R101	229	"The University would enrol me. . ."	226	"Slitely yes."
Q102	229	"If Boom-Sook Kim was such an idle buffoon, how had he attained this holy grail of psychogenomics—stable ascension?"	226	"No, not even by day."
R102	229–30	"Hae-Joo Im's xplanation was. . ."	226–27	"You should go."
Q103	230	"And Boom-Sook Kim stayed unaware of the furore his Ph.D. had triggered?"	227	"Which galleria did you go to?"
R103	230	"Only a fool. . ."	227–28	"Wangshimni Orchard."
Q104	230	"How did you find your new regime in the Unanimity Faculty. . .?"	228	"Did you xperience any negative reactions from consumers in the galleria?"
R104	230	"You will recall I was moved . . ."	229	"No. Many other fabricants were there."
Q105	230	"What was your first lecture?"	229	"So she couldn't believe you *weren't* a pureblood?"
R105	230–31	"Swanti's 'Biomathematics'. . ."	229	"She gave me her card."
Q106	231	"Did Professor Mephi know about the students' unfriendliness?"	229	"So the xcursion helped dislodge your. . . sense of ennui?"
R106	231	"Yes."	229	"In a way, yes."
Q107	231	"It must have taken courage to return."	229	"It could hardly be wise for an ascended server to visit a dinery?"
R107	231–32	"An enforcer escorted me."	229–30	"I do not claim it was wise."

Variant	*P* page	*Cloud Atlas P* text (UK)	*E* page	*Cloud Atlas E* text (US)
Q108	232	"Did you brave any more lectures?"	230	"In case you got separated?"
R108	232	"One, on Lööw's *Fundaments*."	230	"For good luck, I thought. . ."
Q109	232	"Media had been allowed into a state-funded university?"	230	"In what ways?"
R109	232	"No. . ."	230–31	"That spacious dome was so poky."
Q110	233	"How were the morning xperiments you underwent?"	232	"So your visit. . ."
R110	233	"A daily reminder. . ."	232–33	"Perhaps it was anticlimactic."
Q111	233	"Back to lectures?"	233	"How many of these xcursions took place?"
R111	233–34	"Ninth Nite. . ."	233	"Every ninthnite until Corpocracy Day."
Q112	235	"Didn't he irritate you a little?"	233	"Please do."
R112	235	"At first, he irritated me a lot."	233	"A keen passion of Hae-Joo's was disneys. . ."
Q113	235	"Were you nervous about leaving Taemosan?"	233	"You mean Union samizdat from the Production Zones?"
R113	235	"Slitely, yes."	233–34	"No."
Q114	236	"No, nor even by day. Us citizens leave the Tower for the tourists, mostly."	234	"Namely?"
R114	236	"Go."	234	"A picaresque entitled 'The Ghastly Ordeal of Timothy Cavendish'. . ."
Q115	236	"Which galleria did you go to?"	234	"Sweet Corpocracy, no!"

Variant	*P* page	*Cloud Atlas P* text (UK)	*E* page	*Cloud Atlas E* text (US)
R115	236–37	"Wangshimni Orchard."	234	"Is that so? Well, the Juche's stance on historical discourse is riddled with inconsistencies. On the one hand, if historical discourse were permitted, the downstrata could access a bank of human xperience that would rival, and sometimes contradict, that taught by Media. On the other hand, corpocracy funds your Ministry of Archivism, dedicated to preserving a historical record for future ages."
Q116	237	"Did you xperience any negative reactions from consumers in the galleria?"	234	"Yes, but our xistence is kept from the downstrata."
R116	237–38	"Many fabricants could be seen there."	234	"Xcept from those condemned to the Litehouse."
Q117	238	"[...] she couldn't believe you weren't a pureblood?"	234	"Why had Hae-Joo Im chosen to show you this *Ghastly Ordeal*?"
R117	238	"She gave me her card."	234–35	"Perhaps Professor Mephi had instructed him. . ."
Q118	238	"So the xcursion helped dislodge your. . . sense of *ennui*?"	235	"I can tell how fascinated you were."
R118	238–39	"I understood. . ."	235	"Certainly: the vacant disneyarium was a haunting frame for those lost, rainy landscapes. Giants strode the screen, lit by sunlite captured thru a lens when your grandfather's grandfather, Archivist, was kicking in his natural womb. Time is the speed at which the past decays, but disneys enable a brief resurrection."

Variant	*P* page	*Cloud Atlas P* text (UK)	*E* page	*Cloud Atlas E* text (US)
Q119	239	"It could hardly be wise. . ."	235	"Only fifty minutes?"
R119	239	"I am not saying it was wise."	235	"Hae-Joo's handsony purred at a key scene."
Q120	239	"Why?"	235	"Do you remember your thoughts on hearing that?"
R120	239	"For good luck. . ."	235–36	"No. . ."
				Cloud Atlas E breaks here
Q121	239	"In what ways?"	313	"Then who was Hae-Joo Im, if he was not xactly who he said he was?"
R121	239–41	"That spacious dome: so poky. . ."	313	"I surprised myself by answering that question: Union."
Q122	241	"Did you find the 'key' to your ascended self?"	313	"How did you know for sure he wasn't abducting you?"
R122	241–42	"I suppose the key was, there was no key."	313	"I did not know: I was not sure."
Q123	242	"How many of these xcursions took place?"	314	"Unionmen really cut out their own eternal Souls? I always thought it was an urban myth."
R123	242–43	"Every Ninth Nite until Corpocracy Day."	314	"How else can a resistance movement elude Unanimity?"
Q124	243	"As you wish."	314	"What? His own man? Why?"
R124	243	"A keen passion of Hae-Joo's was disneys."	314–15	"Unanimity dumdums combine kalodoxalyn and stimulin."
Q125	243	"You mean Union samizdat from the Production Zones?"	315	"But please describe it for my orison."
R125	243	"No. I mean that zone even more forbidden: the past."	315–16	"Huamdonggil is a noxious maze of low, crooked ramshacks."
Q126	243	"Namely?"	316	"Which was where xactly?"

Variant	*P* page	*Cloud Atlas P* text (UK)	*E* page	*Cloud Atlas E* text (US)
R126	243	"A picaresque entitled 'The Ghastly Ordeal of Timothy Cavendish'. . ."	316–17	"Xactly I cannot say: Huamdonggil is not gridnumbered or charted."
Q127	243	"An eightstratum archivist can't dream of getting such security clearance!"	317	"The parlor?"
R127	243	"Why our corpocratic state outlaws *any* historical discourse is a perplexing question. Is it that history provides a bank of human xperience that rivals Media's? If so, why preserve archives like ministry's, whose very xistence is a state secret?"	317	"A gaproom behind a roaring kitchen and a false wall. . ."
Q128	243	"What was your own opinion of this *Ghastly Ordeal*?"	318	"A carp?"
R128	244	"Its world intrigued me."	318	"A carp, as in the fish."
Q129	244	"It all sounds grimly dystopian."	319	"How was Hae-Joo planning to pass thru a city xit without Souls?"
R129	244	"Time is what stops history happening at once."	319–20	"The Soul implanter was ushered in just minutes later."
Q130	244	"Only fifty minutes?"	320	"So I suppose your next destination was the facescaper?"
R130	244	"Hae-Joo's handsony purred at a key scene."	320–21	"It was."
Q131	244	"What did you think on hearing that?"	321	"So what happened to Madam Ovid's artistry?"
R131	244–45	"I couldn't think."	321–22	"Unanimity refaced me for my peaktime courtroom appearances."
		Cloud Atlas P breaks here		

Variant	*P* page	*Cloud Atlas P* text (UK)	*E* page	*Cloud Atlas E* text (US)
Q132	329	"Then who *was* Hae-Joo Im . . .?"	322	"East Gate One?"
R132	329	"I surprised myself by answering that question: Union."	322	"Yes."
Q133	329	"How did you know for sure he wasn't abducting you?"	322	"That's a dangerously simple crypto, it seems to me."
R133	329	"I didn't know for sure."	322–23	"Meticulous brains will overlook the simple."
Q134	330	"Unionmen *really* cut out their own Juche-given eternal Souls?"	323	"Where did you really curfew that nite? Not a seedy motel?"
R134	330	"How else can a resistance movement elude Unanimity?"	323	"No."
Q135	330	"What? *Why*?"	323	"Wombtanks?"
R135	330–31	"Unanimity dumdums combine kalodoxalyn and giga-stimulin."	323–24	"Yes."
Q136	331	"What did you find there?"	324	"A penthouse? In a fabricant nursery?"
R136	331–32	"Huamdonggil is a noxious maze of crookeds, ramshacks . . ."	324	"The Unionman was fond of irony."
Q137	332	"Which was what, xactly?"	324	"You didn't feel vulnerable . . .?"
R137	332–33	"Huamdonggil is not gridnumbered or charted."	324–25	"I was too toxed."
Q138	333	"The parlor?"	325	"More evasion?"
R138	333	"A gaproom behind a roaring kitchen and a false wall. . ."	325	"No."
Q139	333	"A carp? As in the fish?"	325	"What could replace their labor?"
R139	333–34	"A numinous. . ."	325	"Us. Fabricants."

Variant	*P* page	*Cloud Atlas P* text (UK)	*E* page	*Cloud Atlas E* text (US)
Q140	334	"How was Hae-Joo planning to pass thru a conurb exit without Souls in your indexes?"	325	"And how did Union aim to xtract these. . . alleged 'ills' of our state?"
R140	334–36	"The Soul implanter was ushered in just minutes later."	325	"Revolution."
Q141	336	"So I guess your next destination was the facescaper?"	325–26	"How can any rational organization embrace a creed that opposes corpocracy?"
R141	336–37	"Yes."	326	"All rising suns set, Archivist."
Q142	337	"So what happened to Madam Ovid's artistry?"	326	"Well, you seem to have embraced Union propaganda wholeheartedly, Sonmi~451."
R142	337–38	"Unanimity refaced me for my peaktime courtroom appearances."	326	"And I might observe that you have embraced corpocracy propaganda wholeheartedly, Archivist."
Q143	338	"*East* Gate One?"	326	"Did your new friends mention xactly how Union plans to overthrow a state with a standing pureblood army of 2 million backed by a further 2 million fabricant troops?"
R143	338	"The leader suffixed. . ."	326	"Yes."
Q144	338	"That's a dangerously simple crypto."	326	Fantasy. Lunacy.
R144	338–39	"Meticulous brains often overlook the simple."	326	"All revolutions are, until they happen, then they are historical inevitabilities."
Q145	339	"Where did you curfew that nite? The outer motel?"	326	"How could Union possibly achieve this 'simultaneous ascension'?"
R145	339	"No"	326	"The battlefield, you see, is neuromolecular."

Variant	*P* page	*Cloud Atlas P* text (UK)	*E* page	*Cloud Atlas E* text (US)
Q146	339	"Wombtanks?"	326	"What damage could even 10 million. . .?"
R146	339–40	"We had entered a genomics unit."	326–27	"Who would work factory lines?"
Q147	340	"A penthouse? In a fabricant nursery?"	327	"Unanimity would maintain order."
R147	340	"The Unionman was fond of irony."	327	"Even Yoona~939 chose death over slavery."
Q148	340	"You didn't feel vulnerable . . .?"	327	"And your role in this. . . proposed rebellion?"
R148	340–41	"No."	327	"My first role was. . ."
Q149	341	"More evasion?"	327	How did you feel about being a figurehead for terrorists?
R149	341	"No."	327	"Trepidation: . . ."
Q150	341	"What will replace their valuable labor?"	327	"Weren't you curious about Union's blueprint for the briter tomorrow?"
R150	341–42	"Us. Fabricants [. . .]"	327	"You show xtraordinary erudition for an eighth-stratum, Archivist."
Q151	342	"And how did Union aim to xpunge these. . . alleged 'ills' of our state?"	327	"We're circling a contentious core, Sonmi. Let's return to your journey."
R151	342	"Revolution."	327–28	"We reached Suanbo Plain around hour eleven."
Q152	342	"How can any organization embrace such. . . terrorism?"	328	"Hae-Joo Im wasn't trying to get to Pusan in one day?"
R152	342	"The sun sets."	328–29	"No."
Q153	342	"You seem to have embraced Union propaganda wholeheartedly, Sonmi."	329	"Why did Im take you on this field trip to the middle of nowhere?"

Variant	*P* page	*Cloud Atlas P* text (UK)	*E* page	*Cloud Atlas E* text (US)
R153	342	"I might observe that you have embraced Nea So Copros propaganda wholeheartedly, Archivist."	329	"Every nowhere is somewhere, Archivist."
Q154	342	"Did Hae-Joo mention xactly how Union plans to overthrow a state with a standing army of two million?"	329	"So Union hid its interlocutor, its. . . messiah, in a colony of recidivists?"
R154	342	"He did."	329–30	"Messiah: what a grandiose title for a Papa Song server."
Q155	342	"I don't understand how you didn't recognize this as sheerest fantasy?"	330	"Who were these 'colonists' xactly?"
R155	342	"All revolutions are sheerest fantasy, until they happen; then they become historical inevitabilities."	330	"Each colonist had a different story."
Q156	342	"How could Union possibly achieve this 'simultaneous ascension'?"	330	"But. . . how could people there survive without franchises and gallerias?"
R156	342	"The battlefield was at the molecular level."	330	"Go visit them, Archivist."
Q157	342	"What damage could even six million. . .?"	330	"What about the mountain winters?"
R157	342–43	"Who would work the factory lines?"	330–31	"They survived as fifteen centuries of nuns had before them."
Q158	343	"Unanimity would maintain order."	331	"So what was Union's interest in the colony?"
R158	343	"Even Yoona~939, a fabricant server, chose death over slavery."	331–32	"Simple: . . ."
Q159	343	"Wait, wait, wait. . ."	333	"She knew you weren't pureblood all along? How?"
R159	343	"Unanimity were alerted. . ."	333	"It seemed tactless to ask."

Variant	*P* page	*Cloud Atlas P* text (UK)	*E* page	*Cloud Atlas E* text (US)
Q160	343	"And your role in this . . . *überplan*?"	333	"I presume she meant fabricants?"
R160	343	"My first role. . ."	333	"I did not know. . ."
Q161	343	"How did you feel about such a role in a terrorist organization?"	333	"So day two as a fugitive got under way."
R161	343	"The greatest trepidation: . . ."	333–35	"Yes."
Q162	343–44	"Weren't you curious about Union's blueprint for the briter tomorrow?"	335	"I presume he had discarded a fabricant living doll."
R162	344	"Your study is curiously broad. . ."	335–36	"Yes."
Q163	344	"We're circling a contentious core, Sonmi. Let's return to your journey."	336	"You considered him a murderer?"
R163	344	"We reached Suanbo Plain around hour eleven."	336	"Of course."
Q164	344	"Hae-Joo Im wasn't trying to get to Pusan in one day?"	336	"But hate men like Seer Kwon, and you hate the whole world."
R164	344–45	"No."	336	"Not the whole world, Archivist,. . ."
Q165	345	"What was the purpose of this xpedition into the middle of nowhere?"	336	"When did you finally reach Pusan?"
R165	345–46	"Every nowhere is somewhere."	336–37	"Nitefall."
Q166	346	"So Union hid its interlocutor, its. . . 'messiah', in a colony of recidivists?"	338	"Was she Union?"
R166	346	"'Messiah'. What a grand title for a Papa Song server."	338	"No."
Q167	346	"So who were these squatters xactly?"	338	"Surely, such a distinguished defector as yourself deserved a rather grander reception?"

Variant	*P* page	*Cloud Atlas P* text (UK)	*E* page	*Cloud Atlas E* text (US)
R167	346	"Each colonist had a different story."	338–39	"Grand receptions draw attention."
Q168	347	"But. . . how could they survive without franchises and gallerias?"	339	"You'd never seen it before?"
R168	347	"Their food came from forest and garden. . ."	339	"Only on Papa Song's 3-Ds of life in Xultation."
Q169	347	"What about the mountain winters?"	339	"An illegal transceiver?. . ."
R169	347	"They survived as fifteen centuries of nuns had before them."	339–41	"The sacred is a fine hiding place for the profane."
Q170	347	"So what was Union's interest in the monastery?"	341	"Gaining access to a corp ship was so simple?"
R170	347–49	"Union provides hardware. . ."	341	"Papa Song's Golden Ark is not xactly a magnet for illegal boarders."
Q171	349	"How did she know?"	342	"You sound as if you still envy them."
R171	349	"I didn't ask."	342	"Watching them from the hangway, I envied their certainty about the future."
Q172	349	"Why did she show her hand?"	342	"Weren't you in danger of being seen?"
R172	349	"To xpress solidarity."	342	"No."
Q173	349	"Was she speaking in general terms or specific?"	342	"'Odd' in what way?"
R173	349	"I didn't learn until the following nite."	342–43	"There was only one door."
Q174	350	"So Day Two as a fugitive got under way."	343	"But. . . why would— What would the purpose be of such. . . carnage?"
R174	350–51	"Hae-Joo breakfasted."	343	"The economics of corpocracy . . ."

Variant	*P* page	*Cloud Atlas P* text (UK)	*E* page	*Cloud Atlas E* text (US)
Q175	351	"I presume he had discarded a fabricant living doll."	343–44	"What you describe is beyond the. . . conceivable, Sonmi~451."
R175	351–52	"The xec was keen. . ."	344	"Business is business."
Q176	352	"You considered him a murderer?"	344	"You've described not 'business' but. . . industrialized evil!"
R176	352	"One so shallow he didn't even know it."	344	"You underestimate humanity's ability to bring such evil into being."
Q177	353	"But hate men like Seer Kwon, and you hate the whole world."	344	"No crime of such magnitude could take root in Nea So Copros. [...]"
R177	353	"Not the whole world, Archivist."	344	"Rights are susceptible to subversion, as even granite is susceptible to erosion."
Q178	353	"When did you finally reach Pusan?"	344	"But what about the 3-Ds of Xultation and such?"
R178	353–54	"Nitefall."	344–45	"Xultation is a sony-generated simulacrum dijied in Neo Edo."
Q179	354	"Was she Union?"	345	"How long did you watch this slaughter?"
R179	354–55	"No."	345–46	"I cannot recall, accurately."
Q180	355	"Surely, such a distinguished defector deserved a grander reception?"	346	"Weren't you angry with Union for xposing you to the Golden Ark without adequately preparing you?"
R180	355	"Grand receptions draw attention."	346	"What words could Apis or Hae-Joo have used?"
Q181	355	"You'd never seen it before?"	346	"Many xpert witnesses at your trial denied *Declarations* could be the work of a fabricant."
R181	355–56	"Only on sony, Papa Song's 3Ds of life in Xultation."	346–47	"How lazily 'xperts' dismiss what they fail to understand!"

Variant	*P* page	*Cloud Atlas P* text (UK)	*E* page	*Cloud Atlas E* text (US)
Q182	356	"An illegal transceiver?"	347	"And your capture came shortly after completing your text?"
R182	356–57	"The sacred is a fine hiding place for the profane."	347	"The same afternoon."
Q183	357	"Gaining access to a corp ship was so straitforward?"	347	"You are implying that you xpected the raid, Sonmi?"
R183	357–58	"Papa Song's Golden Ark is not xactly a magnet for illegal boarders."	347	"Once I had finished my manifesto, the next stage could only be my arrest."
Q184	358	"Did you envy them?"	348	"What do you mean?"
R184	358	"I envied their certainty about the future."	348	"Of the theatrical production, set up while I was still a server in Papa Song's."
Q185	358	"Weren't you in danger of being seen?"	348	"Wait, wait, wait. What about.. . everything?"
R185	358	"Brite droplights. . ."	348	"Its key events, yes. . ."
Q186	358	"What was so odd about that?"	348	"Such as?. . ."
R186	358–59	"There was one door. . ."	348	"Wing~027 was as stable an ascendant as I."
Q187	359	"But. . . why would— What would the purpose be of such. . . carnage?"	349	"But what about Xi-Li. . .?"
R187	359–60	"The genomics industry. . ."	348	"Indeed not."
Q188	360	"No."	348	"But. . . Union?"
R188	360	"Business is business."	348	"No."
Q189	360	"But. . .why didn't this emerge during your trial?"	348	"I still can't understand why Unanimity would go to the xpense and trouble of staging this fake. . . "
R189	360	"I must reiterate. . ."	348–49	"To generate the show trial of the decade."
Q190	360	"Yes, but what you allege. . ."	349	"But if you knew about this. . .?"

Variant	*P* page	*Cloud Atlas P* text (UK)	*E* page	*Cloud Atlas E* text (US)
R190	360	"It is. . ."	349	"Why does any martyr cooperate with his judases?"
Q191	360	"What about the 2Ds of Hawaii?"	349	"Tell me."
R191	360	"Xultation is a sony-generated . . ."	349	"We see a game beyond the endgame."
Q192	360	"No, I cannot accept. . ."	349	"But to what end?"
R192	360–61	"My fifth *Declaration* proposes. . ."	349	"As Seneca warned Nero. . ."
Q193	361	"How long did you watch the slaughter you describe?"	349	". . .name it."
R193	361–62	"I don't recall."	349	"Your sony and access codes."
Q194	362	"But weren't you angry. . .?"	349	"What do you wish to download?"
R194	362	"No."	349	"A certain disney I once began, one nite long ago in another age."
Q195	362	"Many xpert witnesses at your trial denied *Declarations* was the work of a fabricant."		***Cloud Atlas E* ends here**
R195	362–63	"How lazily 'xperts' dismiss what they fail to understand!"		
Q196	363	"And your capture came shortly after completing your text?"		
R196	363	"The same afternoon."		
Q197	363	"You are implying that you xpected the raid, Sonmi?"		
R197	363	"Once I had finished my manifesto, the next stage could only be my arrest."		
Q198	363	"What do you mean?"		
R198	363	"Of the theatrical production. . ."		

Variant	*P* page	*Cloud Atlas P* text (UK)	*E* page	*Cloud Atlas E* text (US)
Q199	363	"Wait, wait, wait. What about . . . well, everything?"		
R199	364	"Its key events, yes. . ."		
Q200	364	"Such as?"		
R200	364	"Wing~027. . ."		
Q201	364	"But what about Xi-Li. . .?"		
R201	364	"That poor idealist."		
Q202	364	"But. . . Union. . .?"		
R202	364	"No: . . ."		
Q203	364	"I still can't understand why Unanimity would go to the xpense and trouble of staging this fake. . . "		
R203	364	"To generate a show-trial."		
Q204	364	"But if you knew about this. . .?"		
R204	364	"Why does any martyr cooperate with his judases?"		
Q205	364	"What is yours?"		
R205	364–65	"The *Declarations*."		
Q206	365	"But to what end?"		
R206	365	"To Corpocracy."		
Q207	365	"Two brief last questions."		
R207	365	"How can I?"		
Q208	365	"Did you love Hae-Joo Im?"		
R208	365	"Tell the Chairman of Narcissism he'll have to consult with future historians on that."		
Q209	365	"Very well. . . name it."		
R209	365	"The use of your sony and access codes."		

Variant	*P* page	*Cloud Atlas P* text (UK)	*E* page	*Cloud Atlas E* text (US)
Q210	365	"What do you wish to download?"		
R210	365	"I wish to finish viewing a film."		
		***Cloud Atlas P* ends here**		

Appendix B
LIST OF DIGITAL DATA APPENDIXES

DIGITAL APPENDIX 1: DATA FOR CHAPTER 1

This digital data appendix is available at http://www.sup.org/closereading/ and https://doi.org/10.25740/bd095jt2882.

This appendix is a JavaScript Object Notation (JSON) file that is used to generate figure 2 using the SankeyTextualVariant software.[1]

DIGITAL APPENDIX 2: DATA FOR CHAPTER 2

This digital data appendix is available at http://www.sup.org/closereading/ and https://doi.org/10.25740/bd095jt2882.

This appendix contains:

- The data used to generate figures 5 through 13.
- The data used to make the claims about Melville's texts.
- The part-of-speech tagging outputs of *Cloud Atlas E*.

DIGITAL APPENDIX 3: DATA FOR CHAPTER 3

This digital data appendix is available at http://www.sup.org/closereading/ and https://doi.org/10.25740/bd095jt2882.

This appendix contains the data used to generate figures 14 through 16.

NOTES

ACKNOWLEDGMENTS

1. Andrew J. Read, *Mars and Back* (Great Sampford, Essex: Bright Books, 1993).

INTRODUCTION: CLOSE READING, COMPUTERS, AND *CLOUD ATLAS*

1. See Wendy Hui Kyong Chun et al., "The Dark Side of the Digital Humanities," in *Debates in the Digital Humanities 2016*, ed. Matthew K. Gold and Lauren F. Klein (Minneapolis: University of Minnesota Press, 2016), 493–509, http://dhdebates.gc.cuny.edu/debates/text/89; Richard Grusin, "The Dark Side of Digital Humanities: Dispatches from Two Recent MLA Conventions," *Differences* 25, no. 1 (2014): 79–92, https://doi.org/10.1215/10407391-2420009; Janneke Adema and Gary Hall, "Posthumanities: The Dark Side of 'The Dark Side of the Digital,'" *Journal of Electronic Publishing* 19, no. 2 (2016): http://dx.doi.org/10.3998/3336451.0019.201; and Daniel Allington, Sarah Brouillette, and David Golumbia, "Neoliberal Tools (and Archives): A Political History of Digital Humanities," *Los Angeles Review of Books*, May 1, 2016, https://lareviewofbooks.org/article/neoliberal-tools-archives-political-history-digital-humanities/. For a good range of counterresponses see "Editors' Choice: Round-Up of Responses to 'The LA Neoliberal Tools (and Archives),'" Digital Humanities Now, May 3, 2016, http://digitalhumanitiesnow.org/2016/05/editors-choice-round-up-of-responses-to-the-la-neoliberal-tools-and-archives.

2. See Matthew L. Jockers, *Macroanalysis: Digital Methods and Literary History* (Urbana: University of Illinois Press, 2013); Franco Moretti, *Distant Reading* (London: Verso, 2013); and Franco Moretti, *Graphs, Maps, Trees: Abstract Models for Literary History* (London: Verso, 2007).

3. So many pieces have now been written on how to define the so-called digital humanities that there is even a reader on the topic: Melissa M. Terras, Julianne Nyhan, and Edward Vanhoutte, eds., *Defining Digital Humanities: A Reader* (Surrey: Ashgate, 2013). While I do not opt here for a lengthy overall definition of the digital humanities, the methods to which I will be referring should become clear over this introduction.

4. See Mario Livio, *The Golden Ratio: The Story of Phi, the World's Most Astonishing Number* (New York: Broadway, 2003).

5. Annette Vee, "'Literary Analysis by Computer' Offered at Dartmouth, Winter 1969, Working with *Paradise Lost*. #1960sComputing Pic.Twitter.Com/DPrnY23cpU," Tweet, *@anetv* (blog), Oct. 4, 2017, https://twitter.com/anetv/status/915219418189660160/photo/1.

6. Nicholas Dames, *The Physiology of the Novel: Reading, Neural Science, and the Form of Victorian Fiction* (Oxford: Oxford University Press, 2007), 188; Vernon Lee, *The Handling of Words* (London: Bodley Head, 1923), https://gutenberg.ca/ebooks/lee-handling/lee-handling-00-h.html#ch_VI.

7. W. Moskalew, *Formular Language and Poetic Design in the "Aeneid"* (Leiden: Brill, 1982), 21.

8. See, e.g., Timothy Brennan, "The Digital-Humanities Bust," *Chronicle of Higher Education*, Oct. 15, 2017, www.chronicle.com/article/The-Digital-Humanities-Bust/241424. Brennan argues that counting the word *whale* in *Moby-Dick* tells us nothing more than that there are seventeen hundred occurrences of the word *whale* in *Moby-Dick*. By way of critique, Brennan's article is curious in espousing a need for utility from digital projects that he seems also to claim should not be the aim of the humanities disciplines. For a good response to Brennan see Sarah E. Bond, Hoyt Long, and Ted Underwood, "'Digital' Is Not the Opposite of 'Humanities,'" *Chronicle of Higher Education*, Nov. 1, 2017, www.chronicle.com/article/Digital-Is-Not-the/241634.

9. Laura Miller, "Take Notes, Nate Silver! Reinventing Literary Criticism with Computers," *Salon*, April 23, 2014, www.salon.com/2014/04/23/learning_from_failed_books.

10. See, e.g., Mehrdad Yazdani, Jay Chow, and Lev Manovich, "Quantifying the Development of User-Generated Art During 2001–2010," *PLOS ONE* 12, no. 8 (2017): e0175350, https://doi.org/10.1371/journal.pone.0175350.

11. Franco Moretti, "The Slaughterhouse of Literature," *Modern Language Quarterly* 61, no. 1 (2000): 207–27.

12. Stephen Ramsay, "The Hermeneutics of Screwing Around; or What You Do with a Million Books," in *Pastplay: Teaching and Learning History with Technology*, ed. Kevin Kee (Ann Arbor: University of Michigan Press, 2014), 110–20, https://quod.lib.umich.edu/d/dh/12544152.0001.001/1:5/—pastplay-teaching-and-learning-history-with-technology?g=dculture;rgn=div1;view=fulltext;xc=1; Ted Underwood, "The Life Cycles of Genres," *Journal of Cultural Analytics*, May 23, 2016, https://doi.org/10.22148/16.005; Ted Underwood and Jordan Sellers, "The *Longue Durée* of Literary Prestige," *Modern Language Quarterly* 77, no. 3 (2016): 321–44, https://doi.org/10.1215/00267929-3570634.

13. Richard Rogers, *Digital Methods* (Cambridge, MA: MIT Press, 2015), 1.

14. Lisa Gitelman, ed., *"Raw Data" Is an Oxymoron* (Cambridge, MA: MIT Press, 2013).

15. Wai Chee Dimock, *Through Other Continents: American Literature Across Deep Time* (Princeton, NJ: Princeton University Press, 2008), 79.

16. See Amy Hungerford, *Making Literature Now* (Stanford, CA: Stanford University Press, 2016).

17. For more on these forms see Eileen Gardiner and Ronald G. Musto, *The Digital*

Humanities: A Primer for Students and Scholars (New York: Cambridge University Press, 2015), 142–45; Stephen Ramsay, *Reading Machines: Toward an Algorithmic Criticism* (Urbana: University of Illinois Press, 2011); N. Katherine Hayles, *Writing Machines*, Mediawork pamphlet (Cambridge, MA: MIT Press, 2002); and Johanna Drucker, "Why Distant Reading Isn't," *PMLA* 132, no. 3 (2017): 628–35.

18. For more on these estimates see Erik Fredner, "How Many Novels Have Been Published in English? (An Attempt)," *Stanford Literary Lab* (blog), March 14, 2017, https://litlab.stanford.edu/how-many-novels-have-been-published-in-english-an-attempt/; figures for life expectancy come from the World Health Organization, "Life Expectancy," 2015, www.who.int/gho/mortality_burden_disease/life_tables/situation_trends/en/.

19. Lisa Marie Rhody, "Beyond Darwinian Distance: Situating Distant Reading in a Feminist *Ut Pictura Poesis* Tradition," *PMLA* 132, no. 3 (2017): 659.

20. That said, the development of distant techniques requires the methods to be refined on individual texts. See, e.g., Matthew L. Jockers, "A Novel Method for Detecting Plot," June 5, 2014, www.matthewjockers.net/2014/06/05/a-novel-method-for-detecting-plot, where the author uses a method on a small number of individual texts to refine an automatic technique that could then be used on a grand scale. Note also that there was extensive subsequent discussion and debate around the technicalities of this method, particularly the use of the low-pass filter. For more see Matthew L. Jockers, "Requiem for a Low Pass Filter," April 6, 2015, www.matthewjockers.net/2015/04/06/epilogue; Annie Swafford, "Continuing the Syuzhet Discussion," *Anglophile in Academia: Annie Swafford's Blog* (blog), March 7, 2015, https://annieswafford.wordpress.com/2015/03/07/continuingsyuzhet; Matthew L. Jockers, "Resurrecting a Low Pass Filter (Well, Kind Of)," Jan. 12, 2017, www.matthewjockers.net/2017/01/12/resurrecting/; Benjamin M. Schmidt, "Do Digital Humanists Need to Understand Algorithms?" in *Debates in the Digital Humanities 2016*, ed. Matthew K. Gold and Lauren F. Klein (Minneapolis: University of Minnesota Press, 2016), 546–55, http://dhdebates.gc.cuny.edu/debates/text/99.

21. Richard Jean So, "All Models Are Wrong," *PMLA* 132, no. 3 (2017): 671; see also Andrew Piper, "Think Small: On Literary Modeling," *PMLA* 132, no. 3 (2017): 651–58.

22. Margaret Cohen, *The Sentimental Education of the Novel* (Princeton, NJ: Princeton University Press, 2002), 23.

23. Unbeknownst to me at the time of this writing, Ernesto Priego had made this same observation about the "opposite" of distant reading at a recent conference.

24. G. Rockwell, "What Is Text Analysis, Really?" *Literary and Linguistic Computing* 18, no. 2 (2003): 209–19, https://doi.org/10.1093/llc/18.2.209.

25. See Barbara Herrnstein Smith, "What Was 'Close Reading'? A Century of Method in Literary Studies," *Minnesota Review* 87 (2016): 70–71, https://doi.org/10.1215/00265667-3630844.

26. Close reading has been perceived as under threat from other areas, too, such as the resurgence of literary-historical archival work. See Jane Gallop, "The Historicization of Literary Studies and the Fate of Close Reading," *Profession* (2007): 181–86, https://doi.org/10.1632/prof.2007.2007.1.181.

27. Moretti, *Distant Reading*, 48, 65.

28. Moretti, 67, 48.

29. For more on this see Matthew Wickman, "Theology Still?" *PMLA* 132, no. 3 (2017): 674–80; Robert Alter, *Canon and Creativity: Modern Writing and the Authority of Scripture* (New Haven, CT: Yale University Press, 2000); and Charles Altieri, *Canons and Consequences: Reflections on the Ethical Force of Imaginative Ideals* (Evanston, IL: Northwestern University Press, 1990).

30. Shawna Ross, "In Praise of Overstating the Case: A Review of Franco Moretti, *Distant Reading* (London: Verso, 2013)," *Digital Humanities Quarterly* 8, no. 1 (2014): www.digitalhumanities.org/dhq/vol/8/1/000171/000171.html. My account here of some of the oppositions to close reading in various new media and digital humanities spaces is indebted to this work.

31. Lev Manovich, *The Language of New Media* (Cambridge, MA: MIT Press, 2002), 199.

32. Rafael Alvarado and Paul Humphreys, "Big Data, Thick Mediation, and Representational Opacity," *New Literary History* 48, no. 4 (2017): 729–49, https://doi.org/10.1353/nlh.2017.0037.

33. Matthew Wilkens, "Canons, Close Reading, and the Evolution of Method," in *Debates in the Digital Humanities*, ed. Matthew K. Gold (Minneapolis: University of Minnesota Press, 2012), 256, http://dhdebates.gc.cuny.edu/debates/part/5.

34. Peter Middleton, *Distant Reading: Performance, Readership, and Consumption in Contemporary Poetry* (Tuscaloosa: University of Alabama Press, 2005), 5.

35. Andrew Goldstone, "The *Doxa* of Reading," *PMLA* 132, no. 3 (2017): 641.

36. Jonathan Culler, "The Closeness of Close Reading," *ADE Bulletin* 149 (2010): 20, https://doi.org/10.1632/ade.149.20.

37. Jessica Pressman, *Digital Modernism: Making It New in New Media* (New York: Oxford University Press, 2014), 11.

38. Ted Underwood, *Why Literary Periods Mattered: Historical Contrast and the Prestige of English Studies* (Stanford, CA: Stanford University Press, 2013), 81; see also Franklin E. Court, *Institutionalizing English Literature: Culture and Politics of Literary Study, 1750–1900* (Stanford, CA: Stanford University Press, 1992); and Gerald Graff, *Professing Literature: An Institutional History* (Chicago: University of Chicago Press, 1989).

39. I. A Richards, *Principles of Literary Criticism* (London: Routledge, 2001), 158.

40. I. A. Richards, *How to Read a Page: A Course in Efficient Reading with an Introduction to a Hundred Great Words* (Boston: Beacon, 1959), 15.

41. Nancy Armstrong and Warren Montag, "'The Figure in the Carpet,'" *PMLA* 132, no. 3 (2017): 617.

42. There was certainly a broader *geist* at work around the time of *Reading Capital*, however, that sought to interrogate reading methods, say with the publication of Roland Barthes's *S/Z* (Paris: Seuil, 1970).

43. Louis Althusser et al., *Reading Capital: The Complete Edition*, trans. Ben Brewster and David Fernbach (London: Verso, 2015), 17 (italics in original).

44. Althusser et al., 32.

45. Althusser et al., 27.

46. Althusser et al., 69.

47. David Stewart, "The Hermeneutics of Suspicion," *Literature and Theology* 3, no. 3 (1989): 303; Cathy N. Davidson and David Theo Goldberg, "Engaging the Humanities," *Profession* (2004): 45, www.jstor.org/stable/25595777.

48. Stephen Best and Sharon Marcus, "Surface Reading: An Introduction," *Representations* 108, no. 1 (2009): 2, https://doi.org/10.1525/rep.2009.108.1.1.

49. N. Katherine Hayles, *How We Think: Digital Media and Contemporary Technogenesis* (Chicago: University of Chicago Press, 2012), 59.

50. See Bruce Robbins, "Not So Well Attached," *PMLA* 132, no. 2 (2017): 371–76, https://doi.org/10.1632/pmla.2017.132.2.371.

51. Rita Felski, *The Limits of Critique* (Chicago: University of Chicago Press, 2015), 31; Paul Ricœur, *Freud and Philosophy: An Essay on Interpretation*, trans. Denis Savage (New Haven, CT: Yale University Press, 1979). In its own right Ricœur's work has generated a vast and ongoing body of secondary critical literature, including Hans-Georg Gadamer, "The Hermeneutics of Suspicion," in *Phenomenology and the Human Sciences*, ed. J. N. Mohanty (Dordrecht: Springer Netherlands, 1984), 73–83, https://doi.org/10.1007/978-94-009-5081-8_6; Brian Leiter, "The Hermeneutics of Suspicion: Recovering Marx, Nietzsche, and Freud," SSRN Scholarly Paper (Rochester, NY: Social Science Research Network, March 23, 2005), https://papers.ssrn.com/abstract=691002; and Alison Scott-Baumann, *Ricœur and the Hermeneutics of Suspicion* (London: Continuum, 2009). Anthony C. Thiselton, *New Horizons in Hermeneutics: The Theory and Practice of Transforming Biblical Reading* (Grand Rapids, MI: Zondervan, 1998), 344–51, is unusually sound in its contextualization of the phrase.

52. Felski, *The Limits of Critique*, 31.

53. Scott-Baumann, *Ricœur and the Hermeneutics of Suspicion*, 63; Don Ihde, *Hermeneutic Phenomenology: The Philosophy of Paul Ricoeur* (Evanston, IL: Northwestern University Press, 1980).

54. Paul Ricœur, "Biblical Hermeneutics," *Semeia* 4 (1975): 29–148; Paul Ricœur, *The Rule of Metaphor: Multi-disciplinary Studies of the Creation of Meaning in Language*, trans. R. Czerny (Toronto: University of Toronto Press, 1975), 285; Charles E. Reagan, "Interview with Paul Ricœur (Recorded 1982)," in *Paul Ricoeur: His Life and Work* (Chicago: University Of Chicago Press, 1996), 105; I owe all this research to Scott-Baumann, *Ricœur and the Hermeneutics of Suspicion*, 63–67.

55. Scott-Baumann, 66.

56. The phrases "school of suspicion," "tactic of suspicion," "exercise of suspicion," and "masters of suspicion" appear in Ricœur, *Freud and Philosophy*, 37, 39, 43, 44, 75.

57. Felski, *The Limits of Critique*, 3.

58. Felski, 30.

59. Culler, "The Closeness of Close Reading," 22.

60. For just one example essay on the types of new questions that are being raised by close reading in a digital environment, see David Ciccoricco, "The Materialities of Close Reading: 1942, 1959, 2009," *Digital Humanities Quarterly* 6, no. 1 (2012): www.digitalhumanities.org/dhq/vol/6/1/000113/000113.html.

61. Dimock, *Through Other Continents*, 79.

62. John Burrows, *Computation into Criticism: A Study of Jane Austen's Novels and an Experiment in Method* (London: Clarendon, 1987).

63. My thanks to Ted Underwood for pointing this out. See Eviatar Zerubavel, *The Clockwork Muse: A Practical Guide to Writing Theses, Dissertations, and Books* (Cambridge, MA: Harvard University Press, 1999); and Mark Olsen, "Signs, Symbols and Discourses: A New Direction for Computer-Aided Literature Studies," *Computers and the Humanities* 27, no. 5/6 (1993): 309–14.

64. Catherine Nicholson, "Algorithm and Analogy: Distant Reading in 1598," *PMLA* 132, no. 3 (2017): 643–50.

65. Lisa Pearl, Kristine Lu, and Anousheh Haghighi, "The Character in the Letter: Epistolary Attribution in Samuel Richardson's *Clarissa*," *Digital Scholarship in the Humanities* 32, no. 1 (2016): 123–40, https://doi.org/10.1093/llc/fqw007; Alexander A. G. Gladwin, Matthew J. Lavin, and Daniel M. Look, "Stylometry and Collaborative Authorship: Eddy, Lovecraft, and 'The Loved Dead,'" *Digital Scholarship in the Humanities* 32, no. 1 (2017): 123–40, https://doi.org/10.1093/llc/fqv026.

66. Miyuki Yamada, Yuichi Murai, and Ichiro Kumagai, "Story Visualization of Novels with Multi-theme Keyword Density Analysis," *Journal of Visualization* 16, no. 3 (2013): 247–57, https://doi.org/10.1007/s12650-013-0163-4.

67. Stefanie Posavec, "Writing Without Words," 2009, www.stefanieposavec.com/writing-without-words; Jeff Clark, "Novel Views: *Les Miserables*," Neoformix, 2013, http://neoformix.com/2013/NovelViews.html.

68. Pressman, *Digital Modernism*, 156.

69. Hayles, *Writing Machines*; Hayles, *How We Think*; see also Jessica Pressman, "*House of Leaves*: Reading the Networked Novel," *Studies in American Fiction* 34, no. 1 (2006): 107–28, https://doi.org/10.1353/saf.2006.0015.

70. Zara Dinnen, *The Digital Banal: New Media and American Literature and Culture* (New York: Columbia University Press, 2018).

71. Even so, there are questions as to whether digital humanities is actually a *field*. See Alan Liu, "Is Digital Humanities a Field?—An Answer from the Point of View of Language," *Journal of Siberian Federal University, Humanities and Social Sciences* 7 (2013): 1546–52.

72. Alan Liu, *The Laws of Cool: Knowledge Work and the Culture of Information* (Chicago: University of Chicago Press, 2004), 147.

73. David Hoover, "The End of the Irrelevant Text: Electronic Texts, Linguistics, and Literary Theory," *Digital Humanities Quarterly* 1, no. 2 (2007): para. 4, www.digitalhumanities.org/dhq/vol/1/2/000012/000012.html.

74. Stephen Ramsay, "Toward an Algorithmic Criticism," in *A Companion to Digital Literary Studies*, ed. Ray Siemens and Susan Schreibman (New York: Wiley-Blackwell, 2013), 477–78.

75. Cosima Mattner and Ted Underwood, "They Have Completely Changed My Understanding of Literary History," *Textpraxis* 14, no. 3 (2017): www.uni-muenster.de/Textpraxis/en/cosima-mattner-they-have-completely-changed-my-understanding-of-literary-history.

76. Andrew Jewell and Brian L. Pytlik Zillig, "'Counted Out at Last': Text Analysis

on the Willa Cather Archive," in *American Literature Scholar in the Digital Age*, ed. Amy E. Earhart and Andrew Jewell (Ann Arbor: University of Michigan Press, 2011), 184, https://doi.org/10.3998/etlc.9362034.0001.001.

77. Jewell and Zillig, 181. They offer as an example Tanya E. Clement, "'A Thing Not Beginning and Not Ending': Using Digital Tools to Distant-Read Gertrude Stein's *The Making of Americans*," *Literary and Linguistic Computing* 23, no. 3 (2008): 361–81, https://doi.org/10.1093/llc/fqn020. That said, Earhart and Jewell's *American Literature Scholar in the Digital Age* contains many good examples of close, textual, digital practices.

78. Perhaps the work in the field of digital humanities that comes closest to what I do in this book is Johanna Drucker, *SpecLab: Digital Aesthetics and Projects in Speculative Computing* (Chicago: University of Chicago Press, 2009), which insists on the need for experimental practices in the humanities while also aiming at technologies, such as the "'Patacritical Demon," that could unveil how our interpretative practices work. I also do not intend to rehash a series of debates about the "digital humanities." For more on this see, among many others, Matthew K. Gold and Lauren F. Klein, eds., *Debates in the Digital Humanities 2016* (Minneapolis: University of Minnesota Press, 2016); Susan Schreibman, Raymond George Siemens, and John Unsworth, eds., *A New Companion to Digital Humanities* (Chichester: John Wiley and Sons, 2016); Ray Siemens and Susan Schreibman, eds., *A Companion to Digital Literary Studies* (New York: Wiley-Blackwell, 2013); Ramsay, *Reading Machines*; Adam Koehler, *Composition, Creative Writing Studies and the Digital Humanities* (London: Bloomsbury, 2017); David M. Berry and Anders Fagerjord, *Digital Humanities: Knowledge and Critique in a Digital Age* (Cambridge: Polity, 2017); Julianne Nyhan and Andrew Flinn, *Computation and the Humanities: Towards an Oral History of Digital Humanities* (London: Springer, 2016); and Anne Burdick et al., *Digital Humanities* (Cambridge, MA: MIT Press, 2012).

79. Alan Liu, "The State of the Digital Humanities: A Report and a Critique," *Arts and Humanities in Higher Education* 11, no. 1–2 (2012): 8–41, https://doi.org/10.1177/1474022211427364; Tanya E. Clement, "Text Analysis, Data Mining, and Visualizations in Literary Scholarship," MLA Commons, *Literary Studies in the Digital Age: An Evolving Anthology* (New York: Modern Language Association, 2013): https://dlsanthology.mla.hcommons.org/text-analysis-data-mining-and-visualizations-in-literary-scholarship.

80. Theodor W. Adorno, *Negative Dialectics*, trans. E. B. Ashton (London: Routledge, 1973), 5.

81. For more on literature and singularity see Derek Attridge, *The Singularity of Literature* (London: Routledge, 2004).

82. Alison Booth, "Mid-range Reading: Not a Manifesto," *PMLA* 132, no. 3 (2017): 620.

83. *Cloud Atlas* won the British Book Awards Literary Fiction Award and the Richard & Judy Book of the Year award. The novel was short-listed for the 2004 Booker Prize, the Nebula Award, and the Arthur C. Clarke Award. A film of the book achieved widespread recognition in 2012.

84. "Future Library, 2014–2114," https://www.futurelibrary.no/#/years/2015/.

85. Kristian Shaw, "'Some Magic Is Normality': Fantastical Cosmopolitanism in

David Mitchell's *The Bone Clocks*," *C21 Literature: Journal of 21st Century Writings* 6, no. 3 (2018): https://doi.org/10.16995/c21.52.

86. Casey Shoop and Dermot Ryan, " 'Gravid with the Ancient Future': *Cloud Atlas* and the Politics of Big History," *SubStance* 44, no. 1 (2015): 101, https://doi.org/10.1353/sub.2015.0011.

87. Fredric Jameson, "The Historical Novel Today, or, Is It Still Possible?" in *The Antinomies of Realism* (London: Verso, 2013), 303.

88. Rose Harris-Birtill, " 'Looking Down Time's Telescope at Myself': Reincarnation and Global Futures in David Mitchell's Fictional Worlds," *KronoScope: The Journal for the Study of Time* 17, no. 2 (2017): 163–81, https://doi.org/10.1163/15685241-12341382.

89. For just a small selection see most of the essays in Sarah Dillon, ed., *David Mitchell: Critical Essays* (Canterbury: Gylphi, 2011), esp. Courtney Hopf, "The Stories We Tell: Discursive Identity Through Narrative Form in *Cloud Atlas*" (105–26); Patrick O'Donnell, *A Temporary Future: The Fiction of David Mitchell* (New York: Bloomsbury Academic, 2015); and Scott Dimovitz, "The Sound of Silence: Eschatology and the Limits of the Word in David Mitchell's *Cloud Atlas*," *SubStance* 44, no. 1 (2015): 71–91, https://doi.org/10.1353/sub.2015.0009.

90. Peter Childs and James Green, "The Novels in Nine Parts," in *David Mitchell: Critical Essays*, ed. Sarah Dillon (Canterbury: Gylphi, 2011), 33–34.

91. John Shanahan, "Digital Transcendentalism in David Mitchell's *Cloud Atlas*," *Criticism* 58, no. 1 (2016): 115, https://doi.org/10.13110/criticism.58.1.0115.

92. Stuart Jeffries, "David Mitchell: 'I Don't Want to Project Myself as This Great Experimenter,' " *The Guardian*, Feb. 8, 2013, www.guardian.co.uk/books/2013/feb/08/david-mitchell-project-great-experimenter.

93. But see Chapter 3, below.

94. Brian McHale, "Genre as History: Genre-Poaching in *Against the Day*," *Genre* 42, no. 3–4 (2009): 5–20, https://doi.org/10.1215/00166928-42-3-4-5.

95. Book World, "Q&A: Book World Talks with David Mitchell," *Washington Post*, August 22, 2004, www.washingtonpost.com/wp-dyn/articles/A17231-2004Aug19.html; David Mitchell, "Guardian Book Club: *Cloud Atlas* by David Mitchell," *The Guardian*, June 12, 2010, www.theguardian.com/books/2010/jun/12/book-club-mitchell-cloud-atlas; Adam Begley, "David Mitchell, The Art of Fiction No. 204," *Paris Review*, Summer 2010, www.theparisreview.org/interviews/6034/the-art-of-fiction-no-204-david-mitchell; Martin Paul Eve, " 'some kind of thing it aint us but yet its in us': David Mitchell, Russell Hoban, and Metafiction After the Millennium," *Sage Open* 4, no. 1 (2014): 5–6, https://doi.org/10.1177/2158244014521636.

96. Martin Paul Eve, " 'You Will See the Logic of the Design of This': From Historiography to Taxonomography in the Contemporary Metafiction of Sarah Waters's *Affinity*," *Neo-Victorian Studies* 6, no. 1 (2013): 107.

97. John Mullan, "*Cloud Atlas*: The Multi-genre Novel," *The Guardian*, March 26, 2005, sec. Books, www.theguardian.com/books/2005/mar/26/fiction.davidmitchell.

98. There are also other recent examples of form-jumping docufiction, such as Zinzi Clemmons, *What We Lose* (London: Fourth Estate, 2017); Mark Blacklock, *I'm*

Jack (London: Granta, 2015); and narratives with two converging strands, such as Nicola Barker, *H(A)PPY* (Portsmouth, NH: William Heinemann, 2017).

99. A brilliant genealogy of distant reading, as a whole, is given by Underwood—a genealogy that also notes the importance of feminist literary sociology to its emergence, thereby providing an even more problematic space for my work here. See Ted Underwood, "A Genealogy of Distant Reading," *Digital Humanities Quarterly* 11, no. 2 (2017): www.digitalhumanities.org/dhq/vol/11/2/000317/000317.html.

100. David Mitchell, *Cloud Atlas* (London: Sceptre, 2004), 528 (hereafter *Cloud Atlas P*); David Mitchell, *Cloud Atlas* (New York: Random House, 2004), 508 (hereafter *Cloud Atlas E*).

101. Yet, as Dennis Tenen has recently pointed out, "plain text" turns out to be less than vanilla. See Dennis Tenen, *Plain Text: The Poetics of Computation* (Stanford, CA: Stanford University Press, 2017), 1–7.

102. Comparative legal provisions are made in the USA's Digital Millennium Copyright Act.

103. See Government of the United Kingdom, "Complaints to Secretary of State Under s.296ZE Under the Copyright, Designs and Patents Act 1988," August 15, 2014, https://www.gov.uk/government/publications/complaints-to-secretary-of-state-under-s296ze-under-the-copyright-designs-and-patents-act-1988. The document shows zero successful complaints under this protocol as of 2014.

104. See Lisa Samuels and Jerome J. McGann, "Deformance and Interpretation," *New Literary History* 30, no. 1 (1999): 25–56, https://doi.org/10.1353/nlh.1999.0010.

105. Theodor W. Adorno, *Aesthetic Theory*, trans. C. Lenhardt (London: Routledge, 1984), 447.

106. Ian Hacking, "Do We See Through a Microscope?" *Pacific Philosophical Quarterly* 62, no. 4 (1981): 321, https://doi.org/10.1111/j.1468-0114.1981.tb00070.x.

107. For more on interventionist epistemologies and the digital humanities see Berry and Fagerjord, *Digital Humanities*, 33.

108. Matthew L. Jockers, *Text Analysis with R for Students of Literature* (New York: Springer, 2014).

109. Robert Eaglestone, "Contemporary Fiction in the Academy: Towards a Manifesto," *Textual Practice* 27, no. 7 (2013): 1096, https://doi.org/10.1080/0950236X.2013.840113.

110. Caroline Edwards, "'Strange Transactions': Utopia, Transmigration and Time in *Ghostwritten* and *Cloud Atlas*," in *David Mitchell: Critical Essays*, ed. Sarah Dillon (Canterbury: Gylphi, 2011), 178–200; Hopf, "The Stories We Tell"; O'Donnell, *A Temporary Future*.

111. W. Elliot and R. J. Valenza, "So Many Hardballs, so Few over the Plate," *Computers and the Humanities* 36, no. 4 (2002): 455.

CHAPTER 1: THE CONTEMPORARY HISTORY OF THE BOOK

1. Rita Felski, *The Limits of Critique* (Chicago: University of Chicago Press, 2015), 170.

2. Robert Eaglestone, "Contemporary Fiction in the Academy: Towards a Manifesto," *Textual Practice* 27, no. 7 (2013): 1096, https://doi.org/10.1080/0950236X.2013.840113.

3. Eaglestone, 1093.

4. Eaglestone, 1093.

5. See Roland Barthes, "The Death of the Author," in *Image, Music, Text*, trans. Stephen Heath (London: Fontana, 1987), 142–48; Michel Foucault, "What Is an Author?" in *The Essential Works of Michel Foucault, 1954–1984*, ed. James D Faubion, 3 vols. (London: Penguin, 2000), 2:205–22; Seán Burke, *The Death and Return of the Author: Criticism and Subjectivity in Barthes, Foucault and Derrida*, 3rd rev. ed. (Edinburgh: Edinburgh University Press, 2008).

6. Jerome McGann, *A Critique of Modern Textual Criticism* (Charlottesville: University Press of Virginia, 1983).

7. Tim Groenland, "'A Recipe for a Brick': *The Pale King* in Progress," *Critique: Studies in Contemporary Fiction* 58, no. 4 (2017): 1–12, https://doi.org/10.1080/00111619.2016.1271766; see also John Roache, "'The Realer, More Enduring and Sentimental Part of Him': David Foster Wallace's Personal Library and Marginalia," *Orbit: A Journal of American Literature* 5, no. 1 (2017): https://doi.org/10.16995/orbit.142, which examines Wallace's marginalia.

8. Eaglestone, "Contemporary Fiction in the Academy," 1095.

9. Erik Ketzan and Christof Schöch, "What Changed When Andy Weir's *The Martian* Got Edited?" Digital Humanities 2017 conference, Montreal, August 8–11, https://dh2017.adho.org/abstracts/317/317.pdf.

10. For more on this see Jed Deppman, Daniel Ferrer, and Michael Groden, eds., *Genetic Criticism* (Philadelphia: University of Pennsylvania Press, 2004).

11. See, e.g., in my own field Luc Herman and John M. Krafft, "Fast Learner: The Typescript of Pynchon's *V.* at the Harry Ransom Center in Austin," *Texas Studies in Literature and Language* 49, no. 1 (2007): 1–20, https://doi.org/10.1353/tsl.2007.0005.

12. Luigi Giuliani et al., eds., *Texts in Multiple Versions: Histories of Editions* (Amsterdam: Brill, 2006), v.

13. Bobbie Johnson, "Amazon Kindle Users Surprised by 'Big Brother' Move," *The Guardian*, July 17, 2009, sec. Technology, www.theguardian.com/technology/2009/jul/17/amazon-kindle-1984.

14. John Lavagnino, "Excerpted: Reading, Scholarship, and Hypertext Editions," *Journal of Electronic Publishing* 3, no. 1 (1997): http://dx.doi.org/10.3998/3336451.0003.112.

15. A full concordance of all US and UK editions is beyond the scope of this chapter.

16. I also keep to this schema to remain in line with Martin Paul Eve, "'You Have to Keep Track of Your Changes': The Version Variants and Publishing History of David Mitchell's *Cloud Atlas*," *Open Library of Humanities* 2, no. 2 (2016): 1–34, http://dx.doi.org/10.16995/olh.82.

17. See, e.g., Anne Mangen, "Hypertext Fiction Reading: Haptics and Immersion," *Journal of Research in Reading* 31, no. 4 (2008): 404–19, https://doi.org/10.1111/j.1467-9817.2008.00380.x.

18. Burghard Dedner, "Highlighting Variants in Literary Editions: Techniques and Goals," in *Texts in Multiple Versions: Histories of Editions*, ed. Luigi Giuliani et al. (Amsterdam: Rodopi, 2006), 15–32.

19. For more see Deppman, Ferrer, and Groden, *Genetic Criticism*.

20. See Viktor Šklovskij, *Theory of Prose* (Elmwood Park, IL: Dalkey Archive Press, 1991); and Vladimir Propp, *Morphology of the Folktale* (Austin, TX: University of Texas Press, 1968).

21. I had not initially noticed this difference in Eve, "'You Have to Keep Track of Your Changes.'"

22. David Mitchell, *Cloud Atlas* (London: Sceptre, 2004), 39 (hereafter *Cloud Atlas P*).

23. David Mitchell, *Cloud Atlas* (New York: Random House, 2004), 39 (hereafter *Cloud Atlas E*).

24. Mitchell, *Cloud Atlas P*, 198; Mitchell, *Cloud Atlas E*, 192.

25. Martin Paul Eve, "SankeyTextualVariant," GitHub, 2015, https://github.com/MartinPaulEve/SankeyTextualVariant.

26. David Gorman and Jerome McGann, "An Interview with Jerome McGann on Textual Scholarship as Literary History and Ideology Critique," *Social Epistemology* 1, no. 2 (1987): 166, https://doi.org/10.1080/02691728708578428.

27. Mitchell, *Cloud Atlas P*, 188.

28. Mitchell, 189; Mitchell, *Cloud Atlas E*, 194.

29. Mitchell, *Cloud Atlas P*, 192; Mitchell, *Cloud Atlas E*, 190.

30. Mitchell, *Cloud Atlas P*, 197; Mitchell, *Cloud Atlas E*, 192.

31. Mitchell, *Cloud Atlas P*, 199.

32. Mitchell, *Cloud Atlas E*, 193.

33. Mitchell, *Cloud Atlas P*, 200; Mitchell, *Cloud Atlas E*, 190.

34. Mitchell, *Cloud Atlas P*, 215; Mitchell, *Cloud Atlas E*, 206.

35. Mitchell, *Cloud Atlas P*, 244.

36. Mitchell, 365.

37. Mitchell, *Cloud Atlas E*, 212.

38. Mitchell, 234.

39. Mitchell, 234.

40. See Francis Fukuyama, *The End of History and the Last Man* (London: Penguin, 2012).

41. Perhaps the best-known discourses on the interlinks between history and fiction are Hayden White, *Metahistory: Historical Imagination in Nineteenth Century Europe* (Baltimore: Johns Hopkins University Press, 1975); and Hayden White, "Historical Emplotment and the Problem of Truth," in *Probing the Limits of Representation: Nazism and the "Final Solution,"* ed. S. Friedlander (Cambridge, MA: Harvard University Press, 1992), 37–53.

42. Mitchell, *Cloud Atlas P*, 194; Mitchell, *Cloud Atlas E*, 189.

43. Mitchell, 234–35.

44. Mitchell, 344; Hannah Arendt, *Eichmann in Jerusalem: A Report on the Banality of Evil* (New York: Penguin, 2006).

45. Christopher A. Sims, *Tech Anxiety: Artificial Intelligence and Ontological Awakening in Four Science Fiction Novels* (Jefferson, NC: McFarland, 2013), 217.

46. See Joanna Bourke, *What It Means to Be Human: Reflections from 1791 to the Present* (Berkeley, CA: Counterpoint, 2011), 182–89.

47. Bourke, 187.

48. For more on the dangers of relativity and the Holocaust see Elie Wiesel, *From the Kingdom of Memory: Reminiscences* (New York: Summit, 1990), 166; Robert Eaglestone, *The Holocaust and the Postmodern* (Oxford: Oxford University Press, 2004); and Martin Paul Eve, *Pynchon and Philosophy: Wittgenstein, Foucault and Adorno* (London: Palgrave Macmillan, 2014), 30–31.

49. Mitchell, *Cloud Atlas P*, 187.

50. Mitchell, *Cloud Atlas E*, 185. Note that in David Mitchell, *Cloud Atlas*, Kindle Edition (New York: Random House/Amazon Kindle, 2004) the capitalization is different: "TRUTH IS SINGULAR. ITS 'VERSIONS' ARE MISTRUTHS."

51. For more on historiographic metafiction see Linda Hutcheon, *A Poetics of Postmodernism: History, Theory, Fiction* (New York: Routledge, 1988).

52. Mitchell, *Cloud Atlas P*, 187.

53. Mitchell, *Cloud Atlas E*, 185.

54. For more on this see Eve, "'some kind of thing it aint us but yet its in us': David Mitchell, Russell Hoban, and Metafiction After the Millennium," *Sage Open* 4, no. 1 (2014): https://doi.org/10.1177/2158244014521636.

55. Patrick O'Donnell, *A Temporary Future: The Fiction of David Mitchell* (New York: Bloomsbury Academic, 2015), 76–78.

56. O'Donnell, 94; Mitchell, *Cloud Atlas E*, 330.

57. Nicholas Dunlop, "Speculative Fiction as Postcolonial Critique in *Ghostwritten* and *Cloud Atlas*," in *David Mitchell: Critical Essays*, ed. Sarah Dillon (Canterbury: Gylphi, 2011), 221.

58. It seems to me, though, that Dunlop also mis-cites here, omitting the word *naked* from the sentence. See Dunlop, "Speculative Fiction."

59. See, e.g., Theo D'haen, "European Postmodernism: The Cosmodern Turn," *Narrative* 21, no. 3 (2013): 271–83, https://doi.org/10.1353/nar.2013.0019.

60. Louis Hay, "Does 'Text' Exist?" *Studies in Bibliography* 41 (1988): 73.

61. See N. Katherine Hayles, *How We Think: Digital Media and Contemporary Technogenesis* (Chicago: University of Chicago Press, 2012).

62. Matthew G. Kirschenbaum, *Track Changes: A Literary History of Word Processing* (Cambridge, MA: Belknap Press of Harvard University Press, 2016), 30.

63. David Mitchell to the author, personal correspondence, email, Jan. 18, 2016. Published with permission of David Mitchell.

64. For more on intentionality and copy-text see McGann, *A Critique of Modern Textual Criticism*, chap. 5.

65. It is not my intention in this work to try to recover this original manuscript in any Lachmannesque manner.

66. See Mark Crispin Miller, "The Publishing Industry," in *Conglomerates and the Media*, ed. Patricia Aufderheide et al. (New York: New Press, 1997), 107–34; and David

Finkelstein and Alistair McCleery, *An Introduction to Book History*, 2nd ed. (New York: Routledge, 2013), 127.

67. Claire Larsonneur, "Oblique Translations in David Mitchell's Works," *C21 Literature: Journal of 21st Century Writings* 6, no. 3 (2018), https://doi.org/10.16995/c21.53.

68. David Mitchell, *Cartographie des nuages*, trans. Manuel Berri (Paris: Editions de l'Olivier, 2007), 209.

69. Tom Tykwer, Lana Wachowski, and Lilly (as Andy) Wachowski, *Cloud Atlas* (Warner Bros, 2012).

70. David Mitchell, *Cloud Atlas: L'Atlante delle nuvole*, trans. Luca Scarlini and Lorenzo Borgotallo (Milano: Sperling and Kupfer, 2014).

71. David Mitchell, クラウド・アトラス, trans. Chiho Nakagawa (Tokyo: Kawade Shobo Shinsha, 2013), 137.

72. Mitchell, *Cloud Atlas P*, 122, 99; Mitchell, *Cloud Atlas E*, 120, 98.

73. Mitchell, *Cloud Atlas P*, 52; Mitchell, *Cloud Atlas E*, 52.

74. Sims, *Tech Anxiety*, 232n6.

75. If this was not the case, one could see a literary prize scandal emerging here. In much the same way as charted by James F. English, though, it is most likely that this would in time only bolster the prizes. See James F. English, *The Economy of Prestige Prizes, Awards, and the Circulation of Cultural Value* (Cambridge, MA: Harvard University Press, 2005).

76. For more on the social dynamics of reading groups see Jenny Hartley, *The Reading Groups Book* (Oxford: Oxford University Press, 2002).

77. The same happened in 1963 to Thomas Pynchon's *V.*, to a much smaller extent, according to Albert Rolls. See Albert Rolls, "The Two *V.*s of Thomas Pynchon, or From Lippincott to Jonathan Cape and Beyond," *Orbit: Writing Around Pynchon* 1, no. 1 (2012): https://doi.org/10.7766/orbit.v1.1.33.

78. See McGann, *A Critique of Modern Textual Criticism*, chap. 7.

79. McGann, 81.

80. Hayles, *How We Think*, 212.

81. Mitchell, *Cloud Atlas P*, 245; Mitchell, *Cloud Atlas E*, 236.

82. Jacques Derrida, *Archive Fever: A Freudian Impression*, trans. Eric Prenowitz (Chicago: University of Chicago Press, 1995). I note that this is hyperbolic because there are, surely, many things that are less clear than the meaning of the word *archive*.

83. See Michel Foucault, *The Archaeology of Knowledge*, trans. Alan Sheridan (London: Routledge, 2006).

84. Dominick LaCapra, *History & Criticism* (Ithaca, NY: Cornell University Press, 1985), 92.

85. See Marlene Manoff, "Theories of the Archive from Across the Disciplines," *Portal: Libraries and the Academy* 4, no. 1 (2004): 9–25, for an excellent summary of transdisciplinary concepts of the archive, from which much of this paragraph is derived.

86. Derrida, *Archive Fever*, 17.

87. Mitchell, email.

88. Hélène Machinal, "*Cloud Atlas*: From Postmodernity to the Posthuman," in *David Mitchell: Critical Essays*, ed. Sarah Dillon (Canterbury: Gylphi, 2011), 137.

89. Mitchell, *Cloud Atlas P*, 152; in Mitchell, *Cloud Atlas E*, 150, "MAs" is written as "M.A.s."

90. Some parts of this chapter were previously developed on my blog at Martin Paul Eve, "The Conservatism of *Cloud Atlas*," Dr. Martin Paul Eve, 2015, www.martineve.com/2015/06/21/the-conservatism-of-cloud-atlas/; other parts were also first voiced in Eve, " 'some kind of thing it aint us' "

91. Book World, "Q&A: Book World Talks with David Mitchell," *Washington Post*, August 22, 2004, www.washingtonpost.com/wp-dyn/articles/A17231-2004Aug19.html; David Mitchell, "Guardian Book Club: *Cloud Atlas* by David Mitchell," *The Guardian*, June 12, 2010, www.theguardian.com/books/2010/jun/12/book-club-mitchell-cloud-atlas; Adam Begley, "David Mitchell, The Art of Fiction No. 204," *Paris Review*, Summer 2010, www.theparisreview.org/interviews/6034/the-art-of-fiction-no-204-david-mitchell; Eve, " 'some kind of thing it aint us.' "

92. Courtney Hopf, "The Stories We Tell: Discursive Identity Through Narrative Form in *Cloud Atlas*," in *David Mitchell: Critical Essays*, ed. Sarah Dillon (Canterbury: Gylphi, 2011), 115.

93. Roland Barthes, *Camera Lucida*, trans. Richard Howard (New York: Hill and Wang, 1981).

94. George Orwell, *Nineteen Eighty-Four* (San Diego, CA: Harcourt Brace Jovanovich, 1984), 35.

95. National Information Standards Organization, *Understanding Metadata* (Bethesda, MD: NISO Press, 2004), 1.

96. See Michel Foucault, *Discipline and Punish: The Birth of the Prison*, trans. Alan Sheridan (New York: Vintage, 1997).

97. Hayles, *How We Think*, 212.

98. Mitchell, *Cloud Atlas P*, 243; Mitchell, *Cloud Atlas E*, 234.

CHAPTER 2: READING GENRE COMPUTATIONALLY

1. Jacques Derrida, "The Law of Genre," trans. Avital Ronell, *Critical Inquiry* 7, no. 1 (1980): 55, 57.

2. For more on this and the associated literature see Ludwig Wittgenstein, *Remarks on the Foundations of Mathematics*, 3rd ed. (Oxford: Blackwell, 1978); Saul Kripke, *Wittgenstein on Rules and Private Language* (Oxford: Blackwell, 1982); Crispin Wright, "Wittgenstein's Rule-Following Considerations and the Central Project of Theoretical Linguistics," in *Reflections on Chomsky*, ed. Alexander L. George (Oxford: Blackwell, 1989), 233–64; G. P. Baker and P. M. S. Hacker, *Wittgenstein: Rules, Grammar and Necessity*, vol. 2, *An Analytical Commentary on the Philosophical Investigations* (Oxford: Blackwell, 1985).

3. Robert Stam, "Text and Intertext: Introduction," in *Film Theory: An Anthology*, ed. Robert Stam and Toby Miller (Malden, MA: Blackwell, 2000), 151–52; Martin Paul Eve, *Literature Against Criticism: University English and Contemporary Fiction in Conflict* (Cambridge: Open Book Publishers, 2016), 166.

4. Andrew Tudor, *Theories of Film* (London: British Film Institute, 1974), 135.

5. Martin Paul Eve, "New Rhetorics: Disciplinarity and the Movement from Historiography to Taxonomography," in *Metahistorical Narratives and Scientific Metafictions*, ed. Giuseppe di Episcopo (Naples: Edizioni Cronopio, 2015), 101–22.

6. Lauren Berlant, *Cruel Optimism* (Durham, NC: Duke University Press, 2011), 4–7.

7. Ted Underwood, "The Life Cycles of Genres," *Journal of Cultural Analytics*, May 23, 2016, https://doi.org/10.22148/16.005.

8. For the critique see Brennan, "The Digital-Humanities Bust," *Chronicle of Higher Education*, Oct. 15, 2017, www.chronicle.com/article/The-Digital-Humanities-Bust/241424.

9. See A. Q. Morton's widely discredited *Literary Detection: How to Prove Authorship and Fraud in Literature and Documents* (Epping: Bowker, 1978), 205–6; but also Patrick Juola, "Stylometry and Immigration: A Case Study," *Journal of Law and Policy* 21, no. 2 (2012): 287–98.

10. Anthony Kenny, *The Computation of Style: An Introduction to Statistics for Students of Literature and Humanities* (Oxford: Pergamon, 1982), 1.

11. Ariel Stolerman et al., "Breaking the Closed-World Assumption in Stylometric Authorship Attribution," in *Advances in Digital Forensics X*, ed. Gilbert Peterson and Sujeet Shenoi (Berlin: Springer, 2014), 186.

12. F. Mosteller and D. L. Wallace, *Inference and Disputed Authorship: The Federalist* (Reading, MA: Addison-Wesley, 1964).

13. Patrick Juola, "Authorship Attribution," *Foundations and Trends® in Information Retrieval* 1, no. 3 (2007): 242–43, https://doi.org/10.1561/1500000005.

14. David I. Holmes, "The Evolution of Stylometry in Humanities Scholarship," *Literary and Linguistic Computing* 13, no. 3 (1998): 114; Juola, "Authorship Attribution," 243.

15. C. E. Chaski, "Who's at the Keyboard: Authorship Attribution in Digital Evidence Investigations," *International Journal of Digital Evidence* 4, no. 1 (2005): 0–13, www.utica.edu/academic/institutes/ecii/publications/articles/B49F9C4A-0362-765C-6A235CB8ABDFACFF.pdf.

16. J. M. Farringdon, *Analyzing for Authorship: A Guide to the Cusum Technique* (Cardiff: University of Wales Press, 1996).

17. David Canter, "An Evaluation of 'Cusum' Stylistic Analysis of Confessions," *Expert Evidence* 1, no. 2 (1992): 93–99; R. A. Hardcastle, "Forensic Linguistics: An Assessment of the CUSUM Method for the Determination of Authorship," *Journal of the Forensic Science Society* 33, no. 2 (1993): 95–106, https://doi.org/10.1016/S0015-7368(93)72987-4; R. A. Hardcastle, "CUSUM: A Credible Method for the Determination of Authorship?" *Science and Justice* 37, no. 2 (1997): 129–38, https://doi.org/10.1016/S1355-0306(97)72158-0; M. L. Hilton, "An Assessment of Cumulative Sum Charts for Authorship Attribution," *Literary and Linguistic Computing* 8, no. 2 (1993): 73–80, https://doi.org/10.1093/llc/8.2.73; David I. Holmes and Fiona Tweedie, "Forensic Stylometry: A Review of the Cusum Controversy," *La Revue informatique et statistique dans les sciences humaines* 31, nos. 1–4 (1995): 19–47; Juola, "Authorship Attribution," 233–34.

18. C. E. Chaski, "The Keyboard Dilemma and Forensic Authorship Attribution,"

Advances in Digital Forensics 3 (2007); G. McMenamin, "Disputed Authorship in US Law," *International Journal of Speech, Language and the Law* 11, no. 1 (2004): 73–82.

19. J. W. Grieve, "Quantitative Authorship Attribution: A History and an Evaluation of Techniques" (master's thesis, Simon Fraser University, 2005), http://summit.sfu.ca/item/8840.

20. W. Elliot and R. J. Valenza, "And Then There Were None: Winnowing the Shakespeare Claimants," *Computers and the Humanities* 30 (1996): 191–245; W. Elliot and R. J. Valenza, "The Professor Doth Protest Too Much, Methinks," *Computers and the Humanities* 32 (1998): 425–90; W. Elliot and R. J. Valenza, "So Many Hardballs, so Few over the Plate," *Computers and the Humanities* 36, no. 4 (2002): 455–60.

21. Juola, "Authorship Attribution," 245.

22. John Burrows, "'Delta': A Measure of Stylistic Difference and a Guide to Likely Authorship," *Literary and Linguistic Computing* 17, no. 3 (2002): 267–87, https://doi.org/10.1093/llc/17.3.267.

23. S. Argamon, "Interpreting Burrows's Delta: Geometric and Probabilistic Foundations," *Literary and Linguistic Computing* 23, no. 2 (2007): 131–47, https://doi.org/10.1093/llc/fqn003.

24. David Hoover, "Testing Burrows's Delta," *Literary and Linguistic Computing* 19, no. 4 (2004): 453–75; J. Rybicki and M. Eder, "Deeper Delta Across Genres and Languages: Do We Really Need the Most Frequent Words?" *Literary and Linguistic Computing* 26, no. 3 (2011): 315–21, https://doi.org/10.1093/llc/fqr031.

25. Stefan Evert et al., "Outliers or Key Profiles? Understanding Distance Measures for Authorship Attribution," in *Digital Humanities 2016: Conference Abstracts* (Digital Humanities 2016, Jagiellonian University and Pedagogical University, Kraków), http://dh2016.adho.org/abstracts/253.

26. See, e.g., Hoshiladevi Ramnial, Shireen Panchoo, and Sameerchand Pudaruth, "Authorship Attribution Using Stylometry and Machine Learning Techniques," in *Intelligent Systems Technologies and Applications* (Cham, CH: Springer, 2016), 113–25, https://doi.org/10.1007/978-3-319-23036-8_10.

27. For more on computational modeling and loss see Richard Jean So, "All Models Are Wrong," *PMLA* 132, no. 3 (2017): 668–73.

28. Caroline Levine, "Model Thinking: Generalization, Political Form, and the Common Good," *New Literary History* 48, no. 4 (2017): 644, https://doi.org/10.1353/nlh.2017.0033.

29. Burrows, "'Delta,'" 268.

30. Burrows, 267.

31. My thanks to one of my anonymous readers for this point.

32. Michael Robert Brennan and Rachel Greenstadt, "Practical Attacks Against Authorship Recognition Techniques," in *Proceedings of the Twenty-First Conference on Innovative Applications of Artificial Intelligence* (Palo Alto, CA: AAAI, 2009), www.cs.drexel.edu/~greenie/brennan_paper.pdf.

33. Juola, "Authorship Attribution," 239.

34. See Edward W. Said, *On Late Style* (London: Bloomsbury, 2006).

35. Stolerman et al., "Breaking the Closed-World Assumption."

36. Holmes, "The Evolution of Stylometry," 111.

37. Roland Barthes, "The Death of the Author," in *Image, Music, Text*, trans. Stephen Heath (London: Fontana, 1987), 142–48; Michel Foucault, "What Is an Author?" in *The Essential Works of Michel Foucault, 1954–1984*, 3 vols. (London: Penguin, 2000), 2:205–22; Seán Burke, *The Death and Return of the Author: Criticism and Subjectivity in Barthes, Foucault and Derrida*, 3rd rev. ed. (Edinburgh: Edinburgh University Press, 2008).

38. Matthew L. Jockers, *Macroanalysis: Digital Methods and Literary History* (Urbana: University of Illinois Press, 2013).

39. Sarah Allison et al., *Quantitative Formalism: An Experiment*," Stanford Literary Lab (pamphlet), 2011, https://litlab.stanford.edu/LiteraryLabPamphlet1.pdf.

40. Indeed, in a 2004 competition the delta method met a good standard for competitive accuracy. See Juola, "Authorship Attribution," 297.

41. R Core Team, *R: A Language and Environment for Statistical Computing* (Vienna: R Foundation for Statistical Computing, 2016), www.R-project.org; Maciej Eder, Mike Kestemont, and Jan Rybicki, "Stylometry with R: A Suite of Tools," Digital Humanities 2013, University of Nebraska–Lincoln, July 16–19, 2013, conference abstracts, 487–89, http://dh2013.unl.edu/abstracts/ab-136.html.

42. Replication of the following figures can be achieved by using the Stylo package in R and simply using the existing frequency tables. Alternatively, these raw R commands will reproduce the figures:

```
table <- read.csv('table_with_frequencies.txt', sep = ' ')
distancematrix = dist(t(table))
hierarchicalclusters <- hclust(distancematrix)
plot(hierarchicalclusters)
```

43. Norbert L. Kerr, "HARKing: Hypothesizing After the Results Are Known," *Personality and Social Psychology Review* 2, no. 3 (1998): 196–217, https://doi.org/10.1207/s15327957pspr0203_4.

44. Maciej Eder, "Visualization in Stylometry: Cluster Analysis Using Networks," *Digital Scholarship in the Humanities* 32, no. 1 (2017): 50–64, https://doi.org/10.1093/llc/fqv061.

45. David Mitchell, *Cloud Atlas* (London: Sceptre, 2004), 39 (hereafter *Cloud Atlas P*); David Mitchell, *Cloud Atlas* (New York: Random House, 2004), 39 (hereafter *Cloud Atlas E*).

46. See Appendix B: Digital Appendix 2: Melville.

47. Robert Eighteen-Bisang and Elizabeth Miller, *Bram Stoker's Notes for "Dracula": A Facsimile Edition* (Jefferson, NC: McFarland, 2008), 9.

48. For more on this see Kira Hall and Mary Bucholtz, eds., *Gender Articulated: Language and the Socially Constructed Self* (New York: Routledge, 1995).

49. Kristina Toutanova et al., "Feature-Rich Part-of-Speech Tagging with a Cyclic Dependency Network," in *Proceedings of the 2003 Conference of the North American*

Chapter of the Association for Computational Linguistics on Human Language Technology, vol. 1 (Stroudsburg, PA: Association for Computational Linguistics, 2003), 173–80, http://dl.acm.org/citation.cfm?id=1073478.

50. For an example of how such taggers perform on verbless constructions, see Mark Liberman, "A New Verb: To Thaler," Language Log, May 15, 2004, http://itre.cis.upenn.edu/myl/languagelog/archives/000907.html.

51. Mitchell, *Cloud Atlas P*, 22; Mitchell, *Cloud Atlas E*, 22.

52. Mitchell, *Cloud Atlas P*, 89, 90, 97, 99, 100, 102, 104, 106, 109, 113; Mitchell, *Cloud Atlas E*, 89, 90, 97, 99, 100, 102, 103, 105, 108, 112.

53. Mitchell, *Cloud Atlas P*, 103; Mitchell, *Cloud Atlas E*, 102.

54. Mitchell, *Cloud Atlas P*, 89, 90, 95; Mitchell, *Cloud Atlas E*, 89, 90, 94–95.

55. Mitchell, *Cloud Atlas P*, 92, 98; Mitchell, *Cloud Atlas E*, 92, 98.

56. Mitchell, *Cloud Atlas P*, 4, 8, 28, 6, passim; Mitchell, *Cloud Atlas E*, 5, 8, 27, 6, passim.

57. Mitchell, *Cloud Atlas P*, 93, 133, 437; Mitchell, *Cloud Atlas E*, 93, 131, 420.

58. Mitchell, *Cloud Atlas P*, 14; Mitchell, *Cloud Atlas E*, 14.

59. For more on the premodifier here see Yee Seng Chan and Dan Roth, "Exploiting Syntactico-Semantic Structures for Relation Extraction," in *Proceedings of the 49th Annual Meeting of the Association for Computational Linguistics: Human Language Technologies*, vol. 1 (Stroudsburg, PA: Association for Computational Linguistics, 2011), 554, http://dl.acm.org/citation.cfm?id=2002472.2002542.

60. See Brian Larson, "Gender/Genre: Gender Difference in Disciplinary Communication" (PhD diss., University of Minnesota, 2015), 318, http://conservancy.umn.edu/handle/11299/188945.

61. Rose Harris-Birtill, *David Mitchell's Post-Secular World: Buddhism, Belief and the Urgency of Compassion* (London: Bloomsbury, 2019).

62. See Claire Larsonneur, "Revisiting Dejima (Japan): From Recollections to Fiction in David Mitchell's *The Thousand Autumns of Jacob de Zoet* (2010)," *SubStance* 44, no. 1 (2015): 136–47, https://doi.org/10.1353/sub.2015.0004; Paul A. Harris, "David Mitchell's Fractal Imagination: *The Bone Clocks*," *SubStance* 44, no. 1 (2015): 148–53, https://doi.org/10.1353/sub.2015.0006; and Robin Visel, "Reading Forward: The Fractal Texts of Doris Lessing and David Mitchell," *Doris Lessing Studies* 34 (2016): 12–15.

63. Peter Childs and James Green, "The Novels in Nine Parts," in *David Mitchell: Critical Essays*, ed. Sarah Dillon (Canterbury: Gylphi, 2011), 30; Kathryn Simpson, "'Or Something Like That': Coming of Age in Number9dream," in *David Mitchell: Critical Essays*, ed. Sarah Dillon (Canterbury: Gylphi, 2011), 52; Hélène Machinal, "*Cloud Atlas*: From Postmodernity to the Posthuman," in *David Mitchell: Critical Essays*, ed. Sarah Dillon (Canterbury: Gylphi, 2011), 134. For more on the use of this trope see Harris-Birtill, *Beyond Belief*, to which I am indebted.

64. Some parts of my argument here derive from Martin Paul Eve, *Pynchon and Philosophy: Wittgenstein, Foucault and Adorno* (London: Palgrave Macmillan, 2014), 127–30.

65. Georg Wilhelm Friedrich Hegel, *The Phenomenology of Mind*, trans. J. B. Baillie (London: Harper and Row, 1967), para. 20.

66. Robert Hullot-Kentor, *Things Beyond Resemblance: Collected Essays on Theodor W. Adorno* (New York: Columbia University Press, 2006), 200.

67. Theodor W. Adorno, "Skoteinos, or How to Read Hegel," in *Hegel: Three Studies*, trans. Shierry Weber Nicholsen (Cambridge, MA: MIT Press, 1993), 108.

68. Theodor W. Adorno, *Minima Moralia*, trans. E. F. N. Jephcott (London: NLB, 1974), 50.

69. Theodor W. Adorno, "The Experiential Content of Hegel's Philosophy," in *Hegel: Three Studies*, trans. Shierry Weber Nicholsen (Cambridge, MA: MIT Press, 1993), 87.

70. Theodor W. Adorno, *Negative Dialectics*, trans. E. B. Ashton (London: Routledge, 1973), 5.

71. Georg Wilhelm Friedrich Hegel, *The Science of Logic*, trans. George Di Giovanni (Cambridge: Cambridge University Press, 2010), sec. 21.38.

72. Adorno, *Negative Dialectics*, 5.

CHAPTER 3: HISTORICAL FICTION AND LINGUISTIC MIMESIS

1. David Mitchell, *Cloud Atlas* (London: Sceptre, 2004), 463 (hereafter *Cloud Atlas P*); David Mitchell, *Cloud Atlas* (New York: Random House, 2004), 445 (hereafter *Cloud Atlas E*).

2. Giuliana Adamo, "Twentieth-Century Recent Theories on Beginnings and Endings of Novels," *Annali d'Italianistica* 18 (2000): 49–76.

3. Frank Kermode, *The Sense of an Ending: Studies in the Theory of Fiction: With a New Epilogue* (Oxford: Oxford University Press, 2000).

4. Heather J. Hicks, "'This Time Round': David Mitchell's *Cloud Atlas* and the Apocalyptic Problem of Historicism," *Postmodern Culture* 20, no. 3 (2010): https://doi.org/10.1353/pmc.2010.0012.

5. Mitchell, *Cloud Atlas P*, 64; Mitchell, *Cloud Atlas E*, 64.

6. Mitchell, *Cloud Atlas P*, 527; Mitchell, *Cloud Atlas E*, 506.

7. Michael McKeon, *The Origins of the English Novel, 1600–1740*, 15th anniversary ed. (Baltimore: Johns Hopkins University Press, 2002), 93.

8. Mitchell, *Cloud Atlas P*, 64; Mitchell, *Cloud Atlas E*, 64.

9. Forged diaries have a long and prominent history elsewhere, of course. See Eric Rentschler, "The Fascination of a Fake: The Hitler Diaries," *New German Critique*, no. 90 (2003): 177–92, https://doi.org/10.2307/3211115.

10. Mitchell, *Cloud Atlas P*, 518; Mitchell, *Cloud Atlas E*, 499.

11. Mitchell, *Cloud Atlas P*, 493, 512–13; Mitchell, *Cloud Atlas E*, 39, 493–94.

12. See Jerome de Groot, "Walter Scott Prize for Historical Fiction: The New Time-Travellers." *The Scotsman*, June 19, 2010, www.scotsman.com/lifestyle/books/walter-scott-prize-for-historical-fiction-the-new-time-travellers-1-813580.

13. For just some of the literature on this see Victor Strandberg, "Dimming the Enlightenment: Thomas Pynchon's *Mason & Dixon*," in *Pynchon and "Mason & Dixon,"* ed. Brooke Horvath and Irving Malin (Newark: University of Delaware Press, 2000), 100–111; Christy L. Burns, "Postmodern Historiography: Politics and the Parallactic Method in Thomas Pynchon's *Mason & Dixon*," *Postmodern Culture* 14, no. 1 (2003): http://muse.jhu.

edu/article/48412; Julia Jordan, "'What Arises from This?' The Autostereogrammatical in Thomas Pynchon's *Mason & Dixon*," *Critique: Studies in Contemporary Fiction* 56, no. 3 (2015): 270–83, https://doi.org/10.1080/00111619.2014.897932.

14. Russell Hoban, *Riddley Walker* (London: Bloomsbury, 2002), 1; for more on the use of Hoban as a source see David Mitchell, "The Book of Revelations," *The Guardian*, Feb. 5, 2005, www.guardian.co.uk/books/2005/feb/05/featuresreviews.guardianreview27; and Eve, "'some kind of thing it aint us but yet its in us': David Mitchell, Russell Hoban, and Metafiction After the Millennium," *Sage Open* 4, no. 1 (2014): https://doi.org/10.1177/2158244014521636.

15. Edward Mendelson, "Encyclopedic Narrative: From Dante to Pynchon," *MLN* 91, no. 6 (1976): 1267–75.

16. Mendelson, 1268.

17. Mendelson, 1269.

18. David Letzler, *The Cruft of Fiction: Mega-novels and the Science of Paying Attention* (Lincoln: University of Nebraska Press, 2017), 70–71.

19. Martin Paul Eve, "DateText," GitHub, 2016, https://github.com/MartinPaulEve/dateText.

20. Mitchell, *Cloud Atlas P*, 5; Mitchell, *Cloud Atlas E*, 5.

21. Mitchell, *Cloud Atlas P*, 15, recurring in a more appropriate register at p. 89; Mitchell, *Cloud Atlas E*, 14, recurring in a more appropriate register at p. 90.

22. Mitchell, *Cloud Atlas P*, 9; Mitchell, *Cloud Atlas E*, 9.

23. Mitchell, *Cloud Atlas P*, 31; Mitchell, *Cloud Atlas E*, 30.

24. Mitchell, *Cloud Atlas P*, 29; Mitchell, *Cloud Atlas E*, 28.

25. Mitchell, *Cloud Atlas P*, 6; Mitchell, *Cloud Atlas E*, 6.

26. Mitchell, *Cloud Atlas P*, 27; Mitchell, *Cloud Atlas E*, 26.

27. Mitchell, *Cloud Atlas P*, 6; Mitchell, *Cloud Atlas E*, 6.

28. Mitchell, *Cloud Atlas P*, 21; Mitchell, *Cloud Atlas E*, 20.

29. Mitchell, *Cloud Atlas P*, 16; Mitchell, *Cloud Atlas E*, 16.

30. Mitchell, *Cloud Atlas P*, 37; Mitchell, *Cloud Atlas E*, 36.

31. Mitchell, *Cloud Atlas P*, 53; Mitchell, *Cloud Atlas E*, 53.

32. "Spillage," Online Etymology Dictionary, 2017, www.etymonline.com/word/spillage.

33. Mitchell, *Cloud Atlas P*, 9; Mitchell, *Cloud Atlas E*, 9.

34. Harry E. Shaw, *The Forms of Historical Fiction: Sir Walter Scott and His Successors* (Ithaca, NY: Cornell University Press, 1983), 21.

35. For one of the genre spats surrounding this title, see Sian Cain, "Writer's Indignation: Kazuo Ishiguro Rejects Claims of Genre Snobbery," *The Guardian*, March 8, 2015, www.theguardian.com/books/2015/mar/08/kazuo-ishiguro-rebuffs-genre-snobbery.

36. Kazuo Ishiguro, *The Buried Giant* (London: Faber and Faber, 2015), 213.

37. Ishiguro, 118.

38. Kate Chisholm, "Hilary Mantel Explains the Difference Between Facts and Truths," *The Spectator*, June 17, 2017, www.spectator.co.uk/2017/06/hilary-mantel-remembers-bursting-into-tears-as-she-sat-on-the-floor-in-cardinal-wolseys-closet.

39. Don DeLillo, *Libra* (New York: Penguin, 1989), 339.

40. Sarah Lyall, "Novelists Defend One of Their Own Against a Plagiarism Charge," *New York Times*, Dec. 7, 2006, sec. Books, www.nytimes.com/2006/12/07/books/07pync.html.

41. David Cowart, "Pynchon, Genealogy, History: *Against the Day*," *Modern Philology* 109, no. 3 (2012): 385, 389, https://doi.org/10.1086/663688.

42. Mitchell, *Cloud Atlas P*, 3; Mitchell, *Cloud Atlas E*, 3.

43. Mitchell, *Cloud Atlas P*, 3; Mitchell, *Cloud Atlas E*, 3; Herman Melville, *Moby Dick; or, The Whale* (Project Gutenberg, 2008), chap. 12, para. 1, www.gutenberg.org/files/2701/2701-h/2701-h.htm.

44. Melville, *Moby Dick*, chap. 1, para. 1.

45. Andrew Piper, *Enumerations: Data and Literary Study* (Chicago: University of Chicago Press, 2018), 11.

46. See Samuel S. Cohen, *After the End of History: American Fiction in the 1990s* (Iowa City: University of Iowa Press, 2009), 47.

47. Keith Houston, *Shady Characters: The Secret Life of Punctuation, Symbols, & Other Typographical Marks* (New York: Norton, 2013), 76–77.

48. For the most recent literature on the use of different pronouns in different kinds of fiction, see Alison Gibbons and Andrea Macrae, eds., *Pronouns in Literature* (London: Palgrave Macmillan UK, 2018), https://doi.org/10.1057/978-1-349-95317-2.

49. For more on this see Martin Paul Eve, "'What Was Knowledge for, I Would Ask Myself': Science, Technology, and Identity in David Mitchell's *Cloud Atlas*," in *David Mitchell: Contemporary Critical Perspectives*, ed. Wendy Knepper and Courtney Hopf (London: Bloomsbury, forthcoming).

50. Oxford Dictionaries, "The Oxford English Corpus," Oxford Dictionaries | English, 2017, https://en.oxforddictionaries.com/explore/oxford-english-corpus.

51. J. M. Ellis, "Linguistics, Literature, and the Concept of Style," *WORD* 26, no. 1 (1970): 65–78, https://doi.org/10.1080/00437956.1970.11435581; Berel Lang, ed., *The Concept of Style* (Ithaca, NY: Cornell University Press, 1987).

52. "Interview with David Mitchell," Goodreads, July 5, 2010, www.goodreads.com/interviews/show/537.David_Mitchell.

53. A. Shand, "The Occupation of the Chatham Islands by the Maoris in 1835: Part II, The Migration of Ngatiawa to Chatham Island," *Journal of the Polynesian Society* 1, no. 3 (1892): 154–63; Jared M. Diamond, *Guns, Germs and Steel: A Short History of Everybody for the Last 13,000 Years* (London: Vintage, 2005), 53–57; David Mitchell, "Genesis," *The Guardian*, April 16, 2005, sec. Books, www.theguardian.com/books/2005/apr/16/features reviews.guardianreview23; Wendy Knepper, "Toward a Theory of Experimental World Epic: David Mitchell's *Cloud Atlas*," *Ariel: A Review of International English Literature* 47, no. 1 (2016): 104–5.

54. Mitchell, *Cloud Atlas P*, 64; Mitchell, *Cloud Atlas E*, 64.

55. Mitchell, *Cloud Atlas P*, 523; Mitchell, *Cloud Atlas E*, 503.

56. Mitchell, *Cloud Atlas P*, 37; Mitchell *Cloud Atlas E*, 36.

57. Pratik Chakrabarti, *Medicine and Empire: 1600–1960* (Basingstoke: Palgrave Macmillan, 2014), ix.

58. Chakrabarti, x.

59. Chakrabarti, 141.

60. Michael Worboys, "The Emergence of Tropical Medicine: A Study in the Establishment of a Scientific Speciality," in *Perspectives on the Emergence of Scientific Disciplines*, ed. Gerard Lemaine et al. (The Hague: Mouton, 1976), 76–98.

61. Patrick Manson, "On the Development of Filaria Sanguinis Hominis, and on the Mosquito Considered as a Nurse," *Journal of the Linnean Society of London, Zoology* 14, no. 75 (1878): 304–11, https://doi.org/10.1111/j.1096-3642.1878.tb01837.x; Chakrabarti, *Medicine and Empire*, 141–63.

62. Mitchell, *Cloud Atlas P*, 3, 5; Mitchell, *Cloud Atlas E*, 3, 6.

63. Mitchell, *Cloud Atlas P*, 6; Mitchell, *Cloud Atlas E*, 6.

64. Mitchell, *Cloud Atlas P*, 15, 20; Mitchell, *Cloud Atlas E*, 15, 20.

65. Chakrabarti, *Medicine and Empire*, 144, 159; Mitchell, *Cloud Atlas P*, 22, 37; Mitchell, *Cloud Atlas E*, 22, 36.

66. Mitchell, *Cloud Atlas P*, 33; Mitchell, *Cloud Atlas E*, 32.

67. Mitchell, *Cloud Atlas P*, 35; Mitchell, *Cloud Atlas E*, 35.

68. Jacques Derrida, "Plato's Pharmacy," in *Dissemination*, trans. Barbara Johnson (London: Continuum, 2004), 75.

69. Derrida, 77.

70. Mitchell, *Cloud Atlas P*, 152; Mitchell, *Cloud Atlas E*, 150.

71. Derrida, "Plato's Pharmacy," 101, 127.

72. Derrida, 121.

73. For more on technogenesis and human development see Stanley H. Ambrose, "Paleolithic Technology and Human Evolution," *Science* 291, no. 5509 (2001): 1748–53, https://doi.org/10.1126/science.1059487; and N. Katherine Hayles, *How We Think: Digital Media and Contemporary Technogenesis* (Chicago: University of Chicago Press, 2012), 90–91.

74. Mitchell, *Cloud Atlas P*, 497; Mitchell, *Cloud Atlas E*, 477.

75. Mitchell, *Cloud Atlas P*, 513; Mitchell, *Cloud Atlas E*, 494.

76. Lisa Gitelman, *Paper Knowledge: Toward a Media History of Documents* (Durham, NC: Duke University Press, 2014), 26–27.

77. Rose Harris-Birtill, "'Looking Down Time's Telescope at Myself': Reincarnation and Global Futures in David Mitchell's Fictional Worlds," *KronoScope: The Journal for the Study of Time* 17, no. 2 (2017): 166, https://doi.org/10.1163/15685241-12341382.

78. Scott Dimovitz, "The Sound of Silence: Eschatology and the Limits of the Word in David Mitchell's *Cloud Atlas*," *SubStance* 44, no. 1 (2015): 71, https://doi.org/10.1353/sub.2015.0009.

79. See Linda Hutcheon, *A Theory of Parody: The Teachings of Twentieth-Century Art Forms* (New York: Methuen, 1985).

80. Letzler, *The Cruft of Fiction*, 30–62.

81. For more on this see Nicholas Dunlop, "Speculative Fiction as Postcolonial

Critique in *Ghostwritten* and *Cloud Atlas*," in *David Mitchell: Critical Essays*, ed. Sarah Dillon (Canterbury: Gylphi, 2011), 201–23; and Casey Shoop and Dermot Ryan, "'Gravid with the Ancient Future': *Cloud Atlas* and the Politics of Big History," *SubStance* 44, no. 1 (2015): https://doi.org/10.1353/sub.2015.0011.

82. Mitchell, *Cloud Atlas P*, 490; Mitchell, *Cloud Atlas E*, 471.

CHAPTER 4: INTERPRETATION

1. Peter Brooks, *Reading for the Plot: Design and Intention in Narrative* (Cambridge, MA: Harvard University Press, 1992), 23.

2. For more on this type of critical utopian thinking see Tom Moylan, *Demand the Impossible: Science Fiction and the Utopian Imagination* (New York: Methuen, 1986).

3. Mitchell, *Cloud Atlas P*, 3, 39; Mitchell, *Cloud Atlas E*, 3, 38.

4. See Giuliana Adamo, "Twentieth-Century Recent Theories on Beginnings and Endings of Novels," *Annali d'Italianistica* 18 (2000): 49–76.

5. Mitchell, *Cloud Atlas P*, 7; Mitchell, *Cloud Atlas E*, 7.

6. Mitchell, *Cloud Atlas P*, 28; Mitchell, *Cloud Atlas E*, 27.

7. Mitchell, *Cloud Atlas P*, 521; Mitchell, *Cloud Atlas E*, 501.

8. For more on the background contexts of metafiction see Mark Currie, "Introduction," in *Metafiction*, ed. Mark Currie (London: Longman, 1995); Patricia Waugh, *Metafiction: The Theory and Practice of Self-Conscious Fiction* (London: Methuen, 1984); Linda Hutcheon, *Narcissistic Narrative: The Metafictional Paradox* (Waterloo: Wilfrid Laurier University Press, 2013).

9. Mitchell, *Cloud Atlas P*, 21, 26, 36, 37, 502, 518, 521; Mitchell, *Cloud Atlas E*, 21, 25, 35, 36, 482, 498, 501.

10. Mitchell, *Cloud Atlas P*, 11–16; Mitchell, *Cloud Atlas E*, 11–16.

11. Mitchell, *Cloud Atlas P*, 10; Mitchell, *Cloud Atlas E*, 10.

12. Mitchell, *Cloud Atlas P*, 30–33; Mitchell, *Cloud Atlas E*, 29–32.

13. Mitchell, *Cloud Atlas P*, 511; Mitchell, *Cloud Atlas E*, 492.

14. Mitchell, *Cloud Atlas P*, 18; Mitchell, *Cloud Atlas E*, 18. For more on parrhesia as free speech in relation to confession, see Torben Bech Dyrberg, *Foucault on the Politics of Parrhesia* (London: Palgrave Macmillan, 2014), www.palgraveconnect.com/doifinder/10.1057/9781137368355; Alison Ross, "Why Is 'Speaking the Truth' Fearless? 'Danger' and 'Truth' in Foucault's Discussion of Parrhesia," *Parrhesia*, no. 4 (2008): 62–75; Zacharia Simpson, "The Truths We Tell Ourselves: Foucault on Parrhesia," *Foucault Studies* 13 (March 2012): 99–115; and Elizabeth Markovits, *The Politics of Sincerity: Plato, Frank Speech, and Democratic Judgment* (University Park: Pennsylvania State University Press, 2008).

15. Mitchell, *Cloud Atlas P*, 21; Mitchell, *Cloud Atlas E*, 21.

16. Mitchell, *Cloud Atlas P*, 64; Mitchell, *Cloud Atlas E*, 64.

17. Mitchell, *Cloud Atlas P*, 479; Mitchell, *Cloud Atlas E*, 460.

18. Paul Fussell, *The Great War and Modern Memory* (New York: Oxford University Press, 2000), 272.

19. Mitchell, *Cloud Atlas P*, 458–60; Mitchell, *Cloud Atlas E*, 440–42.

20. Mitchell, *Cloud Atlas P*, 43; Mitchell, *Cloud Atlas E*, 43.

21. Mitchell, *Cloud Atlas P*, 53; Mitchell, *Cloud Atlas E*, 53.

22. Mitchell, *Cloud Atlas P*, 52; Mitchell, *Cloud Atlas E*, 52.

23. For more on which see Joe Bray, *The Epistolary Novel: Representation of Consciousness* (London: Routledge, 2003).

24. Mitchell, *Cloud Atlas P*, 72; Mitchell, *Cloud Atlas E*, 71.

25. Mitchell, *Cloud Atlas P*, 71; Mitchell, *Cloud Atlas E*, 70.

26. Mitchell, *Cloud Atlas P*, 71; Mitchell, *Cloud Atlas E*, 70.

27. See N. Katherine Hayles, *How We Think: Digital Media and Contemporary Technogenesis* (Chicago: University of Chicago Press, 2012), 125; and James W. Carey, "Technology and Ideology: The Case of the Telegraph," in *Communication as Culture: Essays on Media and Society* (New York: Routledge, 1989), 19.

28. Mitchell, *Cloud Atlas P*, 471; Mitchell, *Cloud Atlas E*, 452–53.

29. Mitchell, *Cloud Atlas P*, 78–79; Mitchell, *Cloud Atlas E*, 78–79.

30. Mitchell, *Cloud Atlas P*, 52; Mitchell, *Cloud Atlas E*, 52.

31. Mitchell, *Cloud Atlas P*, 72; Mitchell, *Cloud Atlas E*, 72.

32. Mitchell, *Cloud Atlas P*, 478; Mitchell, *Cloud Atlas E*, 459.

33. Mitchell, *Cloud Atlas P*, 61; Mitchell, *Cloud Atlas E*, 61.

34. This is not consistent, however, even in the *P* edition. There is an instance of the word *half* written fully at Mitchell, *Cloud Atlas P*, 84.

35. Mitchell, 52, 58, 60, 78, 83, 84, 85, 466, 474, 478, 479, 482, 483, 484, 485.

36. Mitchell, 85; Mitchell, *Cloud Atlas E*, 85.

37. Mitchell, *Cloud Atlas P*, 80; Mitchell, *Cloud Atlas E*, 79.

38. Mitchell, *Cloud Atlas P*, 487; Mitchell, *Cloud Atlas E*, 468.

39. The reader is told that the Luisa Rey chapter takes place forty-four years after Frobisher's 1931 letters were written. Mitchell, *Cloud Atlas P*, 453; Mitchell, *Cloud Atlas E*, 436.

40. Mitchell, *Cloud Atlas P*, 91; Mitchell, *Cloud Atlas E*, 91.

41. Mitchell, *Cloud Atlas P*, 409; Mitchell, *Cloud Atlas E*, 392–93.

42. For more on this background see Peter Hühn, "The Detective as Reader: Narrativity and Reading Concepts in Detective Fiction," *MFS Modern Fiction Studies* 3, no. 3 (1987): 451–66, https://doi.org/10.1353/mfs.0.1310; and Charles J. Rzepka, *Detective Fiction* (Cambridge, UK: Polity, 2005).

43. Mitchell, *Cloud Atlas P*, 110, 130, 141, 435; Mitchell, *Cloud Atlas E*, 109, 128, 139, 418.

44. Mitchell, *Cloud Atlas P*, 115, 431, 452; Mitchell, *Cloud Atlas E*, 113, 414–15, 434–35.

45. Mitchell, *Cloud Atlas P*, 100; Mitchell, *Cloud Atlas E*, 99.

46. Mitchell, *Cloud Atlas P*, 90; Mitchell, *Cloud Atlas E*, 90.

47. Mitchell, *Cloud Atlas P*, 92–94; Mitchell, *Cloud Atlas E*, 92–94.

48. Mitchell, *Cloud Atlas P*, 94; Mitchell, *Cloud Atlas E*, 94.

49. Mitchell, *Cloud Atlas P*, 89; Mitchell, *Cloud Atlas E*, 89.

50. Mitchell, *Cloud Atlas P*, 120–21, 425; Mitchell, *Cloud Atlas E*, 119, 408–9.

51. Mitchell, *Cloud Atlas P*, 112; Mitchell, *Cloud Atlas E*, 111.

52. Mitchell, *Cloud Atlas P*, 117; Mitchell, *Cloud Atlas E*, 116.

53. Mitchell, *Cloud Atlas P*, 121.

54. Mitchell, 448; Mitchell, *Cloud Atlas E*, 430.

55. Mitchell, *Cloud Atlas P*, 158; Mitchell, *Cloud Atlas E*, 156.

56. Mitchell, *Cloud Atlas P*, 158; Mitchell, *Cloud Atlas E*, 156.

57. Mitchell, *Cloud Atlas P*, 147–48; Mitchell, *Cloud Atlas E*, 145–46.

58. Mitchell, *Cloud Atlas P*, 150, 158, 167, 178, 182, 183, 370, 372, 374, 375, 387, 393, 404; Mitchell, *Cloud Atlas E*, 148, 156, 165, 176, 179, 180, 354, 356, 358, 359, 371, 377, 387.

59. Mitchell, *Cloud Atlas P*, 365; Mitchell, *Cloud Atlas E*, 349.

60. Mitchell, *Cloud Atlas P*, 150, 179, 180, 181, 371, 389; Mitchell, *Cloud Atlas E*, 148, 177, 178, 179, 354–55, 372–73.

61. Mitchell, *Cloud Atlas P*, 373; Mitchell, *Cloud Atlas E*, 357.

62. Mitchell, *Cloud Atlas P*, 181; Mitchell, *Cloud Atlas E*, 179.

63. Mitchell, *Cloud Atlas P*, 370, 400; Mitchell, *Cloud Atlas E*, 354–55, 384.

64. Mitchell, *Cloud Atlas P*, 251; Mitchell, *Cloud Atlas E*, 241.

65. Mitchell, *Cloud Atlas P*, 318; Mitchell, *Cloud Atlas E*, 302.

66. Mitchell, *Cloud Atlas P*, 311–12; Mitchell, *Cloud Atlas E*, 296–97.

67. See Walter J. Ong, *Orality and Literacy: The Technologizing of the Word* (London: Routledge, 2002); but also the related argument about phono- and logocentrism in Jacques Derrida, *Of Grammatology*, trans. Gayatri Chakravorty Spivak (Baltimore: Johns Hopkins University Press, 1998).

68. Mitchell, *Cloud Atlas P*, 324–25; Mitchell, *Cloud Atlas E*, 308–9.

69. John Barth, "Lost in the Funhouse," in *Lost in the Funhouse: Fiction for Print, Tape, Live Voice* (New York: Anchor, 1988), 73.

70. See Jacques Lacan, "Le Séminaire sur la lettre volée," in *Écrits* (Paris: Seuil, 1966); Jacques Derrida, "Le Facteur de la vérité," *Poetics*, no. 21 (1975): 96–147; Barbara Johnson, "The Frame of Reference: Poe, Lacan, Derrida," *Yale French Studies*, no. 55/56 (1977): 457–505, https://doi.org/10.2307/2930445.

71. Michael McKeon, *The Origins of the English Novel, 1600–1740*, 15th anniversary ed. (Baltimore: Johns Hopkins University Press, 2002), 54, 93; Sean Latham, *The Art of Scandal: Modernism, Libel Law, and the Roman à Clef* (Oxford: Oxford University Press, 2009), 21–42.

72. Lisa Gitelman, *Paper Knowledge: Toward a Media History of Documents* (Durham, NC: Duke University Press, 2014), 27–28.

73. Lennard J. Davis, *Factual Fictions: The Origins of the English Novel* (New York: Columbia University Press, 1983), 42–70, 85–101.

74. Gitelman, *Paper Knowledge*, 27.

75. Mitchell, *Cloud Atlas P*, 457; Mitchell, *Cloud Atlas E*, 439.

76. Mitchell, *Cloud Atlas P*, 523; Mitchell, *Cloud Atlas E*, 502.

77. Mitchell, *Cloud Atlas P*, 33; Mitchell, *Cloud Atlas E*, 32.

78. Mitchell, *Cloud Atlas P*, 6; Mitchell, *Cloud Atlas E*, 6.

79. For more on how ideal/model readers are constructed, see the well-known

Umberto Eco, "Overinterpreting Texts," in *Interpretation and Overinterpretation*, ed. Stefan Collini (Cambridge: Cambridge University Press, 1992), 64; and Umberto Eco, *The Role of the Reader: Explorations in the Semiotics of Texts* (Bloomington: Indiana University Press, 1997), 7–11.

80. Diletta De Cristofaro, "'Time, No Arrow, No Boomerang, but a Concertina': *Cloud Atlas* and the Anti-apocalyptic Critical Temporalities of the Contemporary Post-apocalyptic Novel," *Critique: Studies in Contemporary Fiction* 59, no. 2 (2018): 6, https://doi.org/10.1080/00111619.2017.1369386.

81. See, e.g., Rose Harris-Birtill, "'Looking Down Time's Telescope at Myself': Reincarnation and Global Futures in David Mitchell's Fictional Worlds," *KronoScope: The Journal for the Study of Time* 17, no. 2 (2017): https://doi.org/10.1163/15685241-12341382; and Paul A. Harris, "David Mitchell's Fractal Imagination: *The Bone Clocks*," *SubStance* 44, no. 1 (2015): https://doi.org/10.1353/sub.2015.0006.

82. Francis Fukuyama, *The End of History and the Last Man* (London: Penguin, 2012). For more on how Fukuyama remains dialectical, see Timothy Burns, "Modernity's Irrationalism," in *After History? Francis Fukuyama and His Critics*, ed. Timothy Burns (Lanham, MD: Rowman and Littlefield, 1994), 131–32.

83. Fukuyama, *The End of History*, 103.

84. Peter Fenves, "The Tower of Babel Rebuilt: Some Remarks on 'The End of History,'" in *After History? Francis Fukuyama and His Critics*, ed. Timothy Burns (Lanham, MD: Rowman and Littlefield, 1994), 230.

85. Mitchell, *Cloud Atlas E*, 234.

86. Fukuyama, *The End of History*, 290.

87. Among the most well-known of the critics is, perhaps, Jacques Derrida, *Specters of Marx: The State of the Debt, the Work of Mourning, and the New International*, trans. Peggy Kamuf (New York: Routledge, 1994).

88. Derrida, 106.

89. See, e.g., Theodore H. Von Laue, "From Fukuyama to Reality: A Critical Essay," in *After History? Francis Fukuyama and His Critics*, ed. Timothy Burns (Lanham, MD: Rowman and Littlefield, 1994), 26–28.

90. Fukuyama, *The End of History*, 71; International Labour Organization and Walk Free Foundation, "Global Estimates of Modern Slavery, Forced Labour, and Forced Marriage" (Geneva, 2017), 19, www.ilo.org/wcmsp5/groups/public/@dgreports/@dcomm/documents/publication/wcms_575479.pdf.

91. Joanna Bourke, *What It Means to Be Human: Reflections from 1791 to the Present* (Berkeley, CA: Counterpoint, 2011), 4–5.

92. Fukuyama, *The End of History*, 72, 88.

93. Fukuyama, 82.

94. Mitchell, *Cloud Atlas P*, 324; Mitchell, *Cloud Atlas E*, 308.

95. Francis Fukuyama, "Reflections on the End of History, Five Years Later," *History and Theory* 34, no. 2 (1995): 27–43, https://doi.org/10.2307/2505433.

CONCLUSION

1. Notably, such pieces rarely, if ever, define what they mean by *neoliberalism*, which I take to be the replacement of politics by economic quantification, following William Davies, *The Limits of Neoliberalism: Authority, Sovereignty and the Logic of Competition* (Thousand Oaks, CA: SAGE, 2014); and Wendy Brown, *Undoing the Demos: Neoliberalism's Stealth Revolution* (New York: Zone, 2015). Perhaps most important, here, however, is that there are ways in which economic thinking about literary texts has already permeated traditional literary studies. Consider, for instance, the ways in which the canon can be thought of as part of a scarcity situation, itself a type of economic model of attention.

2. Caroline Levine, *Forms: Whole, Rhythm, Hierarchy, Network* (Princeton, NJ: Prince-ton University Press, 2015).

3. Melissa Dinsman and Alexander R. Galloway, "The Digital in the Humanities: An Interview with Alexander Galloway," *Los Angeles Review of Books*, March 27, 2016, https://lareviewofbooks.org/article/the-digital-in-the-humanities-an-interview-with-alexander-galloway.

4. Stanley Fish, "Being Interdisciplinary Is so Very Hard to Do," *Profession*, Jan. 1, 1989, 15–22, www.jstor.org/stable/25595433.

APPENDIX B: LIST OF DIGITAL DATA APPENDIXES

1. Martin Paul Eve, "SankeyTextualVariant," GitHub, 2015, https://github.com/MartinPaulEve/SankeyTextualVariant.

BIBLIOGRAPHY

Adamo, Giuliana. "Twentieth-Century Recent Theories on Beginnings and Endings of Novels." *Annali d'Italianistica* 18 (2000): 49–76.

Adema, Janneke, and Gary Hall. "Posthumanities: The Dark Side of 'The Dark Side of the Digital.'" *Journal of Electronic Publishing* 19, no. 2 (2016): http://dx.doi.org/10.3998/3336451.0019.201.

Adorno, Theodor W. *Aesthetic Theory*. Translated by C. Lenhardt. London: Routledge, 1984.

———. "The Experiential Content of Hegel's Philosophy." In *Hegel: Three Studies*, translated by Shierry Weber Nicholsen, 53–88. Cambridge, MA: MIT Press, 1993.

———. *Minima Moralia*. Translated by E. F. N. Jephcott. London: NLB, 1974.

———. *Negative Dialectics*. Translated by E. B. Ashton. London: Routledge, 1973.

———. "Skoteinos, or How to Read Hegel." In *Hegel: Three Studies*, translated by Shierry Weber Nicholsen, 89–148. Cambridge, MA: MIT Press, 1993.

Allington, Daniel, Sarah Brouillette, and David Golumbia. "Neoliberal Tools (and Archives): A Political History of Digital Humanities." *Los Angeles Review of Books*, May 1, 2016. https://lareviewofbooks.org/article/neoliberal-tools-archives-political-history-digital-humanities.

Allison, Sarah, Ryan Heuser, Matthew Jockers, Franco Moretti, and Michael Witmore. *Quantitative Formalism: An Experiment*. Stanford Literary Lab (pamphlet), 2011. https://litlab.stanford.edu/LiteraryLabPamphlet1.pdf.

Alter, Robert. *Canon and Creativity: Modern Writing and the Authority of Scripture*. New Haven, CT: Yale University Press, 2000.

Althusser, Louis, Étienne Balibar, Roger Establet, Pierre Machery, and Jacques Rancière. *Reading Capital: The Complete Edition*. Translated by Ben Brewster and David Fernbach. London: Verso, 2015.

Altieri, Charles. *Canons and Consequences: Reflections on the Ethical Force of Imaginative Ideals*. Evanston, IL: Northwestern University Press, 1990.

Alvarado, Rafael, and Paul Humphreys. "Big Data, Thick Mediation, and Representational Opacity." *New Literary History* 48, no. 4 (2017): 729–49. https://doi.org/10.1353/nlh.2017.0037.

Ambrose, Stanley H. "Paleolithic Technology and Human Evolution." *Science* 291, no. 5509 (2001): 1748–53. https://doi.org/10.1126/science.1059487.

Arendt, Hannah. *Eichmann in Jerusalem: A Report on the Banality of Evil*. New York: Penguin, 2006.

Argamon, S. "Interpreting Burrows's Delta: Geometric and Probabilistic Foundations." *Literary and Linguistic Computing* 23, no. 2 (2007): 131–47. https://doi.org/10.1093/llc/fqn003.

Armstrong, Nancy, and Warren Montag. " 'The Figure in the Carpet.' " *PMLA* 132, no. 3 (2017): 613–19.

Attridge, Derek. *The Singularity of Literature*. London: Routledge, 2004.

Baker, G. P., and P. M. S. Hacker. *Wittgenstein: Rules, Grammar and Necessity*. Vol. 2, *An Analytical Commentary on the Philosophical Investigations*. Oxford: Blackwell, 1985.

Barker, Nicola. *H(A)PPY*. Portsmouth, NH: William Heinemann, 2017.

Barth, John. "Lost in the Funhouse." In *Lost in the Funhouse: Fiction for Print, Tape, Live Voice*, 72–97. New York: Anchor, 1988.

Barthes, Roland. *Camera Lucida*. Translated by Richard Howard. New York: Hill and Wang, 1981.

———. "The Death of the Author." In *Image, Music, Text*, translated by Stephen Heath, 142–48. London: Fontana, 1987.

Begley, Adam. "David Mitchell, The Art of Fiction No. 204." *Paris Review*, Summer 2010. www.theparisreview.org/interviews/6034/the-art-of-fiction-no-204-david-mitchell.

Berlant, Lauren. *Cruel Optimism*. Durham, NC: Duke University Press, 2011.

Berry, David M., and Anders Fagerjord. *Digital Humanities: Knowledge and Critique in a Digital Age*. Cambridge: Polity, 2017.

Best, Stephen, and Sharon Marcus. "Surface Reading: An Introduction." *Representations* 108, no. 1 (2009): 1–21. https://doi.org/10.1525/rep.2009.108.1.1.

Blacklock, Mark. *I'm Jack*. London: Granta, 2015.

Bond, Sarah E., Hoyt Long, and Ted Underwood. " 'Digital' Is Not the Opposite of 'Humanities.' " *Chronicle of Higher Education*, Nov. 1, 2017. www.chronicle.com/article/Digital-Is-Not-the/241634.

Book World. "Q&A: Book World Talks with David Mitchell." *Washington Post*, August 22, 2004. www.washingtonpost.com/wp-dyn/articles/A17231-2004Aug19.html.

Booth, Alison. "Mid-Range Reading: Not a Manifesto." *PMLA* 132, no. 3 (2017): 620–27.

Bourke, Joanna. *What It Means to Be Human: Reflections from 1791 to the Present*. Berkeley, CA: Counterpoint, 2011.

Bray, Joe. *The Epistolary Novel: Representation of Consciousness*. London: Routledge, 2003.

Brennan, Michael Robert, and Rachel Greenstadt. "Practical Attacks Against Authorship Recognition Techniques." In *Proceedings of the Twenty-First Conference on Innova-*

tive Applications of Artificial Intelligence. Palo Alto, CA: AAAI, 2009. www.cs.drexel.edu/~greenie/brennan_paper.pdf.

Brennan, Timothy. "The Digital-Humanities Bust." *Chronicle of Higher Education*, Oct. 15, 2017. www.chronicle.com/article/The-Digital-Humanities-Bust/241424.

Brooks, Peter. *Reading for the Plot: Design and Intention in Narrative*. Cambridge, MA: Harvard University Press, 1992.

Brown, Wendy. *Undoing the Demos: Neoliberalism's Stealth Revolution*. New York: Zone, 2015.

Burdick, Anne, Johanna Drucker, Peter Lunenfeld, Todd Presner, and Jeffrey Schnapp. *Digital Humanities*. Cambridge, MA: MIT Press, 2012.

Burke, Seán. *The Death and Return of the Author: Criticism and Subjectivity in Barthes, Foucault and Derrida*. 3rd rev. ed. Edinburgh: Edinburgh University Press, 2008.

Burns, Christy L. "Postmodern Historiography: Politics and the Parallactic Method in Thomas Pynchon's *Mason & Dixon*." *Postmodern Culture* 14, no. 1 (2003): https://muse.jhu.edu/article/48412.

Burns, Timothy, ed. *After History? Francis Fukuyama and His Critics*. Lanham, MD: Rowman and Littlefield, 1994.

———. "Modernity's Irrationalism." In Burns, *After History?* 131–70.

Burrows, John. *Computation into Criticism: A Study of Jane Austen's Novels and an Experiment in Method*. London: Clarendon, 1987.

———. "'Delta': A Measure of Stylistic Difference and a Guide to Likely Authorship." *Literary and Linguistic Computing* 17, no. 3 (2002): 267–87. https://doi.org/10.1093/llc/17.3.267.

Cain, Sian. "Writer's Indignation: Kazuo Ishiguro Rejects Claims of Genre Snobbery." *The Guardian*, March 8, 2015. www.theguardian.com/books/2015/mar/08/kazuo-ishiguro-rebuffs-genre-snobbery.

Canter, David. "An Evaluation of 'Cusum' Stylistic Analysis of Confessions." *Expert Evidence* 1, no. 2 (1992): 93–99.

Carey, James W. "Technology and Ideology: The Case of the Telegraph." In *Communication as Culture: Essays on Media and Society*, 201–30. New York: Routledge, 1989.

Carré, John le. *A Delicate Truth*. New York: Viking, 2013.

Chakrabarti, Pratik. *Medicine and Empire: 1600–1960*. Basingstoke: Palgrave Macmillan, 2014.

Chan, Yee Seng, and Dan Roth. "Exploiting Syntactico-Semantic Structures for Relation Extraction." In *Proceedings of the 49th Annual Meeting of the Association for Computational Linguistics: Human Language Technologies*. Vol. 1, 551–60. Stroudsburg, PA: Association for Computational Linguistics, 2011. http://dl.acm.org/citation.cfm?id=2002472.2002542.

Chaski, C. E. "The Keyboard Dilemma and Forensic Authorship Attribution." *Advances in Digital Forensics* 3 (2007): 133–46.

———. "Who's at the Keyboard: Authorship Attribution in Digital Evidence Investigations." *International Journal of Digital Evidence* 4, no. 1 (2005): 0–13, www.utica

.edu/academic/institutes/ecii/publications/articles/B49F9C4A-0362-765C-6A235CB8ABDFACFF.pdf.

Childs, Peter, and James Green. "The Novels in Nine Parts." In Dillon, *David Mitchell*, 25–47.

Chisholm, Kate. "Hilary Mantel Explains the Difference Between Facts and Truths." *The Spectator*, June 17, 2017. www.spectator.co.uk/2017/06/hilary-mantel-remembers-bursting-into-tears-as-she-sat-on-the-floor-in-cardinal-wolseys-closet.

Chun, Wendy Hui Kyong, Richard Grusin, Patrick Jagoda, and Rita Raley. "The Dark Side of the Digital Humanities." In Gold and Klein, *Debates in the Digital Humanities 2016*, 493–509. http://dhdebates.gc.cuny.edu/debates/text/89.

Ciccoricco, David. "The Materialities of Close Reading: 1942, 1959, 2009." *Digital Humanities Quarterly* 6, no. 1 (2012). www.digitalhumanities.org/dhq/vol/6/1/000113/000113.html.

Clark, Jeff. "Novel Views: *Les Miserables*." Neoformix, 2013. http://neoformix.com/2013/NovelViews.html.

Clement, Tanya E. "Text Analysis, Data Mining, and Visualizations in Literary Scholarship." MLA Commons. *Literary Studies in the Digital Age: An Evolving Anthology* (New York: Modern Language Association, 2013): https://dlsanthology.mla.hcommons.org/text-analysis-data-mining-and-visualizations-in-literary-scholarship.

———. "'A Thing Not Beginning and Not Ending': Using Digital Tools to Distant-Read Gertrude Stein's *The Making of Americans*." *Literary and Linguistic Computing* 23, no. 3 (2008): 361–81. https://doi.org/10.1093/llc/fqn020.

Clemmons, Zinzi. *What We Lose*. London: Fourth Estate, 2017.

Cohen, Margaret. *The Sentimental Education of the Novel*. Princeton, NJ: Princeton University Press, 2002.

Cohen, Samuel S. *After the End of History: American Fiction in the 1990s*. Iowa City: University of Iowa Press, 2009.

Court, Franklin E. *Institutionalizing English Literature: Culture and Politics of Literary Study, 1750–1900*. Stanford, CA: Stanford University Press, 1992.

Cowart, David. "Pynchon, Genealogy, History: *Against the Day*." *Modern Philology* 109, no. 3 (2012): 385–407. https://doi.org/10.1086/663688.

Culler, Jonathan. "The Closeness of Close Reading." *ADE Bulletin* 149 (2010): 20–25. https://doi.org/10.1632/ade.149.20.

Currie, Mark. "Introduction." In *Metafiction*, edited by Mark Currie. London: Longman, 1995.

Dames, Nicholas. *The Physiology of the Novel: Reading, Neural Science, and the Form of Victorian Fiction*. Oxford: Oxford University Press, 2007.

Davidson, Cathy N., and David Theo Goldberg. "Engaging the Humanities." *Profession* (2004): 42–62, www.jstor.org/stable/25595777.

Davies, William. *The Limits of Neoliberalism: Authority, Sovereignty and the Logic of Competition*. Thousand Oaks, CA: Sage, 2014.

Davis, Lennard J. *Factual Fictions: The Origins of the English Novel*. New York: Columbia University Press, 1983.

De Cristofaro, Diletta. "'Time, No Arrow, No Boomerang, but a Concertina': *Cloud Atlas* and the Anti-apocalyptic Critical Temporalities of the Contemporary Post-apocalyptic Novel." *Critique: Studies in Contemporary Fiction* 59, no. 2 (2018): 1–15. https://doi.org/10.1080/00111619.2017.1369386.

Dedner, Burghard. "Highlighting Variants in Literary Editions: Techniques and Goals." In Giuliani et al., *Texts in Multiple Versions*, 15–32.

DeLillo, Don. *Libra*. New York: Penguin, 1989.

Deppman, Jed, Daniel Ferrer, and Michael Groden, eds. *Genetic Criticism*. Philadelphia: University of Pennsylvania Press, 2004.

Derrida, Jacques. *Archive Fever: A Freudian Impression*. Translated by Eric Prenowitz. Chicago: University of Chicago Press, 1995.

———. "The Law of Genre." Translated by Avital Ronell. *Critical Inquiry* 7, no. 1 (1980): 55–81.

———. "Le Facteur de la vérité." *Poetics*, no. 21 (1975): 96–147.

———. *Of Grammatology*. Translated by Gayatri Chakravorty Spivak. Baltimore: Johns Hopkins University Press, 1998.

———. "Plato's Pharmacy." In *Dissemination*, translated by Barbara Johnson, 67–186. London: Continuum, 2004.

———. *Specters of Marx: The State of the Debt, the Work of Mourning, and the New International*. Translated by Peggy Kamuf. New York: Routledge, 1994.

D'haen, Theo. "European Postmodernism: The Cosmodern Turn." *Narrative* 21, no. 3 (2013): 271–83. https://doi.org/10.1353/nar.2013.0019.

Diamond, Jared M. *Guns, Germs and Steel: A Short History of Everybody for the Last 13,000 Years*. London: Vintage, 2005.

Dillon, Sarah, ed. *David Mitchell: Critical Essays*. Canterbury: Gylphi, 2011.

Dimock, Wai Chee. *Through Other Continents: American Literature Across Deep Time*. Princeton, NJ: Princeton University Press, 2008.

Dimovitz, Scott. "The Sound of Silence: Eschatology and the Limits of the Word in David Mitchell's *Cloud Atlas*." *SubStance* 44, no. 1 (2015): 71–91. https://doi.org/10.1353/sub.2015.0009.

Dinnen, Zara. *The Digital Banal: New Media and American Literature and Culture*. New York: Columbia University Press, 2018.

Dinsman, Melissa, and Alexander R. Galloway. "The Digital in the Humanities: An Interview with Alexander Galloway." *Los Angeles Review of Books*, March 27, 2016. https://lareviewofbooks.org/article/the-digital-in-the-humanities-an-interview-with-alexander-galloway/.

Drucker, Johanna. *SpecLab: Digital Aesthetics and Projects in Speculative Computing*. Chicago: University of Chicago Press, 2009.

———. "Why Distant Reading Isn't." *PMLA* 132, no. 3 (2017): 628–35.

Dunlop, Nicholas. "Speculative Fiction as Postcolonial Critique in *Ghostwritten* and *Cloud Atlas*." In Dillon, *David Mitchell*, 201–23.

Dyrberg, Torben Bech. *Foucault on the Politics of Parrhesia*. London: Palgrave Macmillan, 2014. www.palgraveconnect.com/doifinder/10.1057/9781137368355.

Eaglestone, Robert. "Contemporary Fiction in the Academy: Towards a Manifesto." *Textual Practice* 27, no. 7 (2013): 1089–1101. https://doi.org/10.1080/0950236X.2013.840113.

———. *The Holocaust and the Postmodern*. Oxford: Oxford University Press, 2004.

Earhart, Amy E., and Andrew Jewell, eds. *American Literature Scholar in the Digital Age*. Ann Arbor: University of Michigan Press, 2011. https://doi.org/10.3998/etlc.9362034.0001.001.

Eco, Umberto. "Overinterpreting Texts." In *Interpretation and Overinterpretation*, edited by Stefan Collini, 45–66. Cambridge: Cambridge University Press, 1992.

———. *The Role of the Reader: Explorations in the Semiotics of Texts*. Bloomington: Indiana University Press, 1997.

Eder, Maciej. "Visualization in Stylometry: Cluster Analysis Using Networks." *Digital Scholarship in the Humanities* 32, no. 1 (2017): 50–64. https://doi.org/10.1093/llc/fqv061.

Eder, Maciej, Mike Kestemont, and Jan Rybicki. "Stylometry with R: A Suite of Tools." Digital Humanities 2013, University of Nebraska–Lincoln, July 16–19, 2013. Conference Abstracts. http://dh2013.unl.edu/abstracts/ab-136.html.

"Editors' Choice: Round-Up of Responses to 'The LA Neoliberal Tools (and Archives).'" Digital Humanities Now. http://digitalhumanitiesnow.org/2016/05/editors-choice-round-up-of-responses-to-the-la-neoliberal-tools-and-archives.

Edwards, Caroline. "'Strange Transactions': Utopia, Transmigration and Time in *Ghostwritten* and *Cloud Atlas*." In Dillon, *David Mitchell*, 178–200.

Eighteen-Bisang, Robert, and Elizabeth Miller, *Bram Stoker's Notes for "Dracula": A Facsimile Edition* (Jefferson, NC: McFarland, 2008).

Elliot, W., and R. J. Valenza. "And Then There Were None: Winnowing the Shakespeare Claimants." *Computers and the Humanities* 30, no. 3 (1996): 191–245.

———. "The Professor Doth Protest Too Much, Methinks." *Computers and the Humanities* 32, no. 6 (1998): 425–90.

———. "So Many Hardballs, so Few over the Plate." *Computers and the Humanities* 36, no. 4 (2002): 455–60.

Ellis, J. M. "Linguistics, Literature, and the Concept of Style." *WORD* 26, no. 1 (1970): 65–78. https://doi.org/10.1080/00437956.1970.11435581.

English, James F. *The Economy of Prestige Prizes, Awards, and the Circulation of Cultural Value*. Cambridge, MA: Harvard University Press, 2005.

Eve, Martin Paul. "The Conservatism of *Cloud Atlas*." 2015. www.martineve.com/2015/06/21/the-conservatism-of-cloud-atlas.

———. "DateText." GitHub, 2016. https://github.com/MartinPaulEve/dateText.

———. *Literature Against Criticism: University English and Contemporary Fiction in Conflict*. Cambridge: Open Book Publishers, 2016.

———. "New Rhetorics: Disciplinarity and the Movement from Historiography to Taxonomography." In *Metahistorical Narratives and Scientific Metafictions*, edited by Giuseppe di Episcopo, 101–22. Naples: Edizioni Cronopio, 2015.

———. *Pynchon and Philosophy: Wittgenstein, Foucault and Adorno*. London: Palgrave Macmillan, 2014.

———. "SankeyTextualVariant." GitHub, 2015. https://github.com/MartinPaulEve/SankeyTextualVariant.

———. "'some kind of thing it aint us but yet its in us': David Mitchell, Russell Hoban, and Metafiction After the Millennium." *Sage Open* 4, no. 1 (2014): https://doi.org/10.1177/2158244014521636.

———. "'What Was Knowledge for, I Would Ask Myself': Science, Technology, and Identity in David Mitchell's *Cloud Atlas*." In *David Mitchell: Contemporary Critical Perspectives*, edited by Wendy Knepper and Courtney Hopf. London: Bloomsbury, forthcoming.

———. "'You Have to Keep Track of Your Changes': The Version Variants and Publishing History of David Mitchell's *Cloud Atlas*." *Open Library of Humanities* 2, no. 2 (2016): 1–34. http://dx.doi.org/10.16995/olh.82.

———. "'You Will See the Logic of the Design of This': From Historiography to Taxonomography in the Contemporary Metafiction of Sarah Waters's *Affinity*." *Neo-Victorian Studies* 6, no. 1 (2013): 105–25.

Evert, Stefan, Fotis Jannidis, Thomas Proisl, Thorsten Vitt, Christof Schöch, Steffen Pielström, and Isabella Reger. "Outliers or Key Profiles? Understanding Distance Measures for Authorship Attribution." In *Digital Humanities 2016: Conference Abstracts*. Jagiellonian University and Pedagogical University, Kraków. http://dh2016.adho.org/abstracts/253.

Farringdon, J. M. *Analyzing for Authorship: A Guide to the Cusum Technique*. Cardiff: University of Wales Press, 1996.

Felski, Rita. *The Limits of Critique*. Chicago: University of Chicago Press, 2015.

Fenves, Peter. "The Tower of Babel Rebuilt: Some Remarks on 'The End of History.'" In Burns, *After History?* 217–37.

Finkelstein, David, and Alistair McCleery. *An Introduction to Book History*. 2nd ed. New York: Routledge, 2013.

Fish, Stanley. "Being Interdisciplinary Is So Very Hard to Do." *Profession* (1989): 15–22. www.jstor.org/stable/25595433.

Foucault, Michel. *The Archaeology of Knowledge*. Translated by Alan Sheridan. London: Routledge, 2006.

———. *Discipline and Punish: The Birth of the Prison*. Translated by Alan Sheridan. New York: Vintage, 1997.

———. "What Is an Author?" In *The Essential Works of Michel Foucault, 1954–1984*, edited by James D Faubion, 2:205–22. London: Penguin, 2000.

Fredner, Erik. "How Many Novels Have Been Published in English? (An Attempt)." *Stanford Literary Lab* (blog), March 14, 2017. https://litlab.stanford.edu/how-many-novels-have-been-published-in-english-an-attempt.

Fukuyama, Francis. *The End of History and the Last Man*. London: Penguin, 2012.

———. "Reflections on the End of History, Five Years Later." *History and Theory* 34, no. 2 (1995): 27–43. https://doi.org/10.2307/2505433.

Fussell, Paul. *The Great War and Modern Memory*. New York: Oxford University Press, 2000.

"Future Library, 2014–2114." n.d. https://www.futurelibrary.no.

Gadamer, Hans-Georg. "The Hermeneutics of Suspicion." In *Phenomenology and the Human Sciences*, edited by J. N. Mohanty, 73–83. Dordrecht: Springer Netherlands, 1984. https://doi.org/10.1007/978-94-009-5081-8_6.

Gallop, Jane. "The Historicization of Literary Studies and the Fate of Close Reading." *Profession* (2007): 181–86. https://doi.org/10.1632/prof.2007.2007.1.181.

Gardiner, Eileen, and Ronald G. Musto. *The Digital Humanities: A Primer for Students and Scholars*. New York: Cambridge University Press, 2015.

Gibbons, Alison, and Andrea Macrae, eds. *Pronouns in Literature*. London: Palgrave Macmillan, 2018. https://doi.org/10.1057/978-1-349-95317-2.

Gitelman, Lisa. *Paper Knowledge: Toward a Media History of Documents*. Durham, NC: Duke University Press, 2014.

———, ed. *"Raw Data" Is an Oxymoron*. Cambridge, MA: MIT Press, 2013.

Giuliani, Luigi, Herman Brinkman, Geert Lernour, and Marita Mathijsen, eds. *Texts in Multiple Versions: Histories of Editions*. Amsterdam: Brill, 2006.

Gladwin, Alexander A. G., Matthew J. Lavin, and Daniel M. Look. "Stylometry and Collaborative Authorship: Eddy, Lovecraft, and 'The Loved Dead.'" *Digital Scholarship in the Humanities* 32, no. 1 (2017): 123–40. https://doi.org/10.1093/llc/fqv026.

Gold, Matthew K., and Lauren F. Klein, eds. *Debates in the Digital Humanities 2016*. Minneapolis: University of Minnesota Press, 2016.

Goldstone, Andrew. "The *Doxa* of Reading." *PMLA* 132, no. 3 (2017): 636–42.

Gorman, David, and Jerome McGann. "An Interview with Jerome McGann on Textual Scholarship as Literary History and Ideology Critique." *Social Epistemology* 1, no. 2 (1987): 163–73. https://doi.org/10.1080/02691728708578428.

Government of the United Kingdom. "Complaints to Secretary of State Under s.296ZE Under the Copyright, Designs and Patents Act 1988," August 15, 2014. www.gov.uk/government/publications/complaints-to-secretary-of-state-under-s296ze-under-the-copyright-designs-and-patents-act-1988.

Graff, Gerald. *Professing Literature: An Institutional History*. Chicago: University of Chicago Press, 1989.

Grieve, J. W. "Quantitative Authorship Attribution: A History and an Evaluation of Techniques." Master's thesis, Simon Fraser University, 2005. http://summit.sfu.ca/item/8840.

Groenland, Tim. "'A Recipe for a Brick': *The Pale King* in Progress." *Critique: Studies in Contemporary Fiction* 58, no. 4 (2017): 1–12. https://doi.org/10.1080/00111619.2016.1271766.

Groot, Jerome de. "Walter Scott Prize for Historical Fiction: The New Time-Travellers." *The Scotsman*, June 19, 2010. www.scotsman.com/lifestyle/books/walter-scott-prize-for-historical-fiction-the-new-time-travellers-1-813580.

Grusin, Richard. "The Dark Side of Digital Humanities: Dispatches from Two Recent MLA Conventions." *Differences* 25, no. 1 (2014): 79–92. https://doi.org/10.1215/10407391-2420009.

Hacking, Ian. "Do We See Through a Microscope?" *Pacific Philosophical Quarterly* 62, no. 4 (1981): 305–22. https://doi.org/10.1111/j.1468-0114.1981.tb00070.x.

Hall, Kira, and Mary Bucholtz, eds. *Gender Articulated: Language and the Socially Constructed Self.* New York: Routledge, 1995.

Hardcastle, R. A. "CUSUM: A Credible Method for the Determination of Authorship?" *Science and Justice* 37, no. 2 (1997): 129–38. https://doi.org/10.1016/S1355-0306(97)72158-0.

———. "Forensic Linguistics: An Assessment of the CUSUM Method for the Determination of Authorship." *Journal of the Forensic Science Society* 33, no. 2 (1993): 95–106. https://doi.org/10.1016/S0015-7368(93)72987-4.

Harris, Paul A. "David Mitchell's Fractal Imagination: *The Bone Clocks.*" *SubStance* 44, no. 1 (2015): 148–53. https://doi.org/10.1353/sub.2015.0006.

Harris, Robert. *An Officer and a Spy*. London: Arrow, 2014.

Harris-Birtill, Rose. *David Mitchell's Post-Secular World: Buddhism, Belief and the Urgency of Compassion*. London: Bloomsbury, 2019.

———. "'Looking Down Time's Telescope at Myself': Reincarnation and Global Futures in David Mitchell's Fictional Worlds." *KronoScope: The Journal for the Study of Time* 17, no. 2 (2017): 163–81. https://doi.org/10.1163/15685241-12341382.

Hartley, Jenny. *The Reading Groups Book*. Oxford: Oxford University Press, 2002.

Hay, Louis. "Does 'Text' Exist?" *Studies in Bibliography* 41 (1988): 64–76.

Hayles, N. Katherine. *How We Think: Digital Media and Contemporary Technogenesis*. Chicago: University of Chicago Press, 2012.

———. *Writing Machines*. Mediawork pamphlet. Cambridge, MA: MIT Press, 2002.

Hegel, Georg Wilhelm Friedrich. *The Phenomenology of Mind*. Translated by J. B. Baillie. London: Harper and Row, 1967.

———. *The Science of Logic*. Translated by George Di Giovanni. Cambridge: Cambridge University Press, 2010.

Herman, Luc, and John M. Krafft. "Fast Learner: The Typescript of Pynchon's *V.* at the Harry Ransom Center in Austin." *Texas Studies in Literature and Language* 49, no. 1 (2007): 1–20. https://doi.org/10.1353/tsl.2007.0005.

Hicks, Heather J. "'This Time Round': David Mitchell's *Cloud Atlas* and the Apocalyptic Problem of Historicism." *Postmodern Culture* 20, no. 3 (2010): https://doi.org/10.1353/pmc.2010.0012.

Hilton, M. L. "An Assessment of Cumulative Sum Charts for Authorship Attribution." *Literary and Linguistic Computing* 8, no. 2 (1993): 73–80. https://doi.org/10.1093/llc/8.2.73.

Hoban, Russell. *Riddley Walker*. London: Bloomsbury, 2002.

Holmes, David I. "The Evolution of Stylometry in Humanities Scholarship." *Literary and Linguistic Computing* 13, no. 3 (1998): 111–17.

Holmes, David I., and Fiona Tweedie. "Forensic Stylometry: A Review of the Cusum Controversy." *La Revue informatique et statistique dans les sciences humaines* 31, nos. 1–4 (1995): 19–47.

Hoover, David. "The End of the Irrelevant Text: Electronic Texts, Linguistics, and Literary Theory." *Digital Humanities Quarterly* 1, no. 2 (2007): www.digitalhumanities.org/dhq/vol/1/2/000012/000012.html.

———. "Testing Burrows's Delta." *Literary and Linguistic Computing* 19, no. 4 (2004): 453–75.

Hopf, Courtney. "The Stories We Tell: Discursive Identity Through Narrative Form in *Cloud Atlas*." In Dillon, *David Mitchell*, 105–26.

Houston, Keith. *Shady Characters: The Secret Life of Punctuation, Symbols, & Other Typographical Marks*. New York: Norton, 2013.

Hühn, Peter. "The Detective as Reader: Narrativity and Reading Concepts in Detective Fiction." *MFS Modern Fiction Studies* 3, no. 3 (1987): 451–66. https://doi.org/10.1353/mfs.0.1310.

Hullot-Kentor, Robert. *Things Beyond Resemblance: Collected Essays on Theodor W. Adorno*. New York: Columbia University Press, 2006.

Hungerford, Amy. *Making Literature Now*. Stanford, CA: Stanford University Press, 2016.

Hutcheon, Linda. *Narcissistic Narrative: The Metafictional Paradox*. Waterloo: Wilfrid Laurier University Press, 2013.

———. *A Poetics of Postmodernism: History, Theory, Fiction*. New York: Routledge, 1988.

———. *A Theory of Parody: The Teachings of Twentieth-Century Art Forms*. New York: Methuen, 1985.

Ihde, Don. *Hermeneutic Phenomenology: The Philosophy of Paul Ricoeur*. Evanston, IL: Northwestern University Press, 1980.

International Labour Organization and Walk Free Foundation. "Global Estimates of Modern Slavery, Forced Labour, and Forced Marriage." Geneva, 2017. www.ilo.org/wcmsp5/groups/public/@dgreports/@dcomm/documents/publication/wcms_575479.pdf.

"Interview with David Mitchell." Goodreads, July 5, 2010. www.goodreads.com/interviews/show/537.David_Mitchell.

Ishiguro, Kazuo. *The Buried Giant*. London: Faber and Faber, 2015.

Jameson, Fredric. "The Historical Novel Today, or, Is It Still Possible?" In *The Antinomies of Realism*, 259–313. London: Verso, 2013.

Jeffries, Stuart. "David Mitchell: 'I Don't Want to Project Myself as This Great Experimenter.'" *The Guardian*, Feb. 8, 2013. www.guardian.co.uk/books/2013/feb/08/david-mitchell-project-great-experimenter.

Jewell, Andrew, and Brian L. Pytlik Zillig. "'Counted Out at Last': Text Analysis on the Willa Cather Archive." In Earhart and Jewell, *American Literature Scholar in the Digital Age*, 170–84.

Jockers, Matthew L. *Macroanalysis: Digital Methods and Literary History*. Urbana: University of Illinois Press, 2013.

———. "A Novel Method for Detecting Plot." June 5, 2014. www.matthewjockers.net/2014/06/05/a-novel-method-for-detecting-plot.

———. "Requiem for a Low Pass Filter." April 6, 2015. www.matthewjockers.net/2015/04/06/epilogue.

———. "Resurrecting a Low Pass Filter (Well, Kind Of)." Jan. 12, 2017. www.matthewjockers.net/2017/01/12/resurrecting.

———. *Text Analysis with R for Students of Literature*. New York: Springer, 2014.

Johnson, Barbara. "The Frame of Reference: Poe, Lacan, Derrida." *Yale French Studies*, no. 55/56 (1977): 457–505. https://doi.org/10.2307/2930445.

Johnson, Bobbie. "Amazon Kindle Users Surprised by 'Big Brother' Move." *The Guardian*, July 17, 2009, sec. Technology. www.theguardian.com/technology/2009/jul/17/amazon-kindle-1984.

Jordan, Julia. "'What Arises from This?' The Autostereogrammatical in Thomas Pynchon's *Mason & Dixon*." *Critique: Studies in Contemporary Fiction* 56, no. 3 (2015): 270–83. https://doi.org/10.1080/00111619.2014.897932.

Juola, Patrick. "Authorship Attribution." *Foundations and Trends® in Information Retrieval* 1, no. 3 (2007): 233–334. https://doi.org/10.1561/1500000005.

———. "Stylometry and Immigration: A Case Study." *Journal of Law and Policy* 21, no. 2 (2012): 287–98.

Kenny, Anthony. *The Computation of Style: An Introduction to Statistics for Students of Literature and Humanities*. Oxford: Pergamon, 1982.

Kermode, Frank. *The Sense of an Ending: Studies in the Theory of Fiction: With a New Epilogue*. Oxford: Oxford University Press, 2000.

Kerr, Norbert L. "HARKing: Hypothesizing After the Results Are Known." *Personality and Social Psychology Review* 2, no. 3 (1998): 196–217. https://doi.org/10.1207/s15327957pspr0203_4.

Ketzan, Erik, and Christof Schöch. "What Changed When Andy Weir's *The Martian* Got Edited?" Digital Humanities 2017 conference, Montreal, August 8–11. https://dh2017.adho.org/abstracts/317/317.pdf.

Kirschenbaum, Matthew G. *Track Changes: A Literary History of Word Processing*. Cambridge, MA: Belknap Press of Harvard University Press, 2016.

Knepper, Wendy. "Toward a Theory of Experimental World Epic: David Mitchell's *Cloud Atlas*." *Ariel: A Review of International English Literature* 47, no. 1 (2016): 93–126.

Koehler, Adam. *Composition, Creative Writing Studies and the Digital Humanities*. London: Bloomsbury, 2017.

Kripke, Saul. *Wittgenstein on Rules and Private Language*. Oxford: Blackwell, 1982.

Lacan, Jacques. "Le Séminaire sur la lettre volée." In *Écrits*. Paris: Seuil, 1966.

LaCapra, Dominick. *History & Criticism*. Ithaca, NY: Cornell University Press, 1985.

Lang, Berel, ed. *The Concept of Style*. Ithaca, NY: Cornell University Press, 1987.

Larson, Brian. "Gender/Genre: Gender Difference in Disciplinary Communication." PhD diss., University of Minnesota, 2015. http://conservancy.umn.edu/handle/11299/188945.

Larsonneur, Claire. "Oblique Translations in David Mitchell's Works." *C21 Literature: Journal of 21st Century Writings* 6, no. 3 (2018): https://doi.org/10.16995/c21.53.

———. "Revisiting Dejima (Japan): From Recollections to Fiction in David Mitchell's *The Thousand Autumns of Jacob de Zoet* (2010)." *SubStance* 44, no. 1 (2015): 136–47. https://doi.org/10.1353/sub.2015.0004.

Latham, Sean. *The Art of Scandal: Modernism, Libel Law, and the Roman à Clef*. Oxford: Oxford University Press, 2009.

Laue, Theodore H. Von. "From Fukuyama to Reality: A Critical Essay." In Burns, *After History?* 23–37.

Lavagnino, John. "Excerpted: Reading, Scholarship, and Hypertext Editions." *Journal of Electronic Publishing* 3, no. 1 (1997): http://dx.doi.org/10.3998/3336451.0003.112.

Lee, Vernon. *The Handling of Words*. London: Bodley Head, 1923. https://gutenberg.ca /ebooks/lee-handling/lee-handling-00-h.html#ch_VI.

Leiter, Brian. "The Hermeneutics of Suspicion: Recovering Marx, Nietzsche, and Freud." SSRN Scholarly Paper. Rochester, NY: Social Science Research Network, March 23, 2005. https://papers.ssrn.com/abstract=691002.

Letzler, David. *The Cruft of Fiction: Mega-novels and the Science of Paying Attention*. Lincoln: University of Nebraska Press, 2017.

Levine, Caroline. *Forms: Whole, Rhythm, Hierarchy, Network*. Princeton, NJ: Princeton University Press, 2015.

Liberman, Mark. "A New Verb: To Thaler." Language Log, May 15, 2004. http://itre.cis.upenn.edu/myl/languagelog/archives/000907.html.

Liu, Alan. "Is Digital Humanities a Field?—An Answer from the Point of View of Language." *Journal of Siberian Federal University, Humanities and Social Sciences* 7 (March 2013): 1546–52.

———. *The Laws of Cool: Knowledge Work and the Culture of Information*. Chicago: University of Chicago Press, 2004.

———. "The State of the Digital Humanities: A Report and a Critique." *Arts and Humanities in Higher Education* 11, no. 1–2 (2012): 8–41. https://doi.org/10.1177/1474022211427364.

Livio, Mario. *The Golden Ratio: The Story of Phi, the World's Most Astonishing Number*. New York: Broadway, 2003.

Lyall, Sarah. "Novelists Defend One of Their Own Against a Plagiarism Charge." *New York Times*, Dec. 7, 2006, sec. Books. www.nytimes.com/2006/12/07/books/07pync.html.

Machinal, Hélène. "*Cloud Atlas*: From Postmodernity to the Posthuman." In Dillon, *David Mitchell*, 127–54.

Mangen, Anne. "Hypertext Fiction Reading: Haptics and Immersion." *Journal of Research in Reading* 31, no. 4 (2008): 404–19. https://doi.org/10.1111/j.1467-9817.2008.00380.x.

Manoff, Marlene. "Theories of the Archive from Across the Disciplines." *Portal: Libraries and the Academy* 4, no. 1 (2004): 9–25.

Manovich, Lev. *The Language of New Media*. Cambridge, MA: MIT Press, 2002.

Manson, Patrick. "On the Development of Filaria Sanguinis Hominis, and on the Mosquito Considered as a Nurse." *Journal of the Linnean Society of London, Zoology* 14, no. 75 (1878): 304–11. https://doi.org/10.1111/j.1096-3642.1878.tb01837.x.

Markovits, Elizabeth. *The Politics of Sincerity: Plato, Frank Speech, and Democratic Judgment*. University Park: Pennsylvania State University Press, 2008.

Mattner, Cosima, and Ted Underwood. "They Have Completely Changed My Understanding of Literary History." *Textpraxis* 14, no. 3 (2017): www.uni-muenster.de /Textpraxis/en/cosima-mattner-they-have-completely-changed-my-understanding -of-literary-history.

McGann, Jerome. *A Critique of Modern Textual Criticism*. Charlottesville: University Press of Virginia, 1983.

McHale, Brian. "Genre as History: Genre-Poaching in *Against the Day*." *Genre* 42, no. 3–4 (2009): 5–20. https://doi.org/10.1215/00166928-42-3-4-5.

McKeon, Michael. *The Origins of the English Novel, 1600–1740*. 15th anniversary ed. Baltimore: Johns Hopkins University Press, 2002.

McMenamin, G. "Disputed Authorship in US Law." *International Journal of Speech, Language and the Law* 11, no. 1 (2004): 73–82.

Melville, Herman. *Moby Dick; or, The Whale*. Project Gutenberg, 2008. www.gutenberg.org/files/2701/2701-h/2701-h.htm.

Mendelson, Edward. "Encyclopedic Narrative: From Dante to Pynchon." *MLN* 91, no. 6 (1976): 1267–75.

Middleton, Peter. *Distant Reading: Performance, Readership, and Consumption in Contemporary Poetry*. Tuscaloosa: University of Alabama Press, 2005.

Miller, Laura. "Take Notes, Nate Silver! Reinventing Literary Criticism with Computers." Salon, April 23, 2014. www.salon.com/2014/04/23/learning_from_failed_books.

Miller, Mark Crispin. "The Publishing Industry." In *Conglomerates and the Media*, edited by Patricia Aufderheide, Erik Barnouw, Richard M. Cohen, Thomas Frank, David Lieberman, Mark Crispin Miller, Gene Roberts, and Thomas Shatz, 107–34. New York: New Press, 1997.

Mitchell, David. *Black Swan Green*. London: Sceptre, 2006.

———. *The Bone Clocks*. London: Sceptre, 2014.

———. "The Book of Revelations." *The Guardian*, Feb. 5, 2005. www.guardian.co.uk/books/2005/feb/05/featuresreviews.guardianreview27.

———. *Cartographie des nuages*. Translated by Manuel Berri. Paris: Editions de l'Olivier, 2007.

———. *Cloud Atlas*. London: Sceptre, 2004.

———. *Cloud Atlas*. New York: Random House, 2004.

———. *Cloud Atlas*. Kindle Edition. New York: Random House/Amazon Kindle, 2004.

———. *Cloud Atlas: L'Atlante delle nuvole*. Translated by Luca Scarlini and Lorenzo Borgotallo. Milano: Sperling and Kupfer, 2014.

———. *Der Wolkenatlas*. Translated by Volker Oldenburg. Reinbeck: Rowohlt Taschenbuch, 2012.

———. "Genesis." *The Guardian*, April 16, 2005, sec. Books. www.theguardian.com/books/2005/apr/16/featuresreviews.guardianreview23.

———. "Guardian Book Club: *Cloud Atlas* by David Mitchell." *The Guardian*, June 12, 2010. www.theguardian.com/books/2010/jun/12/book-club-mitchell-cloud-atlas.

———. *Number9Dream*. London: Random House, 2003.

———. *The Thousand Autumns of Jacob de Zoet*. Repr. ed. New York: Random House Trade Paperbacks, 2011.

———. クラウド・アトラス. Translated by Chiho Nakagawa. Tokyo: Kawade Shobo Shinsha, 2013.

Moretti, Franco. *Distant Reading*. London: Verso, 2013.

———. *Graphs, Maps, Trees: Abstract Models for Literary History*. London: Verso, 2007.

———. "The Slaughterhouse of Literature." *Modern Language Quarterly* 61, no. 1 (2000): 207–27.

Morton, A. Q. *Literary Detection: How to Prove Authorship and Fraud in Literature and Documents*. Epping: Bowker, 1978.

Moskalew, W. *Formular Language and Poetic Design in the "Aeneid."* Leiden: Brill, 1982.

Mosteller, F., and D. L. Wallace. *Inference and Disputed Authorship: The Federalist*. Reading, MA: Addison-Wesley, 1964.

Moylan, Tom. *Demand the Impossible: Science Fiction and the Utopian Imagination*. New York: Methuen, 1986.

Mullan, John. "*Cloud Atlas*: The Multi-genre Novel." *The Guardian*, March 26, 2005, sec. Books. www.theguardian.com/books/2005/mar/26/fiction.davidmitchell.

National Information Standards Organization. *Understanding Metadata*. Bethesda, MD: NISO, 2004.

Nicholson, Catherine. "Algorithm and Analogy: Distant Reading in 1598." *PMLA* 132, no. 3 (2017): 643–50.

Nyhan, Julianne, and Andrew Flinn. *Computation and the Humanities: Towards an Oral History of Digital Humanities*. London: Springer, 2016.

O'Donnell, Patrick. *A Temporary Future: The Fiction of David Mitchell*. New York: Bloomsbury Academic, 2015.

Olsen, Mark. "Signs, Symbols and Discourses: A New Direction for Computer-Aided Literature Studies." *Computers and the Humanities* 27, no. 5/6 (1993): 309–14.

Ong, Walter J. *Orality and Literacy: The Technologizing of the Word*. London: Routledge, 2002.

Orwell, George. *Nineteen Eighty-Four*. San Diego: Harcourt Brace Jovanovich, 1984.

Oxford Dictionaries. "The Oxford English Corpus." Oxford Dictionaries | English, 2017. https://en.oxforddictionaries.com/explore/oxford-english-corpus.

Pearl, Lisa, Kristine Lu, and Anousheh Haghighi. "The Character in the Letter: Epistolary Attribution in Samuel Richardson's *Clarissa*." *Digital Scholarship in the Humanities* 32, no. 1 (2016): 123–40. https://doi.org/10.1093/llc/fqw007.

Piper, Andrew. *Enumerations: Data and Literary Study*. Chicago: University of Chicago Press, 2018.

———. "Think Small: On Literary Modeling." *PMLA* 132, no. 3 (2017): 651–58.

Posavec, Stefanie. "Writing Without Words." 2009. www.stefanieposavec.com/writing-without-words.

Pressman, Jessica. *Digital Modernism: Making It New in New Media*. New York: Oxford University Press, 2014.

———. "House of Leaves: Reading the Networked Novel." *Studies in American Fiction* 34, no. 1 (2006): 107–28. https://doi.org/10.1353/saf.2006.0015.

Propp, Vladimir. *Morphology of the Folktale*. Austin: University of Texas Press, 1968.

R Core Team. *R: A Language and Environment for Statistical Computing*. Vienna: R Foundation for Statistical Computing, 2016. https://www.R-project.org.

Ramnial, Hoshiladevi, Shireen Panchoo, and Sameerchand Pudaruth. "Authorship Attribution Using Stylometry and Machine Learning Techniques." In *Intelligent Systems Technologies and Applications*, 113–25. Cham, CH: Springer, 2016. https://doi.org/10.1007/978-3-319-23036-8_10.

Ramsay, Stephen. "The Hermeneutics of Screwing Around; or What You Do with a Million Books." In *Pastplay: Teaching and Learning History with Technology*, edited by Kevin Kee, 110–20. Ann Arbor: University of Michigan Press, 2014. https://quod.lib.umich.edu/d/dh/12544152.0001.001/1:5/—pastplay-teaching-and-learning-history-with-technology?g=dculture;rgn=div1;view=fulltext;xc=1.

———. *Reading Machines: Toward an Algorithmic Criticism*. Urbana: University of Illinois Press, 2011.

———. "Toward an Algorithmic Criticism." In *A Companion to Digital Literary Studies*, edited by Ray Siemens and Susan Schreibman, 477–91. New York: Wiley-Blackwell, 2013.

Rankin, Ian. *Tooth and Nail*. London: Orion, 2008.

Read, Andrew J. *Mars and Back*. Great Sampford, Essex: Bright Books, 1993.

Reagan, Charles E. "Interview with Paul Ricœur (Recorded 1982)." In *Paul Ricoeur: His Life and Work*, 105. Chicago: University Of Chicago Press, 1996.

Rentschler, Eric. "The Fascination of a Fake: The Hitler Diaries." *New German Critique*, no. 90 (2003): 177–92. https://doi.org/10.2307/3211115.

Rhody, Lisa Marie. "Beyond Darwinian Distance: Situating Distant Reading in a Feminist *Ut Pictura Poesis* Tradition." *PMLA* 132, no. 3 (2017): 659–67.

Richards, I. A. *How to Read a Page: A Course in Efficient Reading with an Introduction to a Hundred Great Words*. Boston: Beacon, 1959.

———. *Principles of Literary Criticism*. London: Routledge, 2001.

Ricœur, Paul. "Biblical Hermeneutics." *Semeia* 4 (1975): 29–148.

———. *Freud and Philosophy: An Essay on Interpretation*. Translated by Denis Savage. New Haven, CT: Yale University Press, 1979.

———. *The Rule of Metaphor: Multi-disciplinary Studies of the Creation of Meaning in Language*. Translated by R. Czerny. Toronto: University of Toronto Press, 1975.

Roache, John. "'The Realer, More Enduring and Sentimental Part of Him': David Foster Wallace's Personal Library and Marginalia." *Orbit: A Journal of American Literature* 5, no. 1 (2017): https://doi.org/10.16995/orbit.142.

Robbins, Bruce. "Not So Well Attached." *PMLA* 132, no. 2 (2017): 371–76. https://doi.org/10.1632/pmla.2017.132.2.371.

Rockwell, G. "What Is Text Analysis, Really?" *Literary and Linguistic Computing* 18, no. 2 (2003): 209–19. https://doi.org/10.1093/llc/18.2.209.

Rogers, Richard. *Digital Methods*. Cambridge, MA: MIT Press, 2015.

Rolls, Albert. "The Two *V.*s of Thomas Pynchon, or From Lippincott to Jonathan Cape and Beyond." *Orbit: Writing Around Pynchon* 1, no. 1 (2012): https://doi.org/10.7766/orbit.v1.1.33.

Ross, Alison. "Why Is 'Speaking the Truth' Fearless? 'Danger' and 'Truth' in Foucault's Discussion of Parrhesia." *Parrhesia*, no. 4 (2008): 62–75.

Ross, Shawna. "In Praise of Overstating the Case: A Review of Franco Moretti, *Distant*

Reading (London: Verso, 2013)." *Digital Humanities Quarterly* 8, no. 1 (2014): www.digitalhumanities.org/dhq/vol/8/1/000171/000171.html.

Rybicki, J., and M. Eder. "Deeper Delta Across Genres and Languages: Do We Really Need the Most Frequent Words?" *Literary and Linguistic Computing* 26, no. 3 (2011): 315–21. https://doi.org/10.1093/llc/fqr031.

Rzepka, Charles J. *Detective Fiction*. Cambridge, UK: Polity, 2005.

Said, Edward W. *On Late Style*. London: Bloomsbury, 2006.

Samuels, Lisa, and Jerome J. McGann. "Deformance and Interpretation." *New Literary History* 30, no. 1 (1999): 25–56. https://doi.org/10.1353/nlh.1999.0010.

Schmidt, Benjamin M. "Do Digital Humanists Need to Understand Algorithms?" In Gold and Klein, *Debates in the Digital Humanities 2016*, 546–55. http://dhdebates.gc.cuny.edu/debates/text/99.

Schreibman, Susan, Raymond George Siemens, and John Unsworth, eds. *A New Companion to Digital Humanities*. Chichester: John Wiley and Sons, 2016.

Scott-Baumann, Alison. *Ricœur and the Hermeneutics of Suspicion*. London: Continuum, 2009.

Shanahan, Jonathan. "Digital Transcendentalism in David Mitchell's *Cloud Atlas*." *Criticism* 58, no. 1 (2016): 115–45. https://doi.org/10.13110/criticism.58.1.0115.

Shand, A. "The Occupation of the Chatham Islands by the Maoris in 1835: Part II, The Migration of Ngatiawa to Chatham Island." *Journal of the Polynesian Society* 1, no. 3 (1892): 154–63.

Shaw, Harry E. *The Forms of Historical Fiction: Sir Walter Scott and His Successors*. Ithaca, NY: Cornell University Press, 1983.

Shaw, Kristian. " 'Some Magic Is Normality': Fantastical Cosmopolitanism in David Mitchell's *The Bone Clocks*." *C21 Literature: Journal of 21st Century Writings* 6, no. 3 (2018): https://doi.org/10.16995/c21.52.

Shoop, Casey, and Dermot Ryan. " 'Gravid with the Ancient Future': *Cloud Atlas* and the Politics of Big History." *SubStance* 44, no. 1 (2015): 92–106. https://doi.org/10.1353/sub.2015.0011.

Siemens, Ray, and Susan Schreibman, eds. *A Companion to Digital Literary Studies*. New York: Wiley-Blackwell, 2013.

Simpson, Kathryn. " 'Or Something Like That': Coming of Age in *Number9dream*." In Dillon, *David Mitchell*, 49–76.

Simpson, Zacharia. "The Truths We Tell Ourselves: Foucault on Parrhesia." *Foucault Studies* 13 (March 2012): 99–115.

Sims, Christopher A. *Tech Anxiety: Artificial Intelligence and Ontological Awakening in Four Science Fiction Novels*. Jefferson, NC: McFarland, 2013.

Šklovskij, Viktor. *Theory of Prose*. Elmwood Park, IL: Dalkey Archive Press, 1991.

Smith, Barbara Herrnstein. "What Was 'Close Reading'? A Century of Method in Literary Studies." *Minnesota Review* 87 (2016): 57–75. https://doi.org/10.1215/00265667-3630844.

So, Richard Jean. "All Models Are Wrong." *PMLA* 132, no. 3 (2017): 668–73.

"Spillage." Online Etymology Dictionary, 2017. https://www.etymonline.com/word/spillage.

Stam, Robert. "Text and Intertext: Introduction." In *Film Theory: An Anthology*, edited by Robert Stam and Toby Miller, 145–56. Malden, MA: Blackwell, 2000.

Stewart, David. "The Hermeneutics of Suspicion." *Literature and Theology* 3, no. 3 (1989): 296–307.

Stolerman, Ariel, Rebekah Overdorf, Sadia Afroz, and Rachel Greenstadt. "Breaking the Closed-World Assumption in Stylometric Authorship Attribution." In *Advances in Digital Forensics X*, edited by Gilbert Peterson and Sujeet Shenoi, 184–205. Berlin: Springer, 2014.

Strandberg, Victor. "Dimming the Enlightenment: Thomas Pynchon's *Mason & Dixon*." In *Pynchon and "Mason & Dixon,"* edited by Brooke Horvath and Irving Malin, 100–111. Newark: University of Delaware Press, 2000.

Swafford, Annie. "Continuing the Syuzhet Discussion." *Anglophile in Academia: Annie Swafford's Blog* (blog), March 7, 2015. https://annieswafford.wordpress.com/2015/03/07/continuingsyuzhet/.

Tenen, Dennis. *Plain Text: The Poetics of Computation*. Stanford, CA: Stanford University Press, 2017.

Terras, Melissa M., Julianne Nyhan, and Edward Vanhoutte, eds. *Defining Digital Humanities: A Reader*. Surrey: Ashgate, 2013.

Thiselton, Anthony C. *New Horizons in Hermeneutics: The Theory and Practice of Transforming Biblical Reading*. Grand Rapids, MI: Zondervan, 1998.

Toutanova, Kristina, Dan Klein, Christopher D. Manning, and Yoram Singer. "Feature-Rich Part-of-Speech Tagging with a Cyclic Dependency Network." In *Proceedings of the 2003 Conference of the North American Chapter of the Association for Computational Linguistics on Human Language Technology*. Vol. 1, 173–80. Stroudsburg, PA: Association for Computational Linguistics, 2003. http://dl.acm.org/citation.cfm?id=1073478.

Tudor, Andrew. *Theories of Film*. London: British Film Institute, 1974.

Tykwer, Tom, Lana Wachowski, and Lilly (as Andy) Wachowski, dirs. *Cloud Atlas*. Warner Bros, 2012.

Underwood, Ted. "A Genealogy of Distant Reading." *Digital Humanities Quarterly* 11, no. 2 (2017): www.digitalhumanities.org/dhq/vol/11/2/000317/000317.html.

———. "The Life Cycles of Genres." *Journal of Cultural Analytics*, May 23, 2016. https://doi.org/10.22148/16.005.

———. *Why Literary Periods Mattered: Historical Contrast and the Prestige of English Studies*. Stanford, CA: Stanford University Press, 2013.

Underwood, Ted, and Jordan Sellers. "The *Longue Durée* of Literary Prestige." *Modern Language Quarterly* 77, no. 3 (2016): 321–44. https://doi.org/10.1215/00267929-3570634.

Vee, Annette. "'Literary Analysis by Computer' Offered at Dartmouth, Winter 1969, Working with *Paradise Lost*. #1960sComputing Pic.Twitter.Com/DPrnY23cpU." Tweet. *@anetv* (blog), Oct. 4, 2017. https://twitter.com/anetv/status/915219418189660160/photo/1.

Visel, Robin. "Reading Forward: The Fractal Texts of Doris Lessing and David Mitchell." *Doris Lessing Studies* 34 (2016): 12–15.

Waugh, Patricia. *Metafiction: The Theory and Practice of Self-Conscious Fiction*. London: Methuen, 1984.

White, Hayden. "Historical Emplotment and the Problem of Truth." In *Probing the Limits of Representation: Nazism and the "Final Solution,"* edited by S. Friedlander, 37–53. Cambridge, MA: Harvard University Press, 1992.

———. *Metahistory: Historical Imagination in Nineteenth-Century Europe*. Baltimore: Johns Hopkins University Press, 1975.

Wickman, Matthew. "Theology Still?" *PMLA* 132, no. 3 (2017): 674–80.

Wiesel, Elie. *From the Kingdom of Memory: Reminiscences*. New York: Summit, 1990.

Wilkens, Matthew. "Canons, Close Reading, and the Evolution of Method." In *Debates in the Digital Humanities*, edited by Matthew K. Gold, 249–58. Minneapolis: University of Minnesota Press, 2012. http://dhdebates.gc.cuny.edu/debates/part/5.

Wittgenstein, Ludwig. *Remarks on the Foundations of Mathematics*. 3rd ed. Oxford: Blackwell, 1978.

Worboys, Michael. "The Emergence of Tropical Medicine: A Study in the Establishment of a Scientific Speciality." In *Perspectives on the Emergence of Scientific Disciplines*, edited by Gerard Lemaine, Roy Macleod, Michael Mulkay, and Peter Weingart, 76–98. The Hague: Mouton, 1976.

World Health Organization. "Life Expectancy." 2015. www.who.int/gho/mortality_burden_disease/life_tables/situation_trends/en/.

Wright, Crispin. "Wittgenstein's Rule-Following Considerations and the Central Project of Theoretical Linguistics." In *Reflections on Chomsky*, edited by Alexander L. George, 233–64. Oxford: Blackwell, 1989.

Yamada, Miyuki, Yuichi Murai, and Ichiro Kumagai. "Story Visualization of Novels with Multi-theme Keyword Density Analysis." *Journal of Visualization* 16, no. 3 (2013): 247–57. https://doi.org/10.1007/s12650-013-0163-4.

Yazdani, Mehrdad, Jay Chow, and Lev Manovich. "Quantifying the Development of User-Generated Art During 2001–2010." *PLOS ONE* 12, no. 8 (2017): e0175350. https://doi.org/10.1371/journal.pone.0175350.

Zerubavel, Eviatar. *The Clockwork Muse: A Practical Guide to Writing Theses, Dissertations, and Books*. Cambridge, MA: Harvard University Press, 1999.

INDEX

Page numbers in italics refer to figures.